KEY STAGE 3

GERMAN

Reich and McKeane

LONGMAN

HOMEWORK HANDBOOKS

Series editors:

Geoff Black and Stuart Wall

Other titles in the series:

ENGLISH

FRENCH

MATHEMATICS

SCIENCE

Addison Wesley Longman
Edinburgh Gate, Harlow
Essex CM20 2JE
England

First published 1996

ISBN 0852 29329-4

British Cataloguing in Publication Data
A catalogue record for this title is available from the British Library

Set in Stone by 36

Produced by Longman Singapore Publishers Pte

Printed in Great Britain by Short Run Press Ltd., Exeter

Contents

USING THIS BOOK

This book will help you in your homework and other activities throughout your Key Stage 3 studies in German. In particular it will help you develop your abilities in the four key skills, namely:

- Listening
- Reading
- Speaking
- Writing

The book is divided into five sections:

Section 1: **The National Curriculum and Study Skills**

Section 2: **Grammar**

Section 3: **Practice exercises with solutions**

Section 4: **Vocabulary**

Section 5: **Mini-dictionary**
– German–English
– English–German

At the start of each section there is an easy-to-use chart showing you at a glance what you can find in that section, and where you can find it.

Sections 2, 4 and 5 are also arranged **alphabetically** to help you find what you want to know more easily.

Section

one

The National Curriculum and Study Skills

The National Curriculum in Modern Foreign Languages is the same for all modern languages. It lays down for teachers how each language, in this case German, is to be taught.

In this section we give you an idea of what is required of you in each of the four language skills of listening, reading, speaking and writing. We also look at a number of useful study techniques which will help you reach the highest possible level in your study of German.

The box below will help you see at a glance what you can find in this section.

The four language skills

The **four language skills** are called Attainment Targets (ATs).

AT1 Listening
AT2 Reading
AT3 Speaking
AT4 Writing

At the end of Key Stage 3, all four attainment targets have equal weight in the assessment of how well each pupil has done. So if you are quite good at speaking German, this can balance out being not quite so good at writing it. This can be difficult for parents to understand, mainly because when they learned a foreign language, writing was all-important. For most people, though, understanding and speaking a foreign language is more useful than writing it. That is why there is now increased emphasis on reading, listening and speaking.

The **learning activities** which teachers have to use include such obvious things as listening and responding, asking and answering questions, and so on. You should also expect to redraft your writing, learn things by heart, use dictionaries and reference materials, take part in imaginative and creative activities, and use your knowledge to experiment with language.

It is likely that most of your lessons will have very little English spoken in them. This is because it is important to use German for such real purposes as calling the register, saying which page to read, etc.

The **descriptions of performance** in each of the skills are quite technical, and are intended for teachers' use in assessing how well you have done. However, the different levels do reflect real progress. The government performance targets for most Year 9 pupils at the end of Key Stage 3 are that they should be between Levels 4 and 6. Clearly some pupils may be performing at Levels 7, 8 or at 'exceptional performance' at that age, while a few will be performing at levels 1–3.

If Level 8 seems difficult – it is meant to be. It was originally intended to be equivalent to GCSE Grade B, which is a good result for a 16-year-old. So there is no shame in not having reached that level by age 14 at the end of Year 9. Whatever level you do actually reach, remember that you can always improve with practice.

Achieving levels 1–8 in each skill

AT1: Listening

LEVEL 1

Pupils show understanding of	simple classroom commands short statements questions
Pupils understand speech	spoken clearly face to face from a clear tape recording
Pupils may need support	from repetition from gesture

LEVEL 2

Pupils show understanding of	simple classroom commands and instructions for setting tasks familiar statements familiar questions
Pupils understand speech	in standard German
Pupils may need support	from repetition

LEVEL 3

Pupils show understanding of	short passages messages dialogues
Pupils	identify main points identify likes, dislikes and feelings
Pupils may need support	from some repetition of short sections

LEVEL 4

Pupils show understanding of	longer passages made up of simple sentences
Pupils understand speech	at near normal speed with little interference
Pupils may need support	from repetition of some items

LEVEL 5

Pupils show understanding of	longer passages made up of familiar material past, present and future events
Pupils understand speech	at near normal speed in everyday circumstances with little interference
Pupils note	main points specific details
Pupils may need support	from some repetition

LEVEL 6

Pupils show understanding of	short narratives familiar language in unfamiliar contexts
Pupils understand speech	at normal speed in everyday circumstances with some hesitancy and interference
Pupils note	main points specific details points of view
Pupils may need support	from occasional repetition

AT1: Listening continued

LEVEL 7

Pupils show understanding of	some complex materials some unfamiliar language
Pupils understand speech	at normal speed of brief news items of other TV and radio items
Pupils need little support	

LEVEL 8

Pupils show understanding of	a wide range of spoken materials unfamiliar material
Pupils	draw inferences report attitudes and emotions need little repetition

Exceptional performance

Pupils show understanding of	a wide range of materials, factual and imaginative material with a variety of points of view
Pupils	listen independently organise their own listening

AT2: Reading

LEVEL 1

Pupils show understanding of	single words
Pupils may need support	from visuals

LEVEL 2

Pupils show understanding of	short phrases
Pupils can	match sound to print read aloud familiar words and phrases use books and glossaries to look new words up

LEVEL 3

Pupils show understanding of	printed or word-processed short dialogues and texts
Pupils	identify main points identify likes, dislikes and feelings
Pupils	use bilingual dictionary or glossary
Pupils	choose simple texts to read independently

LEVEL 4

Pupils show understanding of	printed or clearly handwritten short stories and other texts
Pupils	identify details and main points
Pupils sometimes	use context to deduce meaning

LEVEL 5

Pupils show understanding of	longer passages made up of familiar material past, present and future events
Pupils note	main points, specific details and opinions
Pupils	read aloud with some confidence
Pupils	use reference materials with more confidence

LEVEL 6

Pupils show understanding of	a variety of texts familiar language in unfamiliar contexts
Pupils	select their reading independently
Pupils	use context and grammatical understanding to infer meaning

LEVEL 7

Pupils show understanding of	some complex materials some unfamiliar language
Pupils	use language from their reading in their speaking and writing
Pupils	are confident with reference materials

LEVEL 8

Pupils show understanding of	a wide range of written materials unfamiliar material
Pupils	draw inferences report attitudes and emotions
Pupils	read for personal interest and for information

Exceptional performance

Pupils	understand a wide range of imaginative and factual texts can cope with formal and official material can summarise and explain orally and in writing

AT3: Speaking

LEVEL 1

Pupils respond	to single words and short phrases
Pupils' pronunciation	is approximate
Pupils may need support	from visual clues from the teacher's model

LEVEL 2

Pupils respond	in short and simple ways
Pupils	name and describe objects, places and people
Pupils' pronunciation	is approximate but does not obscure meaning

LEVEL 3

Pupils take part in	brief role-plays with visual or written clues
Pupils	briefly express likes, dislikes and feelings
Pupils usually	use memorised phrases
Pupils sometimes	vary memorised phrases

LEVEL 4

Pupils take part in	simple structured conversations
Pupils	adapt phrases by substituting single words
Pupils' pronunciation is usually	accurate with reasonable intonation

LEVEL 5

Pupils take part in	short conversations
Pupils	briefly express likes, dislikes and feelings
Pupils refer to	past, present and future events
Pupils	are easily understood despite some errors

LEVEL 6

Pupils initiate	short conversations including past, present and future events
Pupils	improvise and paraphrase
Pupils	routinely use German for giving and receiving information
Pupils	are easily understood despite some hesitancy

LEVEL 7

Pupils	discuss matters of topical interest
Pupils	give and justify opinions
Pupils	deal with some unprepared situations by adapting language
Pupils' pronunciation	is good, as is their intonation

LEVEL 8

Pupils deal increasingly confidently	with the unpredictable
Pupils discuss	facts, ideas and experiences
Pupils' language and pronunciation	is generally accurate

Exceptional performance

Pupils discuss	a wide range of topics, factual and imaginative
Pupils speak fluently	with few errors
Pupils	vary intonation

AT4: Writing

LEVEL 1

Pupils copy	single words

LEVEL 2

Pupils write and copy	short familiar phrases
Pupils	write classroom signs and instructions
Pupils' spelling is approximate	when writing from memory

LEVEL 3

Pupils write	a couple of sentences on familiar topics
Pupils	briefly express likes, dislikes and feelings
Pupils sometimes	use help when writing
Pupils write	short phrases from memory
Pupils' spelling is readily understandable	when writing from memory

LEVEL 4

Pupils write	short paragraphs using memorised language
Pupils	adapt phrases by substituting single words
Pupils use	dictionaries and glossaries

AT4: Writing continued

LEVEL 5

Pupils write	briefly, expressing likes, dislikes and feelings
Pupils refer to	past, present and future events
Pupils	are generally understood despite some errors
Pupils	apply grammar in new contexts
Pupils	use dictionaries and glossaries to look up unknown words

LEVEL 6

Pupils write	descriptive paragraphs about past, present and future events
Pupils use informal language	in diaries and personal letters
Pupils use formal language	in letters booking accommodation
Pupils	are easily understood despite some errors

LEVEL 7

Pupils	write on real or imaginary subjects
	use paragraphs
	improve, edit and re-draft work, using reference sources as a guide
Pupils make	only occasional errors

LEVEL 8

Pupils discuss	facts, ideas and experiences and points of view
Pupils produce	longer, developed pieces of writing
Pupils' language	is generally accurate
Pupils use	reference materials to extend their linguistic range

Exceptional performance

Pupils write coherently	on a wide range of topics, factual and imaginative
Pupils choose the form of their writing	to suit the task
Pupils write fluently	with few errors

Study skills

This section is intended to point out two aspects of how to learn German.

1. Study skills to help you to make the best possible use of your valuable time in school. These will also be of general use in preparing for other subjects.
2. Hints and tips to improve your performance in the four language skills tested in Key Stage 3 German: Listening, Speaking, Reading and Writing.

   Because performance in German is a skill, it is improved by practice. And any good musician or sporting star will confirm that the best forms of practice contain variety.

Some students find school work difficult. Sometimes this is because the work they are being asked to do really is too difficult for them. However, in our experience this is relatively rare. What is much more likely is that the student has not organised his or her attitude or priorities well in order to get the best out of the learning experience. This is a real shame, as learning a foreign language to a good standard is much easier to do at school than in later life. One reason for this is that in school the teaching has to match a nationally agreed way of learning which is known to work.

Good and poor students

So the foundations of success in German are laid early in your course, not so much by your teacher, as by how you personally approach your work. Let us compare a good student and a poor student, seen from the teacher's point of view.

Good student	Poor student
Is a regular attender.	Is often absent.
Catches up with work after absence – usually without prompting.	Makes no effort to catch up. Needs to be 'chased'.
Always writes notes in lessons.	Lets teacher's explanations wash over him/her. Has lost notebook and/or pen.
Tries his/her best during pairwork.	Chats in English during pairwork.
Sits with a good view of board and teacher.	Sits at the back or in corners.
Asks when stuck.	Gives up if stuck. Claims he/she doesn't understand.
Does homework on time.	Does homework late, or not at all.
Works at a regular time.	Works when he/she feels like it.
Presents work – rough or neat – tidily, with dates, page numbers, titles, etc.	Work is messy.
Writes legibly, with clear Umlauts.	Hard to read. Umlauts could be ink splodges.
Has obviously done a rough draft of homework.	Hands in first draft with altered letters, crossings-out, etc. A pain to mark.

Continued on page 6

continued from page 5

Good student	Poor student
Re-reads corrected homework, notes errors and resolves to act on comments and corrections.	Never looks at anything teacher writes except the mark at the bottom of work.
When no homework is set, finds something extra to do in German.	When no homework is set, does nothing except cheer.
Is basically interested in most aspects of the subject.	Only took German because there was no other option.
Quite enjoys German. Improving.	Hates German. Getting worse at it.

The key to a successful approach is motivation. You know your reasons for taking German. Whatever they are, look for ways to succeed.

Getting organised

Observation suggests that successful students are organised. Many students fail to reach their full potential because they approach the mechanics of studying the wrong way.

Here are some practical ways you can get yourself organised. Parents, too, may find this useful.

1. Have set routines for work. If you have a fixed time or times in the day or week when you do homework, then you don't have to spend time deciding when to do it. Your school, after all, has a set timetable for lessons for that very reason. Set times save you time.
2. Have set times when you do not work. This ensures that you get enough leisure time. 'All work and no play makes Jack a dull boy', says the proverb. Again, you save time on decision-making.
3. Do assignments as they are set. This is particularly important in German, where one piece of work often builds on the previous one, and where you need detailed, early feedback from your teacher to support your learning. By doing work immediately, you also save the time you might spend worrying about how and when to do the work. Do it **NOW**!
4. Have a suitable place for study. The ideal location is free from distractions. Aim for a table or desk free from clutter, with good lighting, and pens, pencils, paper and reference books within reach (so you don't have to keep getting up).
5. Do a reasonable amount of study per week. This might, perhaps, be in the range 30–40 hours weekly, including the 25–27 hours or so spent in lessons in school. Many adults work about that number of hours. You may, of course, work longer if you can do so effectively.
6. Approach topics on the 'before, during and after' principle.
   Before a new topic – read ahead in your textbook to prepare yourself
   During the lesson – take notes or take part, as appropriate.
   After the lesson – go over the notes and the textbook material as soon as possible.

Being organised doesn't take any more time than being disorganised. In fact, it saves time. And most importantly, it makes you a more efficient learner who will certainly do better than your disorganised fellow-students.

Listening

This often seems difficult. Many students feel that 'they speak too fast' or 'I don't understand a word' when they hear German in class. This is especially so when they are listening to a cassette recording.

However, there are hints for making it more enjoyable.

1. Don't be put off easily. You cannot expect to understand every word at first. Concentrate on picking out words you **do** understand. Many teachers will want you to practise comprehension, or to listen out for the familiar among the unfamiliar. This is, after all, what you did when learning English as a baby. You are probably still learning new words in English (perhaps during Science or Technology lessons) and may not understand them the first time you hear them. The same is true of German.
2. Make sure you have read the tasks you are asked to do **before** the cassette is played. It is doubly difficult to read and listen at the same time. This may mean being super-attentive in class. On the same theme, it is important to have paper and pen/pencil handy so that you can react quickly when your teacher does a listening exercise.
3. Develop the ability to make quick notes from what you hear. This may be something you need to be able to do in other subjects, too. You need to know whether your listening notes need to be beautifully neat or not. In most cases, speed is more important than presentation. After the cassette has been played you will have time to work on improving presentation.
4. Work through the listening exercises and the cassette which go with this book. They have been designed to follow a typical programme for Key Stage 3 German. If you find them difficult at first, you could follow the transcript of what is being said in the answers section as the cassette plays.
5. Ask if you can use the audio material which goes with your course at lunch times, etc. You might ask to follow the transcripts which are in the teacher's book. This is especially recommended on wet, cold days! You could even make your own copies!
6. If you have a radio which can receive Short Wave, there is a station which plays a lot of music called *Deutsche Welle* which is on the 49 m band at 6.05. It's a change from your local station....
7. BBC and Channel 4 have schools programmes in German which are aimed at young learners. Current titles include: *Deutsch Direkt, Lern express, Hallo aus Berlin, Globo*.
8. If there are German-speaking visitors in your locality (for example an exchange with older pupils), you will probably find that the young German people are pleased to talk to you in German. Ask them about such things as schools and their family and their journey as a starting point. The teachers accompanying such parties, too, are worth approaching.
9. If your school is fortunate enough to have a German Assistant, be sure to take his/her sessions seriously.

Reading

The obvious starting point is your German textbook. It will have a large amount of material in it, specifically chosen to meet the range of topics needed at Key Stage 3. You will certainly benefit from spending time working through texts you have previously done in class, or those which your teacher has decided to miss out. Use the vocabulary at the back to help you. Make a note of words you don't know without looking up – that is the first step to learning them.

Your school or local library may well have a variety of easy books in German. Some are available with English translations of the same stories. Look out for:

- Asterix
- The Mr Men

European Schoolbooks stock these and a very wide range of other material not easily available elsewhere (European Schoolbooks Ltd, The Runnings, Cheltenham, GL51 9PQ, Tel: 01242 245252).

Your teacher may have back numbers of magazines designed for learners of German, or you could subscribe to them direct. Popular suitable titles include, in order of difficulty:

- *DAS RAD*
- *SCHUSS*

Obtainable from: Mary Glasgow Magazines, Building 1, Kineton Road Industrial Estate, Southam, CV33 ODG, Tel: 01926 815560, Fax: 01926 815563.

Many schools have 'reading schemes' which have graded material suitable for beginners. If they are used as part of your regular lessons, do be sure to make the most of the time.

A little German reading daily will pay dividends. And the more you do, the easier you will find it.

Speaking

We say that someone who knows another language 'speaks' it. And speaking a foreign language is certainly the most useful skill in real life.

Some students feel very shy about speaking in German, especially in front of their classmates. However, you are all in the same boat. And your teacher will also have had the experience of learning to pronounce a foreign language. So it is really important right from the start to make sure that you get all the practice you can in speaking.

If the class repeats a word, phrase, or sentence, make sure that you do it as well as you can. You may not get it right first time. But if you don't take the opportunity to practise when there is plenty of 'cover', you are missing a chance you can't get any other way.

If you are asked questions by the teacher, or asked to repeat individually, do the best you can. With time your accent and intonation will improve. While others are being asked, keep quiet to give them the best chance of hearing the teacher's model.

During pairwork, make *Englisch verboten* a rule with your partner. You can chat in English at virtually any time. But you can only practise conversations in German in your German lesson. So don't waste the opportunity. When you have done a role-play task once, do it again and again until you are really good at it and can do it with virtually no prompts.

Take opportunities to learn short conversations by heart. There are many phrases in the vocabulary topics of this book. They have been selected for their usefulness. Be sure you know as many as possible.

Finally, make sure that you practise reading aloud as well as silently. If you can do it well – and you will improve with practice – you will help your ability to understand German, too.

Writing

At Key Stage 3, writing German is worth 25 per cent of the marks. However you will probably spend more than a quarter of your German-learning time writing because it is a useful tool for fixing new material.

At the simplest level you will be asked to copy words, perhaps into a notebook. This is not actually as easy as it sounds, as the spelling rules for German are not the same as English ones. So develop the habit of copying correctly and checking that you have done so.

In the authors' experience, it is noticeable that students who write a date and title for each piece of work, number it clearly and rule off neatly afterwards are better at German than those students who do none of these things. Be sure your work is tidy.

It is important, too, that you have:

- capital letters at the beginning of nouns
- Umlauts where they are needed
- no Umlauts on *e* or *i*
- *ß* and *ss* correct
- *sch* always with a *c*
- *e* and *i* always the correct way round.

Check each of these points for each piece of work.

Avoid the use of ditto marks. Even if an exercise is repetitive, the act of repeating a word or spelling is a learning tool.

Remember, too, that writing set for homework will usually have something to do with the lesson during which it was set. Indeed, there may well be similar material in your textbook from which you can get clues.

When work is handed back, the best students will want to write a fair version of any sentence which contains an error. This really doesn't take long, and makes sure that you have really looked hard at your mistake. If you are lucky, your teacher will have shown you how to correct the work.

Using a dictionary

Knowing how to use a dictionary is a really useful language-learning skill. Dictionaries are not expensive, and you may well find one useful. At GCSE dictionaries will be available to you during some parts of the exam from 1998 onwards. At this stage in your German-learning career you will probably not need to spend more than £10 on a dictionary; many good ones are available for much less. In the English–German, German-English section of this book you should find all the words you might reasonably be expected to know at Key Stage 3. However, it is worth knowing how to look words up and what to look for among the many abbreviations dictionaries contain.

Useful commonly-used abbreviations include:

acc	Accusative
adj/a	adjective
art	article
coll	colloquial
comp	comparative
conj	conjunction
dat	Dative
def art	definite article
esp	especially
f	feminine
gen	Genitive
impers	impersonal
indef art	indefinite article
inf	infinitive
insep	inseparable
irr/irreg	irregular
m	masculine
n	noun
nt	neuter

nom	Nominative
pl	plural
pp	past participle
poss	possessive
prep	preposition
pres	present
pron	pronoun
reg	regular
s.	see
sep	separable
sing/sg	singular
sl	slang
refl	reflexive
vi	intransitive verb
vr	reflexive verb
vt	transitive verb

When you look up a **German** word, you may find a number of possible English translations, listed with the most common first. You will then need to apply common sense to work out which meaning is most likely in the context.

You may find that a word is not listed. This may mean that it is a past participle. Check if it begins with *ge-* or with one of the inseparable prefixes such as *be-*, *emp-*, *ent-* or *ver-*, or if it ends in *-en*. Then see if you can find it in the strong verb table.

When you look up an **English** word to find the German equivalent, follow some or all of these steps:

1. Make sure you know if you want a noun, adjective, verb, etc.
2. After finding the German word, look that up in the German–English section. You should get the word you started with, or one which means the same in the same context.
3. If you are offered a German word which looks very like the English one be careful: sometimes Germans use words borrowed from other languages for much more specialised meanings than they originally had.

phonetic script · *transitive verb* · *slang* · *gender of noun* · *noun (substantive)* · *different meanings* · *examples of idioms*

di-vulge [daɪ'vʌldʒ] *vt. Geheimnis etc.* enthüllen. preisgeben
dix-ie[1] ['dɪksɪ] *s. sl.* **1.** Kochgeschirr *n;* **2.** , 'Gulaschka,none' *f.*
Dix-ie ['dɪksɪ] → ***Dixieland;***
D-mark ['di:ma:k] *s.* Deutsche Mark. (f)
do [du:;dʊ] **I** *v/t.* [*irr.*] **1.** tun, machen: ***what can I ~ for you?*** womit kann ich dienen?; ***what does he ~ for a living?*** womit verdient er sein Brot?; ~ ***right*** recht tun; → ***done*** 1; **2.** tan, ausführen, sich beschäftigen mit. verrichten. vollbringen. erledigen. ***business*** Geschäfte machen; ~ ***one's duty*** s–e Pflicht tun; ~ **German** Deutsch lernen; ~ ***Shakespeare*** Shakespeare durchnehmen *od.* behandeln; ***my work is done*** m–e Arbeit ist getan *od.* fertig; ~ ***60 miles per hour*** 60 Meilen die Stunde fahren; ***It can't be done*** es geht nicht; ~ ***one's best*** sein Bestes tun, sich alle Mühe geben; ~ ***better*** **a)** (et.) Besseres tun *od.* leisten, b) sich verbessern; → ***done;*** **3.** herstellen, anfertigen: ~ ***a translation*** e–e Übersetzung machen; ~ ***a portrait*** ein Porträt malen; **4. *j-m et.*** tun, zufügen, erweisen, gewähren: ~ ***s.o. harm*** j-m schaden; ~ ***s.o. an injustice*** j-m ein Unrecht zufügen, j-m unrecht tun; ***these pills ~ me (no) good*** diese Pillen elfen mir (nicht); **5.** bewirken, erreichen: ***I did it*** ich habe es geschafft;

phonetic script · *optional e in Genitive singular* · *neuter noun* · *adjective* · *adverb* · *plural* · *feminine noun* · *genitive singular* · *medical* · *masculine noun* · *range of translation contexts*

tuberkulös [-ku'lø:s] *adj.* tuberculous, tubercular; ~ **ose** [-ku'lø:zə] *f* (-; -n) tuberculosis; ~ **osenverdächtig** *adj.* suspected of tuberculosis.
Tuch [tu:x] *n* (-[e]s; -e) cloth; fabric; (-[e]s, -er) shawl; scarf, neckerchief, duster; rag; *das wirkt auf ihn wie ein rotes* ~ that's a red rag to him; ~ **ballen** *m* bale of cloth; **~fabrik** *f* cloth factory; **~handel** *m* cloth trade, drapery; ~ **handler** *m* (wool(l)en) draper; ~ **handlung** *f*, ~ **laden** *m* draper's shop; ~ **macher** *m* cloth-maker.
tüchtig ['tyçtiç] **I.** *adj.* able, fit; (cap)able, competent, qualified; efficient; clever, skil(l)ful; proficient, experienced; excellent; good, considerable; powerful, strong; thorough; ~ *in* (*dat.*) good at, proficient (*or* well versed) in; *~er Esser* hearty eater; **II.** *adv.* vigorously, with a vengeance, like mad, thoroughly, well; *coilog* really *~arbeiten* work hard; ~ ***essen*** eat heartily; ~ *verprügeln* give a sound thrashing; ~ **keit** *f* (-) ability, efficiency; cleverness; proficiency; excellence *sportliche* ~ sporting prowess.
Tuch...: ~ **waren** *f/pl.* cloths, drapery *sg.*; ~ **zeichen** *aer. n* ground panel.
Tücke ['tykə] *f* (-; -n) malice, spite; perfidy, insidiousness; trick (*of fate, memory*); **oisch** *adj.* malicious, spiteful; insidious (*a. disease* = malignant); vicious (*a. animal, blow*); treacherous (*a. ice, road, etc.*).
Tugend ['tu:gənt] *f* (-; *-en*) virtue; *es sich zur ~ machen, zu inf.* make a virtue of *doing a th.*, → *Not*; **-haft** *adj.* virtuous; **-reich** *adj.* most virtuous; **-sam** *adj.* virtuous; chaste.
Tüll [tyl] *m* (-s; -e) tulle; **~e** ['tylə] *f* (-; *-n*) socket; spout; ~ **spitzen** *f/pl.* net lace.
Tulpe ['tulpə] *f* (-; *-n*) *bot.* tulip; ~ **nzwiebel** *f* tulipbulb.
Tumor ['tu:mɔr] *med. m* (-s; *-moren*) tumour.
Tumult [tu'mult] *m* (-;[e]s; -e) tumult; riot, uproar; row.
tun [tu:n] *v/t.* (*irr., h.*) do; perform, make; → *machen*; put (*to school, into the bag, etc.*); make (*remark, request*); take (*jump, oath*); nichts ~ do nothing; so ~, *als ob* make *or* act as if, pretend to *inf.*; würdig, *etc.*, ~ assume an air of dignity, *etc.*; ~ *Sie ganz, als ob Sie zu Hause wären* make yourself quite at home!; *was hat er dir getan?* what has he done to you?; *damit ist es nicht getan* that's not enough; *es tut nichts* it doesn't matter, never mind; *es tut sich (et)was* something is going on (*or* is in the wind *or* is brewing); *es tut nichts zur Sache* it is of no significance, that is neither here nor there; *das tut man nicht!* that is not done!; *tu doch nicht so!* don't make a fuss!, *was ist zu ~?* what is to be done?;

Learning vocabulary

This is one of the chores of learning a foreign language. It is best to have a regular time of day (or perhaps two occasions in the day) when you sit down and spend 10–15 minutes learning vocabulary. And the sooner you start, the better – so start today!

This really requires somewhere private, or at least somewhere you won't be disturbed. So your room, somewhere quiet in school at break or lunch-time, or even on public transport would be suitable. What is *not* suitable is trying to do it while talking to or listening to someone else, or watching *Neighbours*. Don't kid yourself you are working when you're not.

As well as having a good place to do it, it's as well to be methodical. Work through the vocabulary topics, changing them daily. Don't try to learn too many words at once. Try to relate them to a situation, rather than just working through an alphabetical list. It's more interesting to learn, say, everything to do with changing money than just 40 words which happen to begin with the same letter.

Begin your sessions with a written test on what you did last time. This could be half German–English and half English–German. Don't cheat, but check your test afterwards with the textbook. If you did well, reward yourself with a treat of some kind. Keep a record of how you have done so you can check your progress.

Rather than simply learning vocabulary in your head from a list, it is better to be **doing** something. The best method is to write out each word or phrase two or three times. (It doesn't matter if you can't read it afterwards. Go for speed!) Make sure of Umlauts. Include the gender for nouns. If you haven't anywhere to write, you can still test yourself using a piece of card or paper cut or folded as shown.

First, cover the English column on your list and see if you can say what the German words mean. Then turn the blind over and see if you can say what the German should

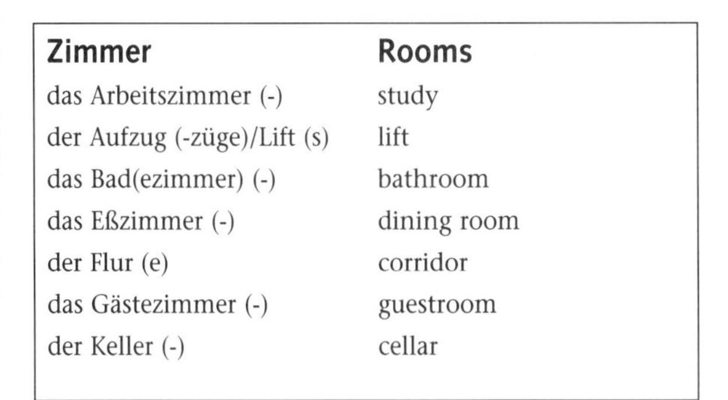

Zimmer	Rooms
das Arbeitszimmer (-)	study
der Aufzug (-züge)/Lift (s)	lift
das Bad(ezimmer) (-)	bathroom
das Eßzimmer (-)	dining room
der Flur (e)	corridor
das Gästezimmer (-)	guestroom
der Keller (-)	cellar

1 Vocabulary to be learned.

2 Cut out shape **blind** as shown here.

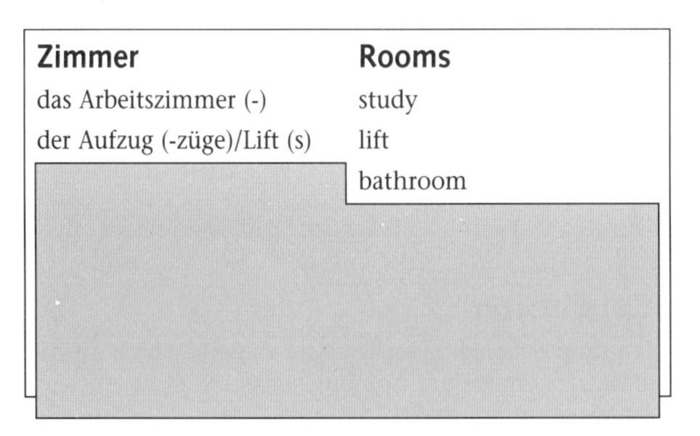

3 Place blind over vocabulary list so that the next English word is shown. See if you can say what the German should be.

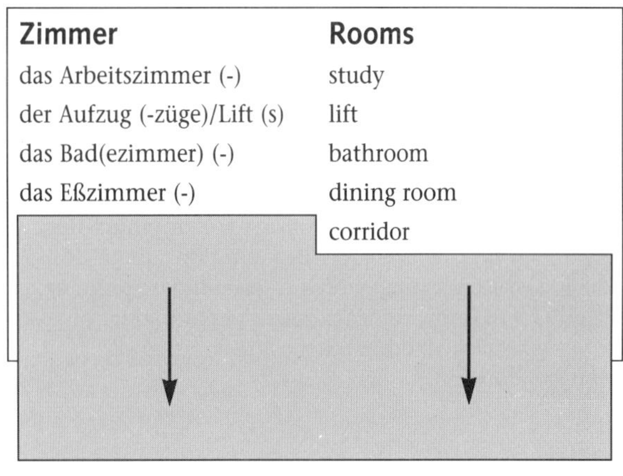

4 Move the blind down to the next English word. See if you were right with the last German word and try the next one, and so on.

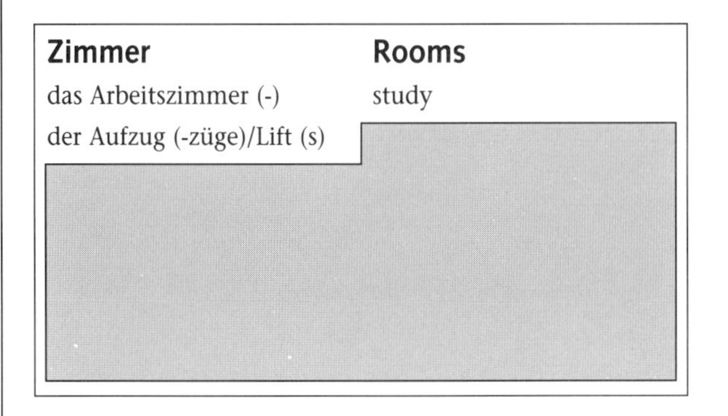

5 Then turn the blind around so that the next German word is shown, and test yourself to see if you know what the English should be.

be (including gender, as before). You can also use the blind to give yourself a written test. You immediately find out if you were right as you move it down to the next word. **No peeping!**

Students often like to learn vocabulary with a friend. This is fine as a way of learning what the English version of German words is, and for checking gender and past participles. However, unless someone is writing, then spelling accuracy is not likely to be improved.

Revising for tests and exams

As we have suggested, being organised produces better results. This applies, of course, to revision as well as normal study. Here are some tips about efficient revision.

The most difficult thing about revision is overcoming boredom. By definition, you have seen things you are revising before, so you need to find ways of making up for the lack of novelty.

Many students revise ineffectively because they merely read through notes and chapters in the textbook and let the information wash over them. This is almost always a waste of time, certainly after the first half-hour or so. The key is to **do** something. Activity is an aid to concentration. In a skill-based subject like German, you will improve your performance by practice.

Try some or all of the following techniques:

1. Write notes. When reading, say, grammar rules again, make yourself skeleton notes which are sufficiently detailed to jog your memory. Some students do this on small pieces of card (index cards or chopped up·pieces of cereal packet) which they carry about with them and consult in odd moments. The same goes for vocabulary. Writing a word down with its gender and meaning will help to fix it in your memory. Another hint is to write down a phrase which contains the word and its gender. When reading texts, make a note of every word you had to look up. As time goes on, you will have to look up fewer and fewer.
2. Work with a friend. This can relieve the boredom. Pick a friend who is about the same standard as you are. Working with someone a lot better can be good for their ego, but not for yours. Similarly, working with someone a lot weaker doesn't teach you anything new. Testing each other is a good idea. But don't forget to include written testing, which is the ultimate proof of whether you know things. Because of the danger of being side-tracked, don't rely on this method of revision alone.
3. Set yourself tests. While learning, make a note of things you found hard, and test yourself later – at the end of your session, then the following day, then the following week. You have to be honest with yourself about how you got on! Keep a chart of your marks as a rough guide to progress.
4. List the topics which you need to revise. Then tick off the ones you have done. Do NOT tick off ones you have missed out! The more you have dealt with, the better you will feel.
5. Set realistic targets. Don't try to do too much in one session – you'll end up frustrated and become more and more depressed. Far better to learn, say, ten words and succeed than to try to learn 56 and fail miserably.
6. Reward yourself. If you have done a reasonable stint of revision, or done well in a test, give yourself a treat – a sweet, or a coffee break, or the chance to watch a favourite soap opera. Having something to look forward to is a great incentive.
7. Don't go too long without a break – 45–50 minutes is probably the longest session most people can concentrate for without a break – even if it's only to stretch your legs for five minutes.
8. Give yourself variety. Vary what you look at – revise different skills in German. Also, vary the subjects you do in any one session – three spells of 45–50 minutes on three different subjects will be more productive than a three-hour 'slog' on one area.
9. Don't be fooled by other students. During the examination season, some fellow-students will be loudly proclaiming either that they 'never do any revision' or that they are 'up till 2 a.m. every evening working'. Ignore them. They are being hysterical, and may well not be telling the truth anyway. What matters to you is not how much or how little revision your friends do, but how much **you** do.
10. Most important of all, don't kid yourself that you are working when you aren't. You can't revise at all while watching TV, chatting to friends, washing your hair or eating a meal. So don't even attempt it. Instead, use these activities to reward yourself after a revision session.

Directed revision pays off. Revise early, and revise often!

Conclusion

Learning a foreign language is an activitiy which can give a great deal of pleasure. You now know the most efficient way to go about it. *Viel Spaß!*

Section two

Grammar

Grammar is often seen as boring or irrelevant. It isn't, as it allows you to generate and understand sentences which you have not come across before, and helps your reading and listening comprehension. Find out how it works, and you have the key to much more German than you could ever hope to learn by heart.

Not all students are taught using formal grammar in their English or German lessons nowadays. There is nothing to be frightened of in the use of grammatical terms. After all, a mechanic wouldn't attempt to describe what a spanner is every time he wanted to have one passed to him. He just uses the technical term, which is 'spanner'. These grammatical terms are the technical 'jargon' of language-learning, which give you access to the patterns of German and other languages to enable you to learn them more quickly.

We have defined the grammatical terms simply at the start of each entry in this section. The entries are arranged alphabetically. The box below will help you to see at a glance the entries presented and the pages on which you can find them.

ADJECTIVES

An **adjective** is a word which describes a noun or pronoun. It gives information about such things as colour, type, character, etc.

1 Adjectives not followed by a noun

Adjectives which stand alone – usually after *sein, werden* and *scheinen* – do not have an adjective ending.

Example:

Die Frau ist groß
The woman is tall

Point to watch: Students also learning French sometimes make adjectives standing alone agree, as they do in French. This is **wrong**.

2 Adjectives followed by a noun

Adjectives in German which are immediately followed by a noun alter their spelling to **agree** with, or 'match' the noun they describe, depending on the article or determiner which comes before them and the case of the noun.

Adjectives followed by a noun take an ending (= agree with the noun) which depends on four factors:

1. the determiner (article) or lack of one in front of the adjective
2. the gender of the noun – masculine, feminine, or neuter
3. whether the noun is singular or plural
4. the case of the noun

If there is more than one adjective before the noun, each one has the appropriate ending. Of course, once you have worked out the ending, all the others in front of the same noun will have the same ending.

There are three sets of adjective endings, depending on which determiner is used:

(a) After *der/die/das*,etc; *dieser; jener; jeder; welcher; solcher; mancher* and *alle* (which is, of course, plural) the adjective has the following endings:

Masculine singular

Nominative:	der groß**e** Mann
Accusative:	den groß**en** Mann
Genitive:	des groß**en** Mann**es**
Dative:	dem groß**en** Mann**(e)**

Feminine singular

Nominative:	die groß**e** Frau
Accusative:	die groß**e** Frau
Genitive:	der groß**en** Frau
Dative:	der groß**en** Frau

Neuter singular

Nominative:	das groß**e** Kind
Accusative:	das groß**e** Kind
Genitive:	des groß**en** Kind**es**
Dative:	dem groß**en** Kind**(e)**

Plural, all genders

Nominative:	die groß**en** Leute
Accusative:	die groß**en** Leute
Genitive:	der groß**en** Leute
Dative:	den groß**en** Leute**n**

Points to watch: All Genitive and Dative singular and all plural endings are *-en.*

Add *-es* or *-s* to masculine and neuter nouns in the Genitive singular.

You can add *-e* to single-syllable masculine and neuter nouns in the Dative singular in formal writing.

Add *-n* to nouns which do not already have one in the Dative plural of all genders (but not to those whose plural ends in *-s*). See ***Nouns***.

(b) After *ein/eine/ein*, etc, *kein, mein, dein, sein, ihr* (= her), *sein, unser, euer, Ihr* and *ihr* (= their) the adjective has the following endings:

Masculine singular

Nominative:	ein groß**er** Mann
Accusative:	einen groß**en** Mann
Genitive:	eines groß**en** Mann**es**
Dative:	einem groß**en** Mann**e**

Feminine singular

Nominative:	eine groß**e** Frau
Accusative:	eine groß**e** Frau
Genitive:	einer groß**en** Frau
Dative:	einer groß**en** Frau

Neuter singular

Nominative:	ein groß**es** Kind
Accusative:	ein groß**es** Kind
Genitive:	eines groß**en** Kind**es**
Dative:	einem groß**en** Kind**(e)**

Plural, all genders

Nominative:	keine groß**en** Leute
Accusative:	keine groß**en** Leute
Genitive:	keiner groß**en** Leute
Dative:	keinen groß**en** Leute**n**

Points to watch: *Ein* itself, for reasons of logic, doesn't have a plural. If 'a' is plural (i.e. 'some'), it follows the plural pattern for the table below.

(c) Adjectives which are used alone before the noun have the following endings:

Masculine singular

Nominative:	kalt**er** Kaffee
Accusative:	kalt**en** Kaffee
Genitive:	kalt**en** Kaffee**s**
Dative:	kalt**em** Kaffee

Feminine singular

Nominative:	kalt**e** Milch
Accusative:	kalt**e** Milch
Genitive:	kalt**er** Milch
Dative:	kalt**er** Milch

Neuter singular

Nominative:	kalt**es** Wasser
Accusative:	kalt**es** Wasser
Genitive:	kalt**en** Wasser**s**
Dative:	kalt**em** Wasser

Plural, all genders

(also after *viele, mehrere* and *einige, ein paar* and numbers)

Nominative:	kalt**e** Getränke
Accusative:	kalt**e** Getränke
Genitive:	kalt**er** Getränke
Dative:	kalt**en** Getränke**n**

Point to watch: In the Genitive singular for masculine and neuter, the ending is *-en*, which might just seem a little unexpected.

(d) Some adjectives do not take an ending:

(i) those formed from town names, which always end in *-er*

Example:

im **Hamburger** Hafen
in Hamburg harbour

(ii) a few words (including some colours) borrowed from other languages

These include:

beige, lila, orange, rosa

3 Adjectives used as nouns

All adjectives and participles can be used as nouns in German. They are then written with a capital letter.

Example:

der Deutsche /die Deutsche – *the German*

Adjective-type nouns take the same endings as they would if they were followed by a noun of the appropriate gender.

Examples:

Masculine singular	*Feminine singular*	*Plural*
der Erwachsen**e**	die Erwachsen**e**	die Erwachsen**en**
den Erwachsen**en**	die Erwachsen**e**	die Erwachsen**en**
des Erwachsen**en**	der Erwachsen**en**	der Erwachsen**en**
dem Erwachsen**en**	der Erwachsen**e**	den Erwachsen**en**

Masculine singular	*Feminine singular*	*Plural*
ein Erwachsen**er**	eine Erwachsen**e**	Erwachsen**e**
einen Erwachsen**en**	eine Erwachsen**e**	Erwachsen**e**
eines Erwachsen**en**	einer Erwachsen**en**	Erwachsen**er**
einem Erwachsen**en**	einer Erwachsen**en**	Erwachsen**en**

4 A large number of adjectives are linked to a noun by means of a preposition. *Auf* and *über* always take the Accusative in this circumstance.

Some common adjective + preposition combinations are:

böse mit + Dat	*cross with*
einverstanden mit + Dat	*agreeable to*
fertig mit + Dat	*finished with*
typisch für + Acc	*typical of*

5 Something and nothing

After *etwas* (something) and *nichts* (nothing) the adjective is written with a capital letter and has *-es* added.

Examples:

etwas Gutes
something good
nichts Schlechtes
nothing bad

Note the idiom:

alles Gute!
best wishes/all the best!

Adverbs

An adverb is a word which describes a verb (which 'adds information to a verb'). It gives information about **how** something is done. Adverbs can also be used to add to adjectives or other adverbs.

In German, adverbs are quite easy. Most adjectives can be used as adverbs without any change.

Example:

Ingrid spielt Beethoven **schön**
Ingrid plays Beethoven nicely

There are different types of adverbs: of place, direction, manner and degree, as well as question-words.

1 Adverbs of place

(a) *Hier, dort* and *da* translate as 'here', 'there' and 'there'.

Example:

Hier im Bild ist meine Mutter, **dort** ist meine Schwester und **da** ist mein Hund
***Here** is my mother in the picture, **there** is my sister and **there** is my dog*

(b) **Unten** and **oben** translate as 'downstairs' and 'upstairs'.

Example:

Unten ist er nicht. Er ist also **nach oben** gegangen
*He isn't **downstairs**. He has therefore gone **upstairs***

2 Adverbs of direction

Many adverbs and prepositions can have *hin-* or *her-* added onto the front of them. As a rule of thumb, the *hin-* prefix is used for motion away from the speaker, with the *her-* prefix being used for motion towards the speaker. *Hin* and *her* are also used as a separable prefix to show movement.

Examples:

Er ist aus Schottland hier**her** gekommen
He came here from Scotland
Wo**hin** gehst du?
Where are you going (to)?
Gib das Buch **her**!
Hand over the book

3 Adverbs of manner

(a) Quite a lot of adverbs of manner do not occur as adjectives.

Examples:

hoffentlich	*hopefully*
leider	*unfortunately*
sonst	*otherwise*
vielleicht	*perhaps*

(b) Many adverbs are formed by adding **-erweise** to adjectives. They convey the additional idea that the speaker didn't expect matters to be as they were.

Examples:

glücklich**erweise**	*fortunately*
komisch**erweise**	*funnily*
normal**erweise**	*normally*

4 Adverbs of degree

Many students seem to know only two or three of these, namely *sehr, etwas* and *ganz*. This is a shame, as very little effort is needed to make your writing seem much more sophisticated. The following are worth learning:

besonders	*especially*
etwas	*rather*
fast	*almost*
genug	*enough*
kaum	*hardly*
relativ	*relatively*
völlig	*completely*
ziemlich	*fairly*
zu	*too*

5 Question words

These include:

wann	*when*
bis wann	*until when, by when*
seit wann	*how long for*
wie lange	*how long*
wie oft	*how often*
wo	*where*
wohin	*where to*
woher	*where from*
wie	*how*
warum	*why*
wozu	*what ... for*

ARTICLES

There are two kinds of articles, **definite** (the) and **indefinite** (a, an or some).

1 The definite article

(a) This translates as 'the' and follows this pattern:

	Masculine	Feminine	Neuter	Plural
Nominative:	der	die	das	die
Accusative:	den	die	das	die
Genitive:	des	der	des	der
Dative:	dem	der	dem	den

In the Genitive singular, for masculine and neuter only, an *-s* is added to the end of the nouns.

In the Dative plural an *-n* is added to the end of the noun unless it has an *-n* or an *-s* already.

(b) Other words which follow this pattern are:

dieser	*this*
jener	*that*
jeder	*each, every*
mancher	*many a*
solcher	*such a*
welcher	*which*

(c) The definite article is usually used just as you would use it in English. However, it is also used in some circumstances when it would not be used in English:

(i) before names of countries which are feminine or plural

Examples:

in der Schweiz	*in Switzerland*
in den Niederlanden	*in the Netherlands*

(ii) before nouns to do with time or mealtimes

Examples:

im September	*in September*
am Sonntag	*on Sunday*
im Sommer	*in summer*
nach dem Abendessen	*after supper/dinner*

(iii) with prices

Example:

2 Mark das Pfund	*2 marks a pound*

(iv) in certain set phrases

Examples:

mit dem Rad	*by bicycle*
in der Schule	*in school*
ins Bett	*to bed*
in die Stadt	*to town*

2 The indefinite article

(a) This translates as 'a' and follows this pattern (*keine* illustrates the plural of this pattern):

Examples:

	Masculine	***Feminine***	***Neuter***	***Plural***
Nominative:	ein	eine	ein	keine
Accusative:	einen	eine	ein	keine
Genitive:	eines	einer	eines	keiner
Dative:	einem	einer	einem	keinen

In the Genitive singular, for masculine and neuter only, an *-s* is added to the end of the noun.

In the Dative plural an *-n* is added to the end of the noun unless it has an *-n* or an -s already.

(b) Other words which follow this pattern are:

mein	*my*
dein	*your*
sein	*his*
ihr	*her*
sein	*its*
unser	*our*
euer	*your*
Ihr	*your*
ihr	*their*
kein	*no, not a*

3 Leaving out the article

Sometimes the article is not used in German where it would probably be used in English.

(a) Before nouns of nationality or profession

Examples:

Frau Krautschneider ist Lehrerin
Frau Krautschneider is a teacher
Sie ist Schottin
She is a Scot

(b) In some common expressions

Examples:

Andrew hat Kopfschmerzen	*Andrew has a headache*
ein Zimmer mit Dusche	*a room with a shower*
Ich habe Durst	*I am thirsty*
Es ist schade	*It's a pity*

CASES AND THEIR USES

German has four **cases**: Nominative, Accusative, Genitive and Dative, which alter the article before the noun, the agreement of the adjective, and occasionally the spelling of the noun. They each are used in specific circumstances.

The four cases in German are one of the principal areas of difficulty for English-speaking learners. But the rules for their use are relatively clear.

1 The Nominative case

The Nominative case is used:

(*a*) for the subject of a verb

Examples:

Ich bin intelligent
I am intelligent
Heute schmeckt **der Fisch** gut
The fish is good today

(*b*) after the verbs *sein, werden, bleiben, heißen* and *scheinen*

Examples:

Jürgen Klinsmann ist **mein Lieblingsfußballspieler**
Jürgen Klinsmann is my favourite footballer
Er scheint **ein wunderbarer Mensch**
He seems a wonderful person
Ich werde **Astronaut**
I am going to be an astronaut
Er bleibt **ein Idiot**
He remains an idiot
Ich heiße **Herr Reich**
My name is Mr Reich

2 The Accusative case

The Accusative is used:

(*a*) for the direct object (the thing that suffers the action of the verb) of active, transitive verbs

Example :

Ich habe **den Mann** gesehen
I saw the man

(*b*) after certain prepositions. Some of them may take the Dative in certain circumstances – see ***Prepositions***.

(*c*) for expressions of definite time

Examples:

nächste Woche
next week
Es hat **den ganzen Monat** geregnet
It rained all month
Donnerstag, **den 19. August 1999**
Thursday 19th August 1999

(*d*) for greetings and wishes

Examples:

Guten Morgen!
Good morning!
Guten Tag!
Good afternoon!, Good day, Hello!
Guten Abend!
Good evening!
Herzlichen Glückwunsch!
Congratulations!
Gute Besserung!
Get well soon!

3 The Genitive case

Note that *von* + Dative is used increasingly in preference to the Genitive.

Example:

Ich bin die Deutschlehrerin **von dieser Klasse**
I am this class's German teacher

(*a*) The Genitive is used in the following phrases:

Das Auto **meiner Eltern**
My parents' car
Das Dach **des Hauses**
The roof of the house
Frau Krechels Mercedes
(Note that there is **no** apostrophe in German)
Frau Krechel's Mercedes
eines schönen Sommertages
one fine summer's day
Einmal **erster Klasse** nach Berlin, bitte
A single first-class ticket to Berlin, please

(*b*) It is also used after certain prepositions – see ***Prepositions***.

4 The Dative case

The Dative is used:

(*a*) for the indirect object of a verb

Example:

Er gab **dem Mann** das Buch
He gave the book ***to the man***

Point to watch: Be careful not to miss the fact that the Dative is needed as it is not always immediately obvious from the English. The example above could be translated as: *He gave the man the book.*

(*b*) after certain prepositions. Some of them may take the Accusative in certain circumstances – see ***Prepositions***.

(*c*) after certain verbs which always take the Dative.The most frequent are *danken, folgen* and *helfen.*

Examples:

Kann ich **dir** helfen?
Can I help you?
Er folgt **seiner Schwester**
He is following his sister
Wir danken **dir** für die Party
We thank you for the party

(*d*) to express advantage or disadvantage for someone

Examples:

Sie kaufte **ihm** eine Banane
She bought a banana ***for him****/She bought* ***him*** *a banana*
Man hat **mir** meinen Wagen gestohlen
They stole my car from me

(*e*) to show possession, especially with parts of the body or with clothing

Examples:

Ich putze **mir** die Zähne
I clean my teeth
Ich ziehe **mir** den grünen Pullover an
I put on my green pullover

Note when it is **not** used:

Ich putzte mein Zimmer
I cleaned my room

(*f*) in certain impersonal constructions expressing sensations

Examples:

Mir ist warm
I am hot
Mir ist kalt
I am cold
Mir ist übel
I feel sick
Mir ist schwindelig
I am dizzy

Comparisons

1 Comparative and superlative

Adverbs and adjectives can be used in **comparative** (e.g. bigger, faster, more beautiful) and **superlative** (e.g. biggest, fastest, most beautiful) forms.

In German, the principle is much the same:

Examples:

schnell	*fast*
schnell**er**	*faster*
der/die/das schnell**ste***	*the fastest*
am schnellsten	*in the fastest manner*

* takes the same endings as any other adjective

2 Common exceptions

(a) A number of common adjectives form comparatives in the usual way, but add an Umlaut.

Examples:

arm	*poor*
ärmer	*poorer*
der ärmste	*the poorest*

These include:

alt	*old*
dumm	*stupid*
groß	*large*
jung	*young*
kalt	*cold*
krank	*ill*
kurz	*short*
lang	*long*
oft	*frequent*
schwach	*weak*
stark	*strong*
warm	*warm*

(b) Some adjectives and adverbs have very irregular comparative and superlative forms.

gern	lieber	am liebsten	*willingly*
gut	besser	der beste	*good*
hoch	höher	der höchste	*high*
nah	näher	der nächste	*near*
viel	mehr	der meiste	*much*

3 Comparative sentence patterns

Note the ways of expressing positive and negative comparisons.

Examples:

Ich bin aber intelligenter **als** du
But I am more intelligent than you
Ich bin **nicht so** intelligent **wie** Albert Einstein
I am not as intelligent as Albert Einstein

4 Superlative sentence patterns

Examples:

Ich spiele am besten Tennis
I play tennis best of all
Ich bin der beste (Tennisspieler)
I am the best (tennis player)

Conditions

See ***Verbs***

Conjunctions

Conjunctions are words which join two clauses, such as 'and', 'that', 'because'. In German, conjunctions are divided into two groups, known as **co-ordinating** conjunctions and **subordinating** conjunctions.

1 Co-ordinating conjunctions

These join two clauses which could otherwise stand as two German sentences in their own right without any alteration. Five of them are common; three of them are very common.

Co-ordinating conjunctions have no effect on the word order. They do **not** send the verb to the end of the clause, and they do **not** count in the '1–2–3' rule (see ***Word order***).

Most of them can also link single words or phrases in lists.

The 'famous five' co-ordinating conjunctions are:

und	*and*
aber	*but*
oder	*or*
sondern	*but* (**after** *not)*
denn	*for*

Example:

Er wohnt in Hamburg **aber** er arbeitet in Bremen
He lives in Hamburg but he works in Bremen

2 Subordinating conjunctions

These are conjunctions which add a subordinate clause (i.e. one which could not stand on its own as a German sentence without alteration) onto a main clause.

They send the verb to the end of the clause. If the verb is an auxiliary it usually comes after the past participle. A subordinate clause always has a comma before the conjunction and after the verb, unless that position is the beginning or end of a sentence. The comma has nothing to do with taking breath, as in English, but merely marks the fact that it is a subordinate clause.

Examples:

Wenn Liverpool gewinnt, bin ich glücklich
Ich bin glücklich, **wenn** Liverpool gewinnt
I am happy if Liverpool wins
Ich bin unglücklich, **weil** Liverpool verloren hat
I am unhappy because Liverpool lost

The most common subordinating conjunctions are:

als	*when (single occasion in the past)*
bis	*until*
nachdem	*after (he had done that)*
obwohl	*although*
weil	*because*
wenn	*if, when, whenever*
wie	*how*

Days, months, dates and times

1 Days

All of these are masculine.

Montag	*Monday*
Dienstag	*Tuesday*
Mittwoch	*Wednesday*

Donnerstag	*Thursday*
Freitag	*Friday*
Samstag	*Saturday*
Sonnabend	*Saturday*
Sonntag	*Sunday*

Note the following usage:

Am Sonntag *on Sunday*

Point to watch: Be wary of missing the correct meaning of *Sonnabend*.

2 Months

All of these are masculine.

Januar	*January*
Februar	*February*
März	*March*
April	*April*
Mai	*May*
Juni	*June*
Juli	*July*
August	*August*
September	*September*
Oktober	*October*
November	*November*
Dezember	*December*

Note the following usage:

im März *in March*

Juni and *Juli* are often pronounced *Juno* and *Julei* on the telephone to reduce confusion.

3 Dates

(a) The major public holidays are:

Neujahr	*New Year's Day*
zu Ostern	*at Easter*
Pfingsten	*Whitsun*
(NB usually the week **after** the British Spring Bank Holiday)	
der Tag der deutschen Einheit	*German Unification Day* (3.10)
der Heilige Abend	*Christmas Eve*
der erste Weihnachtstag	*Christmas Day*
Silvester	*New Year's Eve*

(b) Asking about and giving the date

(i) The following patterns are used in speech:

Der wievielte ist heute? Heute ist der 1. September 1998
What is the date today? It's the 1st September 1998
Am wievielten beginnt das Schuljahr? Am 8. September
When does the school year begin? On the 8th September

(ii) In letters, the date is written on the top right of the page.

Example:

Fulda, den 1.10.98

(c) The year is given as follows:

Either: 1998
Or: im Jahre 1998

Point to watch: Beware of using the English structure of 'in 1998' in German – it's wrong!

4 Times of the clock

There are two ways of telling the time, the everyday way and using the 24-hour clock.

(a) The everyday way

1.00	Es ist ein Uhr
3.00	Es ist drei Uhr
4.05	Es ist fünf (Minuten) nach vier
4.15	Es ist Viertel nach vier
4.30	Es ist halb fünf (beware!!)
4.45	Es ist Viertel vor fünf
4.55	Es ist fünf (Minuten) vor fünf
12.00	Es ist Mittag/Mitternacht

(b) The 24-hour clock

1.00	Es ist ein Uhr
3.00	Es ist drei Uhr
14.05	Es ist vierzehn Uhr fünf
14.15	Es ist vierzehn Uhr fünfzehn
14.30	Es ist vierzehn Uhr dreißig
14.45	Es ist vierzehn Uhr fünfundvierzig
14.55	Es ist vierzehn Uhr fünfundfünfzig
12.00	Es ist zwölf Uhr
00.01	Es ist null Uhr eins

5 Definite and indefinite time

(a) Definite time (which could be found on a calendar if necessary) is shown by using the Accusative case:

(i) to show duration

Example:

Ich war **den ganzen Tag** im Auto
I was in the car all day

(ii) to show a specific time

Examples:

letzte Woche *last week*
nächsten Monat *next month*

(b) Indefinite time (which would be impossible to find exactly on a calendar) is shown by using the Genitive case

Example:

eines schönen Sommertages *one fine summer's day*

(c) Some times are expressed by adverbs, generally ending in *-s*

Examples:

morgens *in the mornings*
werktags *on working days*

Definite Article

See ***Articles***

Future Tense

See ***Verbs***

Imperfect Tense

See ***Verbs***

Indefinite Article

See ***Articles***

INFINITIVES

See ***Verbs***

INSEPARABLE VERBS

See ***Verbs***

IRREGULAR VERBS

See ***Verbs***

MODAL VERBS

See ***Verbs***

NOUNS

Nouns are the names of people, places and things.

1 Gender

All German nouns are grammatically masculine, feminine, or neuter. This presents a real problem for English-speaking learners in knowing which is which. The only real solution is to note the gender and the plural form when you first meet a word. The gender is decided either by the meaning of the word, or by the last few letters. The following guidelines may help.

(a) **Masculine by meaning**

(i) male persons and animals

Examples:

der Lehrer *male teacher*
der Kater *tomcat*

See also (d): ***Unhelpful genders of human beings.***

(ii) seasons, months and days of the week

Examples:

der Frühling *spring*
der Januar *January*
der Montag *Monday*

(iii) points of the compass, winds, most sorts of weather

Examples:

der Norden *the North*
der Wind *wind*
der Frost *frost*

Exceptions:

das Eis *ice*
das Gewitter *thunderstorm*
das Wetter *weather*

(iv) alcoholic drinks

Examples:

der Rotwein *red wine*
der Schnaps *schnaps, spirits*

Exception:

das Bier *beer*

(v) makes of car

Examples:

der Audi *Audi*
der BMW *BMW (car)*
der Mercedes *Mercedes*
der VW *Volkswagen*

(b) **Feminine by meaning**

(i) female persons and animals

Examples:

die Mutter *mother*
die Katze *female cat*

See also (d) ***Unhelpful genders of human beings.***

(ii) aeroplanes, motorcycles and ships

Examples:

die Boeing *Boeing*
die BMW *BMW (motorcycle)*
die Titanic *the Titanic*

Exception:

der Airbus *Airbus*

(iii) names of numerals

Examples:

eine Eins *a one*
die Million *million*
die Milliarde *billion*

(c) **Neuter by meaning**

(i) young persons and animals

Examples:

das Baby *baby*
das Kind *child*
das Kalb *calf*

See also (d) ***Unhelpful genders of human beings.***

(ii) physical units

Examples:

das Atom *atom*
das Pfund *pound*

(iii) letters of the alphabet

Examples:

ein großes A *a big A*
ein scharfes S *ß*

(iv) infinitives of verbs used as nouns

Examples:

das Essen *food*
das Singen *singing*

(v) colours and languages

Examples:

das Rot *red*
das Deutsch *German*

(vi) 'international' words

Examples:

das Café *café*
das Radio *radio*
das Taxi *taxi*
das Telefon *telephone*

(d) **Unhelpful genders of names of human beings**

Examples:

das Fräulein *young lady, 'miss'*
das Mädchen *girl*
das Mitglied *member*
die Person *person*

(e) Masculine by form

Nouns with the following endings are masculine:

-ant (en)	der Passant	*passer-by*
-ig (e)	der Honig	*honey*
-or (en)	der Motor	*motor*
-ast (e)	der Kontrast	*contrast*
-ismus (no pl)	der Kommunismus	*communism*
-us (-en)	der Rhythmus	*rhythm*
-ich (e)	der Teppich	*carpet*
-ling (e)	der Liebling	*darling*

(f) **Feminine by form**
Nouns with the following endings are feminine:

-a (-en)	die Villa	*villa*
-anz (no pl)	die Eleganz	*elegance*
-ei (en)	die Metzgerei	*butcher's shop*
-enz (en)	die Tendenz	*tendency*
-heit (en)	die Freiheit	*freedom*
-ie (n)	die Technologie	*technology*
-ik (en)	die Musik	*music*
-in (nen)	die Lehrerin	*female teacher*
-keit (en)	die Freundlichkeit	*friendliness*
-schaft (en)	die Freundschaft	*friendship*
-sion (en)	die Explosion	*explosion*
-tion (en)	die Situation	*situation*
-tät (en)	die Aktivität	*activity*
-ung (en)	die Landung	*landing*

Exceptions:

der Atlantik	*Atlantic*
der Katholik	*Catholic*
der Papagei	*parrot*
der Pazifik	*Pacific*
das Sofa	*sofa*

(g) **Neuter by form**
Nouns with the following endings are neuter:

-chen (-)	das Mädchen	*girl*
-il (e)	das Krokodil	*crocodile*
-lein	das Fräulein	*young woman, miss*
	das Büchlein	*small book*
-ment (s)	das Apartement	*apartment*
-tel	das Zehntel	*tenth*

(h) **Compound words**
These take the gender and the plurals of the last part.

Examples:

der Stundenplan	*timetable (school)*
der Fahrplan	*timetable (public transport)*
das Rathaus	*town hall*
die Straßenbahnhaltestelle	*tram stop*
das Hallenbad	*indoor pool*

(i) Recent English loan words are mainly masculine, with neuter being the next most common.

Examples:

Masculine:	der Compact Disc	*CD*
	der Computer	*computer*
	der Hit	*hit song*
	der Job	*(part-time) job*
	der Streß	*stress*
	der Trend	*trend*
Neuter:	das Make-up	*make-up*
	das Mountainbike	*mountain bike*
	das Poster	*poster*
Feminine:	die Bar	*bar*
	die Party	*party (not political)*

(j) Some nouns have two or even three genders with different meanings.

Some of the common ones are listed here:

der Band (-¨e) *volume, book*	das Band (-¨er) *ribbon*
	die Band (s) *pop group*
der Pony (no pl) *fringe*	das Pony (s) *pony*
der See (n) *lake*	die See (no pl) *sea*

2 Plural forms

Many attempts have been made to explain how German plural forms work. Here is a simplified version listing rules which always apply, and making some recommendations about what to do if you have to guess. Sadly, the only way to be sure of plural forms is to note them with each new word. Examples have not been given here – the safest way is to check individual words.

In vocabularies, words are usually listed in the plural as follows:

(-)	no change in the plural
(¨)	add an Umlaut over the main vowel
(-e)	add an *-e*
(¨e)	add an Umlaut over the main vowel and an *-e*
(-en)	add *-en*
(¨er)	add an Umlaut over the main vowel and *-er*
(-er)	add *-er*
(-n)	add an *-n*
(s)	add an *-s*
(no plural)	there is no plural

The 'main vowel' is usually the last one.

(a) **Masculine nouns**
There are no foolproof rules concerning the plurals of masculine nouns. The following guidelines might be helpful.

(i) The great majority of masculine nouns form their plural with *-e* or *-¨e*. The Umlaut is added in about half the cases.
(ii) Virtually all masculine nouns ending in *-el*, *-en* or *-er* form their plural with no change.

(b) **Feminine nouns**

(i) Over 90 per cent of feminine nouns have the plural *-en* or *-n*.
(ii) Only *die Mutter* and *die Tochter* have the plural (¨).
(iii) **No** feminine nouns have plurals (-) or (-¨er).

(c) **Neuter nouns**

(i) About 75 per cent of neuter nouns have the plural *-e*.
(ii) Most of the remainder have the plural *-¨er*.

(d) **Loan words from English or French**
Most of these have the plural *-s*.

Spelling changes in nouns

German nouns have slight spelling changes in the following cases:

(a) In the Dative plural in all genders, an *-n* is added if one is not already present, or unless the plural ends in *-s*.

Example:

mit den Schüler**n** *with the school pupils*

(b) In the Genitive singular, an *-s* is added to masculine and neuter nouns or, if single syllable words, often *-es*.

Example:

wegen des schlechten Wetter**s**
because of the bad weather
trotz des Wind**es**
despite the wind

NUMBERS

There are two sorts of numbers, **cardinal numbers** which are counting numbers (ordinary numbers) and **ordinal numbers** which say which order things come in.

1 Cardinal numbers

These are as follows:

0	null
1	eins
2	zwei
3	drei
4	vier
5	fünf
6	sechs
7	sieben
8	acht
9	neun
10	zehn
11	elf
12	zwölf
13	dreizehn
14	vierzehn
15	fünfzehn
16	sechzehn (NB spelling)
17	siebzehn (NB spelling)
18	achtzehn
19	neunzehn
20	zwanzig
21	einundzwanzig
22	zweiundzwanzig etc.
30	dreißig (NB spelling)
40	vierzig
50	fünfzig
60	sechzig (NB spelling)
70	siebzig (NB spelling)
80	achtzig
90	neunzig
100	hundert
101	hunderteins
102	hundertzwei
131	hunderteinunddreißig
200	zweihundert
999	neunhundertneunundneunzig
1000	tausend
1002	tausendzwei
1100	tausendeinhundert/elfhundert/ eintausendeinhundert
654 321	sechshundertvierundfünfzigtausend-dreihunderteinundzwanzig
1 000 000	eine Million (NB spaces every 3 digits, no commas)
42 500 400	zweiundvierzig Millionen fünfhunderttausendvierhundert (NB new word after Millionen)
1 000 000 000	eine Milliarde
2 000 000 000	zwei Milliarden

(a) In practice, complex numbers are never written out in full. Use figures instead.

(b) *Zwo* is used instead of *zwei* where there is any danger of confusion. It is common in public announcements, and on the telephone.

(c) Longer numbers – such as telephone numbers after dialling codes - are often written and read in pairs

Example:

02364/65 54 07 is pronounced as: Null zwo drei sechs vier, fünfundsechzig vierundfünfzig null sieben

(d) Years are usually stated in hundreds:

Example:

1999 = neunzehnhundertneunundneunzig
2000 = zweitausend
2001 = zweitausendeins

(e) Cardinal numbers can be used as nouns, particularly when discussing school grades.

Example:

Ich habe eine Sechs in Englisch
I have a six in English

(f) 7 is usually written with a cross, to distinguish it from 1.

2 Ordinal numbers

(a) Virtually all ordinal numbers are formed as follows:
(i) 2nd, 4th, 6th and 8th–19th add *-te* to the cardinal number

Examples:

der vier**te**
der sechzehn**te**

Exceptions are:

1st	der erste
3rd	der dritte
7th	der siebte

(ii) 20th and upwards add *-ste* to the cardinal number

Examples:

20th	der zwanzig**ste**
23rd	der dreiundzwanzig**ste**
100th	der hundert**ste**
1000th	der tausend**ste**
millionth	der million**ste**

However, if the number above 20 ends with part of the compound derived from a number less than 20, the endings in (i) apply.

Examples:

der hundert**erste**
der tausend**dritte**
der zweihundert**sechzehnte**

(b) The use of ordinal numbers is straightforward.
(i) They are normally used as adjectives, and take the usual endings.
(ii) In writing, they are usually written as an abbreviation which must have a full stop.

Examples:

am 1.10. (pronounced: am ersten zehnten)
on the first of the tenth
der 5. Versuch
the 5th attempt

3 Fractions

(a) Most fractions – except 'half' – are formed by adding *-el* to the ordinal.

Examples:

ein Drittel (-)	*a third*
ein Viertel (-)	*a quarter*
ein Zehntel (-)	*a tenth*

(b) 'Half' can be either the noun *die Hälfte* or the adjective *halb*.
(i) *Die Hälfte* is used as follows:

Example:

Ich habe nur die Hälfte gelesen
I have only read half of it

(ii) *Halb* is used like this:

Example:

Ich aß eine halbe Banane
I ate half a banana

(iii) One and a half is anderthalb or eineinhalb.
The principle of *eineinhalb* continues with *zweieinhalb, dreieinhalb*, etc.

(c) Decimals are written with a comma and not a point in German.

Examples:

Ich habe eine Durchschnittsnote von 3,2
(pronounced drei Komma zwei)
I have an average mark of 3·2

PAST TENSE

See ***Verbs: Perfect and Imperfect***

PERFECT TENSE

See ***Verbs***

PLUPERFECT TENSE

See ***Verbs***

PLURALS

See ***Nouns***

PREPOSITIONS

Prepositions show a relationship between one noun and another, often of position, which accounts for the name.

In German prepositions are followed by different cases. For the majority of prepositions, it is merely a matter of knowing what they 'take'. For example, *mit* 'takes' the Dative. However, some common prepositions take either Accusative or Dative according to their meaning.

(a) Prepositions which always take the Accusative

bis	*as far as; until*
durch	*through; throughout*
für	*for*
gegen	*against; towards; about*
ohne	*without*
um	*at + clock times; round; about; concerning*
pro	*per*

Example:

für meine Mutter *for my mother*
durch die Stadt *through the town*

(b) Prepositions which always take the Dative

aus	*out of; made of*
bei	*by; at; at the house of*
gegenüber*	*opposite; towards*
mit	*with, by*
nach	*to; towards; after + time*
seit	*since; for (uses a more recent tense than in English)*
von	*from; of*
zu	*to; for; as; at; towards; at + price*

* may come before or after the noun

Point to watch: *aus* and *zu* both look as though they might take the Accusative because they imply motion (see below). They **never** take the Accusative.

Point to watch: In the Dative plural, most nouns add an *-n* if they do not already have one. It's easy to forget it.

(c) Prepositions which take either Accusative **or** Dative

Ten common prepositions take either Accusative or Dative. Two basic rules apply to most instances.

(i) If the preposition expresses position, then the Dative is used. If it expresses motion towards, the Accusative is used.

A useful pair of mnemonic sentences is:
D<u>a</u>tive is st<u>a</u>tion<u>a</u>ry or movement <u>a</u>t
Acc<u>u</u>sative is m<u>o</u>vement t<u>o</u>

Examples:

Ich gehe **in die** Stadt (in + Accusative – motion)
I go into town
Ich wohne **in der** Stadt (in + Dative – position)
I live in the town

Verbs of arriving, appearing and disappearing are usually used in conjunction with a Dative.

Example:

Ich bin am Busbahnhof angekommen
I arrived at the bus station

(ii) If the preposition expresses a figurative sense (something which it would be impossible to make a model of, or something which is neither position nor motion) it often takes the Accusative.

Example:

Er weiß viel **über die Stadt**
He knows a lot about the town

Although the above rules can apply to most of the Accusative/Dative prepositions, in practice the majority of them are most frequently found in the cases shown in brackets. It is really *an, auf, in* and *über* which most often require careful thought.

an	*on (the side of); at; of*
auf	*on (top of); at; in*
entlang* *(usually + Acc)*	*along*
hinter *(usually + Dat)*	*behind*
in	*in; inside*
neben *(usually + Dat)*	*next to*
über	*over; about; more than*
unter *(usually + Dat)*	*under; below; among*
vor *(usually + Dat)*	*in front of; before*
zwischen *(usually + Dat)*	*between*

*follows the noun

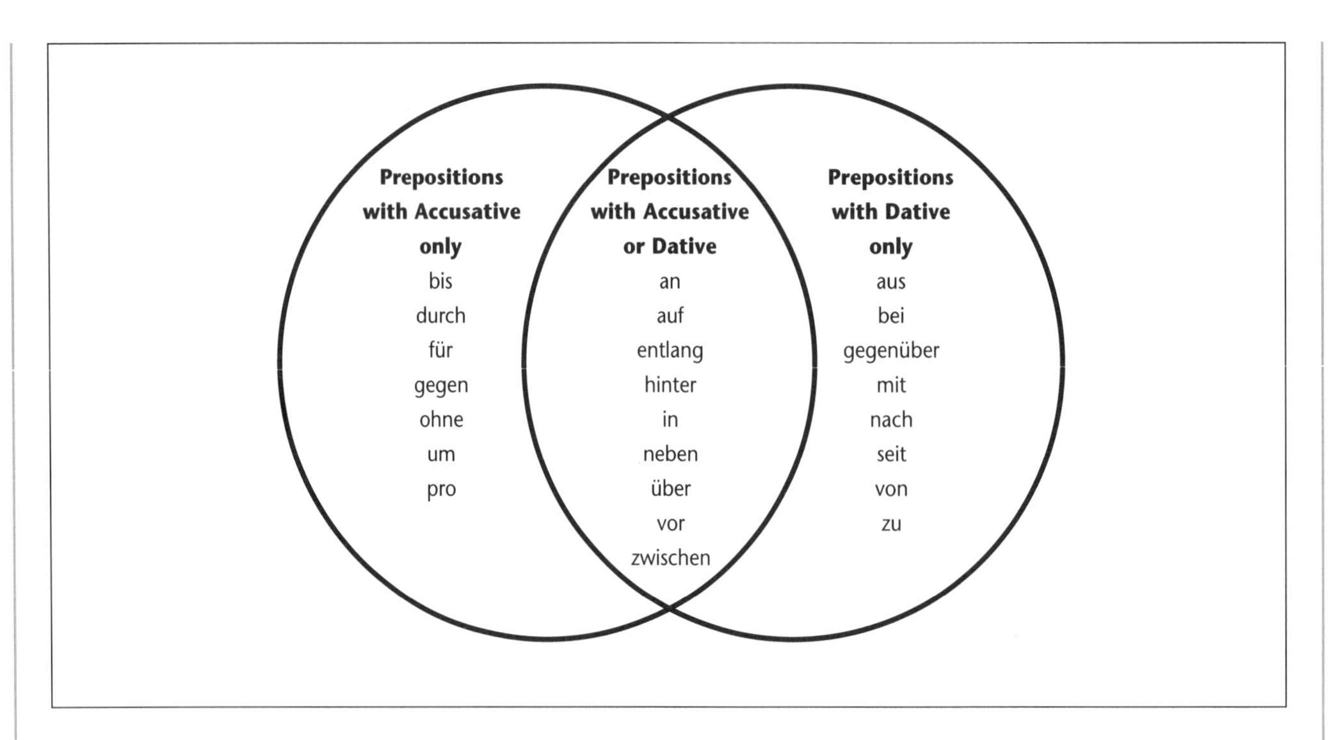

PRESENT TENSE

See ***Verbs***

PRONOUNS

Pronouns stand in the place of a noun, and are used to avoid repeating a noun or a proper name. The case is determined by the pronoun's function in the sentence.

1 Personal pronouns

Nominative		Accusative		Dative	
ich	*I*	mich	*me*	mir	*to me*
du	*you (singular, familiar)*	dich	*you*	dir	*to you*
Sie	*you (singular, formal)*	Sie	*you*	Ihnen	*to you*
er	*he or it*	ihn	*him or it*	ihm	*to him or it*
sie	*she or it*	sie	*her or it*	ihr	*to her or it*
es	*it*	es	*it*	ihm	*to it*
man	*one*	einen	*one*	einem	*to one*
wir	*we*	uns	*us*	uns	*to us*
ihr	*you (plural, familiar)*	euch	*you*	euch	*to you*
Sie	*you (plural, formal)*	Sie	*you*	Ihnen	*to you*
sie	*they*	sie	*them*	ihnen	*to them*

2 Reflexive pronouns

(*a*) The Accusative reflexive pronouns are as in the example below:

ich wasche mich	*I wash myself*
du wäschst dich	*you wash yourself*
Sie waschen sich	*you wash yourself*
er wäscht sich	*he washes himself*
sie wäscht sich	*she washes herself*
es wäscht sich	*it washes itself*
man wäscht sich	*one washes oneself*
wir waschen uns	*we wash ourselves*
ihr wascht euch	*you wash yourselves*
Sie waschen sich	*you wash yourselves*
sie waschen sich	*they wash themselves*

(b) The Dative reflexive pronouns are as follows:

ich wasche **mir** die Haare	*I wash my hair*
du wäschst **dir** die Haare	*you wash your hair*
Sie waschen **sich** die Haare	*you wash your hair*
er wäscht **sich** die Haare	*he washes his hair*
sie wäscht **sich** die Haare	*she washes her hair*
es wäscht **sich** die Haare	*it washes its hair*
man wäscht **sich** die Haare	*one washes one's hair*
wir waschen **uns** die Haare	*we wash our hair*
ihr wascht **euch** die Haare	*you wash your hair*
Sie waschen **sich** die Haare	*you wash your hair*
sie waschen **sich** die Haare	*they wash their hair*

Point to watch: Note that these are only different from the Accusative reflexive pronouns after *ich* and *du.*

3 Du and Sie, ihr and Sie

Germans are very anxious to use the correct form for 'you' for reasons of politeness.

The following are the main rules concerning choice of 'you':

(a) *Du* is used:
   (i) for speaking to a child (up to about 15) and an animal
   (ii) between children, students, relatives and close friends.

(b) *Ihr* is used for speaking to a group of two or more people of which at least some would be addressed as *'du'.* Most commonly it would be used by a teacher to a class or a mother to her children.

(c) *Sie* is used in all other cases, and particularly between adult strangers.

4 Er, sie and es

(a) It should be remembered that 'it' may refer to a masculine or feminine noun in German, and that *er* or *sie, ihn* or *sie, ihm* or *ihr* may be required. *Er* and *sie* do not refer solely to biological gender.

Example:

Hier ist die Banane. Ich habe **sie** gestern gekauft
*Here is the banana. I bought **it** yesterday*

(b) There is sometimes conflict between biological and grammatical gender, particularly with *das Mädchen* and *das Fräulein.* They can be referred to as either *es* or *sie.*

(c) After prepositions, special rules apply. *Es* is never used after a preposition. Instead the preposition has the prefix *da(r)* attached to give *darauf, danach,* etc.

Example:

Hier ist endlich der Bus. Wir haben lang genug darauf gewartet
Here is the bus at last. We've been waiting for it long enough

5 Relative pronouns

Relative pronouns introduce a relative clause, which tells you something more about another part of the sentence.

Relative pronouns correspond to 'who, whom, whose, which or that' in English. It is important to know the test for whether 'that' is in fact a relative pronoun or best translated by *daß.* If 'who' or 'which' can be substituted for 'that' without changing the meaning, it is a relative pronoun. If the substitution cannot be made without generating nonsense, use *daß.*

Examples:

This is the house **that** Jack built
Substitute *which*:
This is the house **which** Jack built
Therefore the original 'that' is a relative pronoun.

I think **that** you should go
Substitute *which*:
I think **which** you should go
This is nonsense, and 'that' should be *daß.*

A further complication is that the relative pronoun is often missed out in English, in such sentences as: This is the book I am reading at the moment. This **never** happens in German.

(a) The form of the relative pronoun

	Masculine	***Feminine***	***Neuter***	***Plural***	***Meaning***
Nominative:	der	die	das	die	*who, which, that*

(b) Agreement

The relative pronoun agrees with the noun to which it refers in number (singular or plural) and gender (masculine, feminine or neuter), but **not** in case. The case of the relative pronoun is determined by its function in the relative clause. However at Key Stage 3, it will usually only be found in the nominative.

Example:

Ich bin eine Lehrerin, **die** oft nach Deutschland fährt
*I am a teacher **who/that** often travels to Germany*

(c) After *alles, nichts, etwas,* the relative pronoun is always *was.*

Example:

Alles, was ich habe, ist mein Hund
All I have left is my dog

(d) Note the idiomatic use of *das, was*:

Example:

Ich habe nur **das, was** ich mitgebracht habe
I only have what I have brought with me

Point to watch: In German the punctuation rules require that relative pronouns have a comma in front of them. This is unlike many English relative clauses

6 Interrogative pronouns

Interrogative pronouns are **question words** which change according to case. The case is determined by their function in the sentence. Their English equivalents mostly begin with 'wh'.

(a) 'Who' declines as follows:

Nominative:	wer	*who*
Accusative:	wen	*who(m)*
Genitive:	wessen	*whose*
Dative:	wem	*to whom*

Examples:

Nominative:	**Wer** hat das gemacht?	***Who*** *did that?*
Accusative:	**Wen** hast du gesehen?	***Who(m)*** *did you see?*

Genitive:	**Wessen** Fahrrad ist das?	***Whose** bike is that?*
Dative:	**Wem** gibt sie das Buch?	***Who** does she give the book **to**?*

7 Demonstrative pronouns

These agree with the noun to which they refer, and decline like this:

	Masculine	***Feminine***	***Neuter***	***Plural***
Nominative:	dies**er**	dies**e**	dies**es**	dies**e**
Accusative:	dies**en**	dies**e**	dies**es**	dies**e**
Genitive:	dies**es**	dies**er**	dies**es**	dies**er**
Dative:	dies**em**	dies**er**	dies**em**	dies**en**

Following this pattern are:

dieser *this*
jener *that*
solcher *such a*

Examples:

Dieser Mann ist immer freundlich
***This** man is always friendly*
Möchtest du **diesen** Rock?
*Would you like **this** skirt?*
Nein, **jenes** Kleid gefällt mir besser
*No, I prefer **that** dress*
Ich habe noch nie einen **solchen** Hund gesehen
*I have never seen **such a** dog*

PUNCTUATION

See ***Spelling and punctuation***

REFLEXIVE VERBS

See ***Verbs***

REGULAR VERBS

See ***Verbs***

SEPARABLE VERBS

See ***Verbs***

SIMPLE PAST TENSE

See ***Verbs: Imperfect***

SPELLING AND PUNCTUATION

1 Spelling

(a) The Umlaut
A common mistake is 'Umlaut blindness', assuming that they have no significance or are mere decoration. In fact they convey important subtleties of meaning. So an Umlaut mistake is a serious one.

(b) ss or ß?
Learn whether a word is spelt with *ss* or *ß* when you first come across it.

(c) The alphabet
(approximate English sound equivalents are given here)

a	ah
b	bay
c	say
d	day
e	eh?
f	eff
g	gay
h	ha!
i	ee
j	yacht
k	car
l	ell
m	emm
n	enn
o	oh!
p	pay
q	coo
r	air
s	ess
t	tay
u	ooo!
v	fow (like foul)
w	vay
x	ekks
y	upsilon
z	tsed
ß	ess tsed or scharfes ess
ä	ah Umlaut
ö	oh Umlaut
ü	ooo Umlaut

2 Punctuation

English punctuation often has a good deal to do with where to breathe, or in separating sense groups. In German there are strict rules which have little to do with either breathing or sense groups.

(a) Capital letters are used:
(i) at the start of sentences
(ii) for all nouns, wherever they occur
(iii) for the 'polite' personal pronouns except *sich* and their related possessives (*Sie, Ihnen, Ihr*)
(iv) in letters, for the 'familiar' personal pronouns and their related possessives (*Du, Dir, Dein, Ihr, Euch, Euer*)
(v) in titles of books, films, etc.

They are not used for nationalities which are adjectives or adverbs.

Example:

Ein **britisches** Schiff hatte ein Poster auf **deutsch**
A British ship had a poster in German

(b) Commas are used:
(i) in lists, but not just before the *und*

Example:

Er hatte zwei Hunde, eine Katze und einen Hamster
He had two dogs, a cat and a hamster

(iii) where there are two main clauses linked by a co-ordinating conjunction

Example:

Mein Vater wohnt in Hamburg, und meine Mutter wohnt in Berlin
My father lives in Hamburg and my mother lives in Berlin

(iii) where there is a subordinate clause

Examples:

Ich wohnte in Flensburg, als ich zweiundzwanzig war
I lived in Flensburg when I was twenty-two
Als ich zweiundzwanzig war, wohnte ich in Flensburg
When I was twenty-two I lived in Flensburg

The second example shows the word order sequence verb – comma – verb which is very common.

(c) Exclamation marks are used:
(i) after commands (even whispered ones!)

Example:

Setzen Sie sich**!**
Sit down

(i) after interjections

Example:

Ach**!** Verdammt**!**
Oh! Bother!

(iii) Often after the opening of a letter

Example:

Lieber Herr Braun**!**
Wie geht es Ihnen?
Dear Mr Brown,
How are you?

This usage is rapidly being replaced by the following punctuation
Lieber Herr Braun**,**
wie geht es Ihnen?

Note the lower case *w* on *wie*.

(d) Direct speech is written as follows:

Ich sagte: „Wie heißt du?"

Tenses

See ***Verbs***

Verbs

A verb is a 'doing word'. It gives information about what is done, who or what does it, and when the action happened, happens, or will happen.

1 Persons

The form of all verbs in German (as in English) is determined in part by the 'subject'. This is generally the person or thing which performs the action of the verb. (But see ***Passive***, below.)

The subject can be one of three possible 'persons'.

The **first** person is used when the speaker performs the action of the verb, e.g. *ich, wir*.

The **second** person is used when the person being spoken to performs the action of the verb, e.g. *du, Sie, ihr*.

The **third** person is used when neither the speaker nor the person being spoken to is performing the action of the verb, i.e. the action is being performed by someone else, e.g. *er, sie* (=she), *es, man, sie* (=they), *Fritz, die Kinder*.

2 Weak, strong and mixed verbs

In German there are two sorts (or conjugations) of verbs, regular (i.e. those which follow a rule) and irregular (i.e. those which do not always follow a rule and which therefore have to be learnt).

Regular verbs are often referred to as **weak** verbs in German, perhaps because they do not have a 'mind of their own'.

Irregular German verbs are often referred to as **strong** verbs, perhaps because they are strong-minded.

In any dictionary most of the verbs are weak. However, in any lengthy piece of German there is probably a majority of strong verbs, which often express common actions.

Some dictionaries and grammars refer to '**mixed verbs**'. These are verbs which are irregular, but behave in some ways like weak verbs. Nevertheless, they are still irregular, and need to be specially mastered.

3 Tenses

These are the different forms of verbs which describe mainly when something takes place, took place, will take place, etc.

There are some differences in the use of tenses between German and English, but future tenses refer to the future, present tenses refer to now or to regular events which are still going on, and past tenses such as the perfect refer to events which have already taken place. The conditional is used for conditions, actual or possible.

4 Forms of German verbs

When a verb is listed in a dictionary, it is given in the infinitive.

Example:

spielen *to play*
fahren *to travel*

In describing how tenses are formed, the infinitive will normally be the starting point.

5 Present tense

Example:

Ich **spiele** Tennis, ich **fahre** nach Hause

It is used with actions which are happening now
actions which habitually happen
actions which will happen in the future.

So *ich spiele Tennis* can mean:
I am playing tennis (implied: now)
I play tennis (implied: regularly)
I am playing tennis (implied: at some point in the future)

Note that the addition of *'nicht'* creates an extra set of meanings in English. So *ich spiele nicht Tennis* can mean:
I do not play tennis
as well as: I am not playing tennis

This is how the present tense is formed:

(a) Weak verbs
Remove *-en* from the infinitive and add the following endings:

1st person: ich	-e	wir	-en
2nd person: du	-st	ihr	-t
		Sie	-en
3rd person: er/sie/es/man	-t	sie	-en

Example:

ich spiel**e**	wir spiel**en**
du spiel**st**	ihr spiel**t**
	Sie spiel**en**
er/sie/es/man spiel**t**	sie spiel**en**

(b) Strong verbs
Check the strong verb table (see p. 35). If there is no

vowel change listed under '3rd person present', then the verb behaves in the same way as weak verbs. If there is a vowel change, it affects the *du* and *er/sie/es/man* forms only.

The endings are the same as for weak verbs.

Example with a vowel change:

ich fahre	wir fahren
du f**ä**hrst	ihr fahrt
	Sie fahren
er/sie/es/man f**ä**hrt	sie fahren

Example without a vowel change:

ich gehe	wir gehen
du gehst	ihr geht
	Sie gehen
er/sie/es/man geht	sie gehen

Verbs (strong or weak) whose infinitives end in *-den, -ten, -chnen, -cknen, -dnen, -fnen, -gnen,* or *-tnen* take the endings *-est* and *-et* in the second and third person singular in order to make pronunciation easier.

Examples:

er arbeit**et**, du öffn**est**, sie trockn**et**

Points to watch:

(a) Remember that the present tense renders not only 'I play' but also 'I am playing' and 'I do (not) play'. Resist the temptation to translate the separate parts of 'I am playing' into German – it's wrong!

(b) The present tense is quite often used to give a future meaning:

Example:

Ich fahre morgen nach München
I am going to Munich tomorrow

6 Future tense

Example:

Ich **werde** Tennis **spielen**, ich **werde** nach Hause **fahren**

It is used to show actions which will happen in the future, often some time from now.

So *ich werde Tennis spielen* can mean:
I shall (will) play tennis
I shall (will) be playing tennis

The future is formed in the same way for both weak and strong verbs.

The verb is in two parts, the present tense of *werden* and, at the end of the clause or sentence, the infinitive of the verb in question.

(a) Weak verbs

Example:

spielen

ich **werde** Tennis **spielen**	wir **werden** Tennis **spielen**
du **wirst** Tennis **spielen**	ihr **werdet** Tennis **spielen**
	Sie **werden** Tennis **spielen**
er/sie/es/man **wird** Tennis **spielen**	sie **werden** Tennis **spielen**

(b) Strong verbs

Example:

fahren

ich **werde** nach Berlin **fahren**	wir **werden** nach Berlin **fahren**
du **wirst** nach Berlin **fahren**	ihr **werdet** nach Berlin **fahren**
	Sie **werden** nach Berlin **fahren**
er/sie/es/man **wird** nach Berlin **fahren**	sie **werden** nach Berlin **fahren**

Point to watch: *werden* itself follows the same pattern.

7 Perfect tense

Example:

Ich **habe** Tennis **gespielt**, ich **bin** nach Hause **gefahren**

The perfect is the most frequent past tense in speech and informal writing such as letters, to talk about actions which are over. It translates a variety of English past tenses.

So *ich habe Tennis gespielt* can mean:
I played tennis
I was playing tennis
I have played tennis
I have been playing tennis

This tense is formed in two parts, with the present tense of *haben* or *sein* and, at the end of the clause or sentence, the past participle of the verb in question. Irregular verbs have irregular past participles.

The present tense of *haben* or *sein* is called the 'auxiliary' verb. Perhaps the German term *Hilfsverb* is clearer!

(a) Weak verbs
The vast majority of weak verbs, including reflexives, form the perfect tense using *haben* as the auxiliary. See **(*c*) Haben *or* sein?**

The past participle is usually formed by adding *ge-* to the infinitive, removing the *-en* and replacing it with *-t*.

Example:

gespiel**t**

If the infinitive ends in *-den, -ten, -chnen, -cknen, -dnen, -fnen, -gnen,* or *-tnen,* then an extra *-e* is added before the final *-t* to make the whole thing pronounceable.

Example:

gearbeit**e**t

However, if the infinitive ends in *-ieren,* then no *ge-* is added.

Example:

repariert
The same applies if the verb starts with a prefix which does not separate. These prefixes are: *be-, ent-, emp-, er-, ge-, miß-, ver-* and *zer-*.

Example:

verkauft

If the verb has a prefix which **does** separate, it is tacked onto the past participle ahead of the *ge-*.

Example:

abgeholt

Once the past participle has been formed, the only change in the verb is to the auxiliary.

Example:

ich **habe** ... **gespielt**	wir **haben** ... **gespielt**
du **hast** ... **gespielt**	ihr **habt** ... **gespielt**
	Sie **haben** ... **gespielt**
er/sie/es/man **hat** ... **gespielt**	sie **haben** ... **gespielt**

(b) Strong and 'mixed'
While many of these verbs form the perfect tense with *haben* as the auxiliary, a good number of them use *sein* as the auxiliary. See **(c) Haben *or* sein?**

Because these verbs are irregular, the only safe way to discover the past participle is to look the verb up in a verb table. If the verb you are looking for does not appear to be in the table, consider the possibility that it is a compound of another verb, with one of the prefixes mentioned above on the front. Compounds like *abfahren* and *losfahren* behave just the same as *fahren*, for example.

Strong verbs proper have a past participle which ends in *-en*, and may or may not have a different main vowel from the infinitive, as in *essen – gegessen* or *gewinnen – gewonnen.*

'Mixed' verbs are verbs which follow the pattern of weak verbs **but** have a vowel change. The past participle of these verbs ends in *-t.*

Example:

bringen – gebrach**t**
wissen – gewuß**t**

The same rules about prefixes which do or do not separate apply as for weak verbs, see **(c) *Weak verbs*** above.

Examples:

essen

ich habe ... gegessen	wir haben ... gegessen
du hast ... gegessen	ihr habt ... gegessen
	Sie haben ... gegessen
er/sie/es/man hat ... gegessen	sie haben ... gegessen

kommen

ich bin ... gekommen	wir sind ... gekommen
du bist ... gekommen	ihr seid ... gekommen
	Sie sind ... gekommen
er/sie/es/man ist ... gekommen	sie sind ... gekommen

wissen

ich habe ... gewußt	wir haben ... gewußt
du hast ... gewußt	ihr habt ... gewußt
	Sie haben ... gewußt
er/sie/es/man hat ... gewußt	sie haben ... gewußt

(c) *'Haben'* or *'sein'*?
The choice of *haben* or *sein* as auxiliary can cause some difficulty, as there is no similar distinction in English. Either learn which verbs take *sein* (in many verb tables, including the ones in the this book, those verbs which require *sein* are marked with *), or use a simple rule which works in most cases:

Verbs of motion, plus *bleiben, sein* and *werden* have *sein* as an auxiliary.

8 Imperfect tense (also known as Simple Past or just Past)

Example:

Ich **spielte** Tennis, ich **fuhr** nach Hause

The imperfect is the most frequent past tense in formal writing such as books and newspapers. Some common verbs are also found in the imperfect tense in speech and informal writing mixed freely with perfect tenses. Like the perfect, it translates a variety of English past tenses.

So *ich spielte Tennis* can mean:
I played tennis
I was playing tennis
I used to play tennis
I would play tennis (on Sundays)

This is how the imperfect tense is formed:

(a) Weak verbs
Remove *-en* from the infinitive and add the following endings:

1st person: ich	-te	wir	-ten
2nd person: du	-test	ihr	-tet
		Sie	-ten
3rd person: er/sie/es/man	-te	sie	-ten

Example:

ich spiel**te**	wir spiel**ten**
du spiel**test**	ihr spiel**tet**
	Sie spiel**ten**
er/sie/es/man spiel**te**	sie spiel**ten**

(b) Strong verbs
Because these verbs are irregular, the only safe way to discover the imperfect tense is to look the verb up in a verb table. If the verb you are looking for does not appear to be in the table, consider the possibility that it is a compound of another verb, with one of the prefixes mentioned above (see ***7 Perfect tense (a)***) on the front. Compounds like *losfahren* and *abfahren* behave just the same as *fahren*, for example.

The form you have looked up is the 3rd (and 1st) person singular. To that, add the following endings:

1st person: ich	**none**	wir	-en
2nd person: du	-st	ihr	-t
		Sie	-en
3rd person: er/sie/es/man	**none**	sie	-en

Example:

fahren – (entry in verb table: *fuhr)*

ich fuhr	wir fuhr**en**
du fuhr**st**	ihr fuhr**t**
	Sie fuhr**en**
er/sie/es/man fuhr	sie fuhr**en**

Points to watch: in practice, because the imperfect tense is mainly used in books and newspapers, it is much more common in the 3rd person singular and plural than in its other forms. Nevertheless, you need to be sure of recognising it in the other persons if it crops up in a text, so be aware of them!

9 Pluperfect tense

Example:

Ich **hatte** Tennis **gespielt**, ich **war** nach Hause **gefahren**

The pluperfect is used together with either the perfect or the imperfect to show actions in the past which happened before other actions in the past. This is similar to English usage.

So *ich hatte Tennis gespielt* can mean:
I had played tennis
I had been playing tennis

This is how the pluperfect is formed:

The pluperfect uses the imperfect tense of *haben* or *sein* as auxiliaries *(Hilfsverben)* and the past participle at the end of the clause or sentence.

The choice of *haben* or *sein* as auxiliary follows the same rules as for the perfect tense.

The past participle is formed in the same way as for the perfect tense. So it has to be looked up for strong and mixed verbs, but can be worked out for weak verbs.

(a) Weak verb

Example:

ich **hatte** ... gespielt	wir **hatten** ... gespielt
du **hattest** ... gespielt	ihr **hattet** ... gespielt
	Sie **hatten** ... gespielt
er/sie/es/man **hatte** ... gespielt	sie **hatten** ... gespielt

(b) Strong verbs

Examples:

essen

ich **hatte** ... gegessen	wir **hatten** ... gegessen
du **hattest** ... gegessen	ihr **hattet** ... gegessen
	Sie **hatten** ... gegessen
er/sie/es/man **hatte** ... gegessen	sie **hatten** ... gegessen

kommen

ich **war** ... gekommen	wir **waren** ... gekommen
du **warst** ... gekommen	ihr **wart** ... gekommen
	Sie **waren** ... gekommen
er/sie/es/man **war** ... gekommen	sie **waren** ... gekommen

wissen

ich **hatte** ... gewußt	wir **hatten** ... gewußt
du **hattest** ... gewußt	ihr **hattet** ... gewußt
	Sie **hatten** ... gewußt
er/sie/es/man **hatte** ... gewußt	sie **hatten** ... gewußt

10 Conditions

You need to know about two sorts of conditions in German. Each sort has a *wenn*-clause and a consequence clause.

(a) Open conditions
The first sort, the open condition, is really a statement of fact. The *wenn*-clause has the present tense; the consequence clause has the future or present tense.

Example:

Wenn du auf der Autobahn schläfst, wirst du sterben
If you sleep on the motorway you will die

(b) Possibilities
The second sort of condition expresses things which might – or might not – happen. It is best to learn a couple of examples of these and change them to suit circumstances. As a rule of thumb, many forms of *haben, werden* and *sein* will have an Umlaut.

Examples:

Wenn ich reich wäre, würde ich in Hollywood wohnen
If I was rich I would live in Hollywood
Wenn ich viel Geld hätte, würde ich einen Swimmingpool im Garten haben
If I had a lot of money I would have a swimming pool in the garden

The modal verbs can be used in their conditional form rather than being used with *werden*:

dürfen	ich dürfte	*I would be allowed to*
können	ich könnte	*I could*
mögen	ich möchte	*I'd like to*
müssen	ich müßte	*I really ought to*
sollen	ich sollte	*I should*
wollen	ich wollte	*I'd like to*

Examples:

Ich könnte nach Berlin kommen, wenn ich Zeit hätte
I could come to Berlin if I had time
Er müßte jetzt gehen, wenn er den Zug erreichen wollte
He would have to go now if he wanted to catch the train
Sie dürfte das nicht machen, wenn sie morgen noch Freunde haben möchte
She shouldn't do that if she wanted to have some friends left tomorrow

11 Command forms (Imperatives)

The command forms of verbs are used when telling people to do something. They include the 'Let's...' sort of command, which is a way of telling yourself and one or more other people to do something.

Every verb has four command forms, based on the present tense. Which form is used depends on who you are talking to.

(a) For those you would normally address as *du*

For both weak and strong verbs, remove the *-st* from the *du*-form of the present tense, and add an exclamation mark! If there is an Umlaut on the vowel of a strong verb, remove it.

Examples:

kaufen	du kaufst	**Kauf**!
kommen	du kommst	**Komm**!
fahren	du fährst	**Fahr** (schneller)!
nehmen	du nimmst	**Nimm** deine Windjacke mit!

Sometimes an *-e* is added after *-d* , *-h* or *-t*.

Examples:

finden	du findest dein Heft	**Finde** dein Heft!
sehen	du siehst oben	**Siehe** oben!

(b) For those you would normally address as *ihr*

For both weak and strong verbs, the *ihr* form of the present tense is used, but without *ihr*.

Examples:

kaufen	ihr kauft	**Kauft**!
kommen	ihr kommt	**Kommt**!
fahren	ihr fahrt	**Fahrt** (schneller)!
nehmen	ihr nehmt	**Nehmt** eure Windjacken mit!

(c) For those you would normally address as *Sie*

For both weak and strong verbs, use the *Sie* form of the present tense, as in the examples:

Examples:

kaufen	Sie kaufen	**Kaufen Sie**!
kommen	Sie kommen	**Kommen Sie**!
fahren	Sie fahren	**Fahren Sie** (schneller)!
nehmen	Sie nehmen	**Nehmen Sie** Ihre Windjacken mit!

(d) To express 'let's', use the wir form as in the examples below. This applies to both weak and strong verbs.

Examples:

kaufen	wir kaufen	**Kaufen wir**!
fahren	wir fahren	**Fahren wir** (schneller)!
nehmen	wir nehmen	**Nehmen wir** unsere Windjacken mit!

12 Modal verbs

(a) There is a group of verbs in German which control the infinitive of another verb (dependent infinitive). These are known as modal verbs, and will be familiar to anyone who has learnt: *Ich kann Tennis spielen* etc. in the first weeks of learning German. They can be used to express a whole variety of subtle meanings.
The modal verbs are:

dürfen
können
mögen
müssen
sollen
wollen

Lassen can behave in much the same way as a modal verb when it means 'to have something done' (as opposed to doing it yourself). See ***13 Infinitives (iii)***.

(i) Formation of the present tense
The plural forms follow the pattern of the regular verbs. The singular forms are as below:

ich darf	ich kann	ich mag	ich muß	ich soll	ich will
du darfst	du kannst	du magst	du mußt	du sollst	du willst
er darf	er kann	er mag	er muß	er soll	er will
sie darf	sie kann	sie mag	sie muß	sie soll	sie will
man darf	man kann	man mag	man muß	man soll	man will

(ii) Modal verbs and word order
In a simple sentence, the modal verb occupies the 'verb' position in the word order, and the dependent infinitive is at the end of the clause.

Example:

Ich **will** Tennis **spielen**, aber ich **muß** meine Hausaufgaben **machen**
I want to play tennis but I have to do my homework

In subordinate clauses, the same principle applies:

Example:

Ich war nicht da, weil ich nicht **ausgehen durfte**
I wasn't there because I wasn't allowed out

In tenses other than the present, only the tense of the modal verb changes. The dependent infinitive doesn't change.

Examples:

Sie **konnte** nicht **kommen**
She couldn't come
Sie **wird** es machen **müssen**
She will have to do it

Sometimes the dependent infinitive is omitted after modal verbs if it is clear from the context what it would have been. This is usually a verb of motion or *tun*.

Examples:

Ich **will** nach Leipzig
I want to go to Leipzig
Wir **könnten** morgen vielleicht ins Kino
We could go to the cinema tomorrow
Das **kann** ich nicht
I can't do that

(b) The meanings of modal verbs are very subtle. In addition, their meaning sometimes changes after *nicht*. The following examples for each modal verb should provide guidance.

(i) dürfen
It most often means 'to be allowed to'.

Example:

Ich darf nicht kommen
I am not allowed to come, I may not come

In the negative, it means 'must not'. See also ***(iv)* müssen**.

Example:

Hier darf man nicht rauchen
You must not smoke here

It is frequently used as a substitute for können when politeness is intended:

Example:

Was darf es sein?
What can I get you?

(iii) können
It most often means 'to be able to'.

Examples:

Ich kann Fußball spielen
I can/am able to play football
Ich konnte leider nicht pünktlich kommen
I am afraid I wasn't able to arrive on time

It can express possibility, like the English 'may, could, might'.

Examples:

Das kann sein
That may be so
Er könnte vielleicht krank sein
He might perhaps be ill

It can mean to know how to do something.

Example:

Sie kann Deutsch
She can speak German
Ich kann Gitarre spielen
I can play the guitar

(iii) mögen
It means 'to like'.

Example:

Ich mag schwimmen
I like swimming
Ich möchte eine Banane
I'd like a banana
Er mochte seine Tante Wilhelmina nicht
He didn't like his Aunt Wilhelmina

(iv) müssen
It most often means 'to have to'.

Examples:

Ich muß jetzt gehen
I have to go now
Das mußte man sehen!
You had to see it!
Muß das sein?
Is that really necessary?

With *nicht*, it corresponds to 'needn't' or 'don't have to'.

Example:

Wir müssen das Buch nicht jetzt lesen
We don't have to/needn't read that book now

Point to watch: 'Mustn't' is usually expressed by *darf nicht*. Germans often use *ich brauche nicht* in preference to the negative of *müssen*.

(v) sollen
It most often means 'to be obliged to, to have to'. There is often an 'external' obligation.

Examples:
Um wieviel Uhr sollen wir bei Fritz sein?
When should we be at Fritz's place?
Du solltest Maria doch vom Bahnhof abholen, oder?
Shouldn't you have picked Maria up from the station?

It can often be the equivalent of a command.

Examples:
Er soll auf mich warten
He is to wait for me
Du sollst nicht stehlen
Thou shalt not steal

It may express an intention, with the meaning 'are to', is supposed to', etc.

Examples:
Hier soll die neue Straße gebaut werden
This is where the new road is to be built
Wann sollen wir uns treffen?
When shall we meet?

(vi) wollen
It most often means 'to want to, to wish to'.

Examples:
Ich wollte früher ankommen
I wanted to arrive earlier
Ich will meinem Sohn helfen
I want to help my son
Machen Sie, was Sie wollen
Do what you like

It can express willingness.

Examples:
Willst du mich in die Stadt fahren?
Will you drive me to town?
Er will das Meerschweinchen nicht verkaufen
He won't sell the guinea pig

It can express intention.

Examples:
Wir wollen nächstes Jahr nach Amerika fahren
We're hoping to go to America next year
Er wollte gerade gehen, als das Telefon klingelte
He was just about to go when the phone rang

13 Infinitives

(a) The infinitive is the part of the verb listed in a dictionary, and means 'to ...'. It doesn't agree with a subject. It may be found in combination with other verbs.

Examples:

kaufen	*to buy*
essen	*to eat*
sein	*to be*

(b) The infinitive without *zu* is found at the end of the clause – see also ***Word order***.

The infinitive is used without *zu*:

(i) with the modal verbs *dürfen, können, mögen, müssen, sollen* and *wollen*

Example:
Sie will Tennis spielen
She wants to play tennis

Much fuller details are given under ***Modals***

(ii) after some verbs of perception: *fühlen, hören, sehen, spüren*

Example:
Ich hörte ihn ankommen
I heard him arrive

(iii) after *lassen*, meaning to have someone do something for you

Example:
Ich ließ meine Uhr reparieren. Ich konnte das selbst nicht machen
I had my watch repaired. I couldn't do it myself.

(iv) after certain verbs of motion: *fahren, gehen, kommen, schicken*. The verb in the infinitive gives the reason for going

Examples:
Ich gehe jetzt schlafen
I am going to bed
Er geht samstags immer tanzen
He always goes dancing on Saturday

(c) The infinitive with *zu* is found at the end of the clause. For separable verbs, the *zu* is inserted between the separable prefix and the verb and written as a single word.

Examples:
Es ist schön, hier zu sein
It is nice to be here
Er hat vor, in der Stadt einzukaufen
He intends to go shopping in town

The infinitive with zu is used:
(i) after certain prepositions
um ... zu – in order to, to

Examples:
Sie hat ihm 1000 DM gegeben, um einen alten Wagen zu kaufen
She gave him 1000 DM to buy an old car
Opa ist zu alt, um Fußball zu spielen
Grandpa is too old to play football

ohne ... zu – without

Example:
Er fuhr nach Dover, ohne zu tanken
He drove to Dover without refuelling

statt ... zu / anstatt ... zu – instead of

Example:
Er spielte Tennis, anstatt seine Hausaufgaben zu machen
He played tennis instead of doing his homework

(ii) after the following verbs:

bekommen	*to get*
bleiben	*to stay*
brauchen	*to need*
scheinen	*to seem*
versprechen	*to promise*
wissen	*to know*

Examples:
Das bleibt noch zu sehen

That remains to be seen
Das brauchst du nicht zu machen
You needn't do that
Der Lehrer scheint den Jungen nicht zu kennen
The teacher doesn't seem to know the boy
Gerlinde hat versprochen zu kommen
Gerlinde has promised to come

(iii) after the adjectives *einfach, interessant, leicht, schwer, schwierig*

Example:

Deutsch ist schwer zu lernen
German is hard to learn

(iv) in small ads

Example:

VW-Golf zu verkaufen
VW Golf for sale

(d) The infinitive used as a noun
(i) The infinitive of almost any German verb can be used as a noun. They are all neuter, don't normally appear in the plural, and have a capital letter. The *sich* from reflexive verbs is usually omitted.

Example:

Das Wandern ist schön
Hiking is lovely

(e) Infinitive nouns are used with prepositions
(i) *beim* + infinitive

Example:

Beim Radfahren hat sie einen Schuh verloren
While cycling she lost a shoe

(ii) *zum* + infinitive

Example:

Zum Tennisspielen ist er viel zu alt
He's far too old to play tennis

14 Verbs followed by the nominative

The following verbs are followed by the Nominative case, or by an adjective standing alone:

bleiben	*to remain*
heißen	*to be called*
scheinen	*to seem*
sein	*to be*
werden	*to become*

Examples:

Du bist mein Freund
You are my friend
Sie wurde rot
She blushed
Er heißt Herr Braun
He is called Herr Braun
Er scheint ein netter Junge zu sein
He seems to be a nice boy

15 Verbs followed by the dative

The following verbs are followed by the Dative case. English-speaking learners of German find this a bit strange, and the only known cure is to learn which they are!

Common verbs taking the Dative include:

danken	*to thank*
folgen	*to follow*
helfen	*to help*

Examples:

Ich habe meiner Mutter im Garten geholfen
I helped my mother in the garden
Ich folge meiner Schwester
I am following my sister
Ich danke dir
I thank you

16 Impersonal verbs

A good number of verbs are used with the subject *es*. These are known as impersonal verbs, because it is not clear who *es* is. They include the following:

(a) Weather verbs

Examples:

Es regnet
It is raining
Es schneit
It is snowing

(b) Verbs referring to other natural occurrences and noises

Examples:

Es riecht stark nach Stinktier
There is a strong odour of skunk
Es klingelt
The bell is ringing

(c) With *sein* and *werden*

Examples:

Es ist zu spät
It is too late
Es wird um vier Uhr morgens hell
It gets light at four in the morning

(d) Various idioms

Examples:

Wie geht es dir?	*How are you?*
Es tut mir leid	*I am sorry*
Es gefällt mir	*I like it*
Es kommt darauf an	*It depends*
Es macht nichts	*It doesn't matter*
Es ist mir kalt	*I am cold*
Es schmeckt mir sehr gut	*It tastes lovely*

17 Reflexive verbs

These are verbs where the person does the action to herself or himself. There are three sorts of reflexive verb in German:

(a) Those which have an accusative reflexive pronoun and cannot be used without it. These include:

sich beeilen	*to hurry*
sich erkälten	*to catch a cold*
sich verabschieden	*to say goodbye*

For reference, the present tense of *sich beeilen* is:

ich beeile mich
du beeilst dich
er/sie/es/man beeilt sich

wir beeilen uns
ihr beeilt euch
Sie beeilen sich
sie beeilen sich

(b) Those verbs which are sometimes reflexive

Examples:

sich fragen	*to wonder*
sich waschen	*to wash oneself*

sich kämmen *to comb oneself*
sich rasieren *to shave oneself*

(c) Those where the reflexive pronoun is Dative and is additional to an Accusative object. For reference, an example is written out below

ich habe mir die Haare gewaschen
du hast dir die Haare gewaschen
er/sie/es/man hat sich die Haare gewaschen
wir haben uns die Haare gewaschen
ihr habt euch die Haare gewaschen
Sie haben sich die Haare gewaschen
sie haben sich die Haare gewaschen

Point to watch: Sometimes these expressions are given as *'sich die Haare waschen'* in vocabularies. Beware! the *sich* is Dative, not Accusative!

18 Verbs followed by a preposition

Many verbs are followed by a particular preposition. The prepositions are listed here alphabetically.

sich erinnern an + Accusative	*to remember*
sich freuen auf + Accusative	*to look forward to*
warten auf + Accusative	*to wait for*
sich interessieren für + Accusative	*to be interested in*
sprechen mit + Dative	*to speak to*
telefonieren mit + Dative	*to speak on the phone with*
schmecken nach	*to taste of (usually something bad)*
sich unterhalten mit + Dative	*to converse with*
suchen nach + Dative	*to search for*
schreiben über + Accusative	*to write about*
sprechen über + Accusative	*to discuss*
sich streiten über + Accusative	*to argue over*
hören von + Dative	*to hear of*
lesen von + Dative	*to read about*
träumen von + Dative	*to dream of*
Angst haben vor + Dative	*to be frightened of*
einladen zu + Dative	*to invite to*

19 Separable and inseparable verbs

Many German verbs have prefixes. The prefixes of separable verbs sometimes separate and appear elsewhere in the sentence. The prefixes of inseparable verbs never separate.

(a) Separable verbs

(i) The common separable prefixes are:
ab-, an-, auf-, aus-, ein-, fern-, her-, hin-, mit-, nach-, vor, vorbei-, weg-, weiter-, zu-, zurück-, zusammen-

(ii) If there is only one verb in a sentence, the separable prefix is the last word in the sentence.

Example:

Ich gehe gern **aus**
I like going out

(iii) If there are two verbs in the sentence, and the separable verb is the second one, it does not separate and comes at the end of the sentence.

Example:

Ich möchte heute abend **fernsehen**
I would like to watch TV this evening

(iv) After a subordinating conjunction, the separable verb has been sent to the end of the clause and does not separate.

Example:

Wenn ich heute abend **fernsehe**
When I watch TV this evening

(v) The past participle of a separable verb is formed by putting *ge* between the separable prefix and the rest of the verb.

Example:

fernsehen fern**ge**sehen

(vi) Because the prefix of separable verbs can separate from the rest of the verb, for strong verbs you may have to check the verb without its prefix in a verb table.

Example:

	ausgehen	*to go out*
Look up	gehen	*to go*

(vii) Common weak separable verbs are:

abholen	*to fetch*
anmachen	*to switch on*
aufmachen	*to open*
aufräumen	*to tidy up*
aufwachen*	*to wake up*
ausmachen	*to switch off*
auspacken	*to unpack*
einkaufen	*to shop*
einpacken	*to pack*
sich hinsetzen	*to sit down*
vorbereiten	*to prepare*
zumachen	*to close*

*takes *sein* in perfect tense

(viii) Common strong separable verbs are:

abfahren*	*to depart*
ankommen*	*to arrive*
anrufen	*to phone*
anziehen	*to put (clothes) on*
aufstehen*	*to get up*
ausgehen*	*to go out*
aussteigen*	*to get out*
einladen	*to invite*
einsteigen*	*to get on*
mitnehmen	*to take with*
stattfinden	*to take place*

*takes *sein* in perfect tense

(b) Inseparable verbs

(i) The common inseparable prefixes are:
be-, ge-, emp-, ent-, er-, miß-, ver-, zer-

Verbs which begin with these prefixes have no *ge-* in the past participle.

Example:

Ich habe nicht verstanden
I didn't understand

(ii) Some prefixes can be either separable or inseparable. These prefixes are:
durch-, hinter-, über-, um-, wider-, wieder-. You have to learn whether a verb with these prefixes is separable or inseparable when you meet the verb for the first time.

Common separable strong verbs like this include:

umsteigen*	*to change (train)*
umziehen*	*to move house*

Common weak verbs with inseparable prefixes include:

übersetzen	*to translate*
wiederholen	*to repeat*
untersuchen	*to investigate*

Common strong verbs with inseparable prefixes include:

überfahren	*to run over*
unterbrechen	*to interrupt*
sich unterhalten	*to talk*

*takes sein in the perfect tense

Regular (weak) verb table

These verbs all follow the pattern of *spielen.*

Infinitive	**Present**	**Imperfect**	**Perfect**	**Meaning**
spielen	ich spiele	ich spielte	ich habe gespielt	*to play*
Infinitive	**Present**	**Imperfect**	**Perfect**	**Meaning**
abholen (sep)	ich hole ab	ich holte ab	ich habe abgeholt	*to fetch*
abräumen (sep)	ich räume ab	ich räumte ab	ich habe abgeräumt	*to clear away*
anmachen (sep)	ich mache an	ich machte an	ich habe angemacht	*to switch on*
antworten	ich antworte	ich antwortete	ich habe geantwortet	*to answer*
arbeiten	ich arbeite	ich arbeitete	ich habe gearbeitet	*to work*
aufmachen (sep)	ich mache auf	ich machte auf	ich habe aufgemacht	*to open*
aufräumen (sep)	ich räume auf	ich räumte auf	ich habe aufgeräumt	*to tidy up*
aufwachen (sep)	ich wache auf	ich wachte auf	ich bin aufgewacht	*to wake up*
ausmachen (sep)	ich mache aus	ich machte aus	ich habe ausgemacht	*to switch off*
auspacken (sep)	ich packe aus	ich packte aus	ich habe ausgepackt	*to unpack*
sich beeilen	ich beeile mich	ich beeilte mich	ich habe mich beeilt	*to hurry*
besichtigen	ich besichtige	ich besichtigte	ich habe besichtigt	*to visit*
bestellen	ich bestelle	ich bestellte	ich habe bestellt	*to order*
besuchen	ich besuche	ich besuchte	ich habe besucht	*to visit*
bezahlen	ich bezahle	ich bezahlte	ich habe bezahlt	*to pay*
brauchen	ich brauche	ich brauchte	ich habe gebraucht	*to need*
buchen	ich buche	ich buchte	ich habe gebucht	*to book*
danken	ich danke	ich dankte	ich habe gedankt	*to thank*
decken	ich decke	ich deckte	ich habe gedeckt	*to set (table)*
drücken	ich drücke	ich drückte	ich habe gedrückt	*to push, press*
einkaufen (sep)	ich kaufe ein	ich kaufte ein	ich habe eingekauft	*to shop*
einpacken (sep)	ich packe ein	ich packte ein	ich habe eingepackt	*to pack*
fragen	ich frage	ich fragte	ich habe gefragt	*to ask*
sich freuen	ich freue mich	ich freute mich	ich habe mich gefreut	*to be pleased*
glauben	ich glaube	ich glaubte	ich habe geglaubt	*to think, believe*
gucken	ich gucke	ich guckte	ich habe geguckt	*to look*
sich hinsetzen (sep)	ich setze mich hin	ich setzte mich hin	ich habe mich hingesetzt	*to sit down*
hoffen	ich hoffe	ich hoffte	ich habe gehofft	*to hope*
hören	ich höre	ich hörte	ich habe gehört	*to hear*

Continued on page 34

Infinitive	Present	Imperfect	Perfect	Meaning
kaufen	ich kaufe	ich kaufte	ich habe gekauft	*to buy*
klingeln	ich klingele	ich klingelte	ich habe geklingelt	*to ring*
kriegen	ich kriege	ich kriegte	ich habe gekriegt	*to get*
lachen	ich lache	ich lachte	ich habe gelacht	*to laugh*
legen	ich lege	ich legte	ich habe gelegt	*to put (down)*
lernen	ich lerne	ich lernte	ich habe gelernt	*to learn*
machen	ich mache	ich machte	ich habe gemacht	*to make, do*
meinen	ich meine	ich meinte	ich habe gemeint	*to think, say*
mieten	ich miete	ich mietete	ich habe gemietet	*to rent*
öffnen	ich öffne	ich öffnete	ich habe geöffnet	*to open*
organisieren	ich organisiere	ich organisierte	ich habe organisiert	*to organise*
parken	ich parke	ich parkte	ich habe geparkt	*to park*
planen	ich plane	ich plante	ich habe geplant	*to plan*
prüfen	ich prüfe	ich prüfte	ich habe geprüft	*to check*
rauchen	ich rauche	ich rauchte	ich habe geraucht	*to smoke*
regnen	es regnet	es regnete	es hat geregnet	*to rain*
reisen*	ich reise	ich reiste	ich bin gereist	*to travel*
reparieren	ich repariere	ich reparierte	ich habe repariert	*to repair*
sagen	ich sage	ich sagte	ich habe gesagt	*to say*
sammeln	ich sammele	ich sammelte	ich habe gesammelt	*to collect*
schauen	ich schaue	ich schaute	ich habe geschaut	*to look*
schicken	ich schicke	ich schickte	ich habe geschickt	*to send*
schmecken	es schmeckt	es schmeckte	es hat geschmeckt	*to taste*
schneien	es schneit	es schneite	es hat geschneit	*to snow*
sparen	ich spare	ich sparte	ich habe gespart	*to save*
spielen	ich spiele	ich spielte	ich habe gespielt	*to play*
stecken	ich stecke	ich steckte	ich habe gesteckt	*to put (in)*
stellen	ich stelle	ich stellte	ich habe gestellt	*to put (upright)*
suchen	ich suche	ich suchte	ich habe gesucht	*to look for*
telefonieren	ich telefoniere	ich telefonierte	ich habe telefoniert	*to phone*
turnen	ich turne	ich turnte	ich habe geturnt	*to do gym*
üben	ich übe	ich übte	ich habe geübt	*to practise*
verkaufen	ich verkaufe	ich verkaufte	ich habe verkauft	*to sell*
vermieten	ich vermiete	ich vermietete	ich habe vermietet	*to rent out*
versuchen	ich versuche	ich versuchte	ich habe versucht	*to try*
vorbereiten (sep)	ich bereite vor	ich bereitete vor	ich habe vorbereitet	*to prepare*
warten	ich warte	ich wartete	ich habe gewartet	*to wait*
wechseln	ich wechsele	ich wechselte	ich habe gewechselt	*to change money*
wiederholen	ich wiederhole	ich wiederholte	ich habe wiederholt	*to repeat*
wohnen	ich wohne	ich wohnte	ich habe gewohnt	*to live*
wünschen	ich wünsche	ich wünschte	ich habe gewünscht	*to wish*
zeigen	ich zeige	ich zeigte	ich habe gezeigt	*to show*

*takes *sein* in the perfect tense

Irregular (strong) verb table

Infinitive	3rd Person Sing *Present*	*Imperfect*	*Perfect*	Meaning
aufstehen*	steht auf	stand auf	ist aufgestanden	*to get up*
beginnen	beginnt	begann	hat begonnen	*to begin*
bekommen	bekommt	bekam	hat bekommen	*to receive, get*
beschreiben	beschreibt	beschrieb	hat beschrieben	*to describe*
bleiben*	bleibt	blieb	ist geblieben	*to stay*
brechen	bricht	brach	hat gebrochen	*to break*
bringen	bringt	brachte	hat gebracht	*to bring*
denken	denkt	dachte	hat gedacht	*to think*
dürfen	darf	durfte		*to be allowed to*
essen	ißt	aß	hat gegessen	*to eat*
fahren*	fährt	fuhr	ist gefahren	*to travel*
fallen*	fällt	fiel	ist gefallen	*to fall*
finden	findet	fand	hat gefunden	*to find*
fliegen*	fliegt	flog	ist geflogen	*to fly*
geben	gibt	gab	hat gegeben	*to give*
gefallen	gefällt	gefiel	hat gefallen	*to please*
gehen*	geht	ging	ist gegangen	*to go*
haben	hat	hatte	hat gehabt	*to have*
halten	hält	hielt	hat gehalten	*to stop, hold*
heißen	heißt	hieß	hat geheißen	*to be called*
helfen	hilft	half	hat geholfen	*to help*
kennen	kennt	kannte	hat gekannt	*to know*
kommen*	kommt	kam	ist gekommen	*to come*
können	kann	konnte		*to be able to*
lassen	läßt	ließ	hat gelassen	*to leave*
laufen*	läuft	lief	ist gelaufen	*to run*
lesen	liest	las	hat gelesen	*to read*
liegen	liegt	lag	hat gelegen	*to lie*
mögen	mag	mochte		*to like to*
müssen	muß	mußte		*to have to*
nehmen	nimmt	nahm	hat genommen	*to take*
rufen	ruft	rief	hat gerufen	*to call*
scheinen	scheint	schien	hat geschienen	*to seem, shine*
schlafen	schläft	schlief	hat geschlafen	*to sleep*
schreiben	schreibt	schrieb	hat geschrieben	*to write*
schwimmen*	schwimmt	schwamm	ist geschwommen	*to swim*
sehen	sieht	sah	hat gesehen	*to see*
sein*	ist	war	ist gewesen	*to be*
singen	singt	sang	hat gesungen	*to sing*
sitzen	sitzt	saß	hat gesessen	*to sit*

Continued on page 36

		3rd Person Sing		
Infinitive	***Present***	***Imperfect***	***Perfect***	**Meaning**
sollen	soll	sollte		*to be supposed to*
sprechen	spricht	sprach	hat gesprochen	*to speak*
stehen	steht	stand	hat gestanden	*to stand*
stehlen	stiehlt	stahl	hat gestohlen	*to steal*
tragen	trägt	trug	hat getragen	*to wear, carry*
trinken	trinkt	trank	hat getrunken	*to drink*
tun	tut	tat	hat getan	*to do*
verbringen	verbringt	verbrachte	hat verbracht	*to spend (time)*
vergessen	vergißt	vergaß	hat vergessen	*to forget*
verlieren	verliert	verlor	hat verloren	*to lose*
verstehen	versteht	verstand	hat verstanden	*to understand*
waschen	wäscht	wusch	hat gewaschen	*to wash*
werden*	wird	wurde	ist geworden	*to become*
wissen	weiß	wußte	hat gewußt	*to know*
wollen	will	wollte		*to want to*
ziehen	zieht	zog	hat gezogen	*to pull*

*takes *sein* in the perfect tense

Word order

Clauses

A **clause** is a part of a sentence which contains a subject and a verb which agrees with that subject. There are **main clauses** which tell you most of the message of the sentence (Example: Er ist sehr krank) and **subordinate clauses** which tell you something more about some other part of the sentence (Example: Der Junge, der sehr krank ist, wohnt in Bonn).

Word order in German, or more exactly the order of certain groups of words, follows a number of rules.

1 Verbs

(a) The verb is the second idea in a simple sentence. It may come after the subject, after another element, or after a subordinate clause. In compound tenses, the auxiliary occupies the position of second idea in the sentence, while the remainder of the sentence is sandwiched between the auxiliary and the past participle or infinitive. This is often called the '1 – 2 – 3 rule'.

Examples:

Ich **kaufe** immer Kleidung mit meiner Mutter
I always buy clothing with my mother
Mit meiner Mutter **kaufe** ich immer Kleidung
Immer **kaufe** ich Kleidung mit meiner Mutter

Als ich jung war, **habe** ich in London gewohnt
When I was young I lived in London

Starting a sentence with an element other than the subject does not change the basic meaning. However, an element other than the subject at the beginning of the sentence is usually being stressed.

(b) If two sentences are joined by a co-ordinating conjunction (e.g. *und, aber, oder*) the conjunction does not count in the word order and has no effect on it.

Example:

Mein Vater spielt Karten **aber** meine Mutter spielt Klavier
My father is playing cards but my mother is playing the piano

(c) Where a clause begins with a subordinating conjunction, the verb or the auxiliary goes to the end of that clause.

Examples:

Meine Mutter bringt mich zur Schule, **wenn** es um 8 Uhr kalt **ist**
My mother brings me to school if it is cold at 8 o'clock
Helmut weiß, **daß** er zu spät angekommen **ist**
Helmut knows he arrived too late
Man kann sehen, **was** in zwei Jahren passieren **wird**
You can see what will happen in a couple of years

(d) If there is only one verb in a sentence or main clause and it is separable, the verb separates. The verb part takes the expected position in the sentence, and the separable prefix goes to the end of the sentence.

Example:

Ich **sehe** oft im Wohnzimmer **fern**
I often watch TV in the living room

If the separable verb is the second verb in a sentence, it does not separate, and goes to the end of the sentence.

Example:

Ich will heute nicht **fernsehen**
I don't wish to watch TV today

In a subordinate clause where the verb is sent to the end of the sentence, the two parts of the verb are joined together.

Example:

Als ich gestern **fernsah** *when I watched TV yesterday*
als sie hier **angekommen ist** *when she arrived here*

(e) Modal verbs follow the same rules as the auxiliary verbs *haben* and *sein*.

Example:

Ich **kann** nicht **schwimmen**
I cannot swim
weil ich nicht **schwimmen kann**
because I can't swim

(f) In questions with a question word the verb comes second.

Example:

Wie **heißt** du? *What is your name?*

In any other questions the verb comes first.

Example:

Heißt sie Sandra oder Brenda?
Is her name Sandra or Brenda?

2 Time, manner, place

In German, time usually comes as early as possible in a sentence, more or less the opposite of the English habit.

(a) The order of adverbs or adverbial phrases which are next to each other is usually Time before Manner (how) before Place:

TIME MANNER PLACE

Example:

Karin kommt am Montag sehr gern zur Schule
Karin likes coming to school on Mondays very much

(b) If there is more than one expression of a particular type, the more general one comes first:

TIME	TIME	PLACE
(general)	(more specific)	

Example:

Sie kommt **jeden Tag um 8 Uhr** in der Schule an
She arrives at school every day at 8

3 Dative and Accusative

The order of Dative and Accusative objects in German is fixed.

(a) If both Dative and Accusative are nouns, the Dative comes first:

DATIVE ACCUSATIVE

Example:

Ich gebe dem Hund einen Ball
I give the dog a ball

(b) If both Dative and Accusative are pronouns, the Accusative comes first:
ACCUSATIVE DATIVE

Example:

Ich gebe es ihm
I give it to him

(a) and *(b)* can be remembered by the mnemonics
DAN (Dative and Accusative for Nouns)
and PAD (Pronouns – Accusative then Dative)
Some learners prefer PADAN as a memory aid (Pronoun before Noun)

(c) If one is a pronoun and the other is a noun, no matter which way round this is, the pronoun comes first.

Examples:

ACCUSATIVE DATIVE
Ich gebe es dem Hund
I give it to the dog

DATIVE ACCUSATIVE
Ich gebe ihm den Ball
I give him the ball

This can be remembered as GROLPEO (Get rid of little pronouns early on).

Section *three*

Practice Exercises with Solutions

In this section we give you many opportunities to check your progress in the four key skills. You will find a range of questions for each of the skills, together with suggested solutions. In the case of listening, you will be instructed, where appropriate, to listen to the accompanying cassette.

The chart below will help you to see, at a glance, where you can find the various materials in this section.

Listening: *questions*

Play the cassette and do the exercises. Use the pause button and the rewind/review button as often as necessary. Then check your answers in the answers section on p.49.

Aufgabe 1 Man stellt sich vor

Höre zu, wie sich die folgenden Leute vorstellen und trage die Information in die Tabelle ein:

Listen to the following people introducing themselves and enter the information in the table below:

Nummer	Vorname	Familienname	Alter (Jahre)
1			
2			
3			
4			
5			
6			
7			
8			
9			

Aufgabe 2 Telefonnummern

Höre zu und trage dann die Telefonnummern in die Tabelle ein:

Listen and enter the phone numbers in the table:

Nummer	Name	Telefonnummer
1	Silke	
2	Max	
3	Frau Roeder	
4	Alexander	
5	Frau Wiesiol	
6	Herr Roth	
7	Herr Fuhrmann	
8	Susanne	
9	Peter	

Aufgabe 3 Wann bist du geboren?

Höre zu, wann die folgenden Leute geboren sind. Schreibe die Daten in die Tabelle:

When were the following people born? Write the dates in the table:

Nummer	Name	Geburtsdatum
1	Silke	
2	Max	
3	Petra	
4	Alexander	
5	Kirsten	
6	Heiner	
7	Dieter	
8	Susanne	
9	Peter	

Aufgabe 4 Ich, Familie und Freunde

Du hast eine Kassette von deinem neuen deutschen Austauschpartner bekommen. Höre zu, was er dir von seiner Familie erzählt.

You have received a cassette from your new German exchange partner. Listen to what he tells you about his family.

1 Fülle das folgende Formular mit den Details deines Austauschpartners aus:

Fill in the following form with the details of your exchange partner:

NAME:

ALTER:

WOHNORT:

GESCHWISTER: a)

b)

HAUSTIERE:

HOBBYS:

2 Höre die Kassette noch einmal und beantworte die Fragen deines Austauschpartners.

Listen to the cassette again and answer the questions your exchange partner asks.

Aufgabe 5 Freizeit

Höre jetzt Max zum zweiten Mal. Er spricht über seine Freizeit und die Hobbys seiner Familie.

Now listen to Max for a second time. He is talking about his free time and his family's hobbies.

Beantworte diese Fragen über Max und seine Familie:

Answer these questions about Max and his family:

1 Welche Bücher liest er?
2 Wann geht er schwimmen?
3 Welches Instrument spielt seine Schwester?
4 Was ist das Hobby seines Bruders?
5 Was ist das Hobby der Eltern?
6 Was macht der Vater?
7 Was malt die Mutter?

Aufgabe 6 Stadt

Dein Austauschpartner Max hat dir ein Prospekt seines Wohnortes Hanau geschickt und spricht auf der Kassette über seine Stadt.

Your exchange partner Max has sent you a leaflet about his home town, Hanau, and is now talking about the town on the cassette.

Richtig oder Falsch? Schreibe R oder F in die Kästchen:

True or false? Write R or F in the boxes:

1 Hanau ist eine kleine Stadt. ☐
2 Hanau liegt in der Nähe von Offenbach. ☐
3 Hanau ist eine Industriestadt. ☐
4 Es gibt keine Geschäfte in Hanau. ☐
5 Hanau hat nur eine Bushaltestelle. ☐
6 Die Eltern von Max fahren nach Frankfurt in die Oper. ☐

Aufgabe 7 Land

Deine Nachbarin gibt dir eine Kassette, auf der ein deutsches Mädchen, Katja, über ihren Bauernhof und das Landleben spricht.

Your neighbour gives you a cassette on which a German girl, Katja, is talking about her farm and life in the country.

A Beantworte jetzt diese Fragen:

Now answer these questions:

1 Wo wohnt Katja?
2 Wieviele Personen leben im Dorf?
3 Was gibt es im Dorf?
4 Was machen die Touristen dort?
5 Welche Tiere hat Katja?

B Sieh dir die vier Bilder an. Welches zeigt Katjas Bauernhof?

Look at the four pictures. Which one shows Katja's farm?

Aufgabe 8 Wetter

Du bist auf Urlaub in Deutschland und hörst im Radio den Wetterbericht.

You are on holiday in Germany and hear the weather forecast on the radio.

Zeichne die Wettersymbole in die Landkarte:

Draw the weather symbols onto the map:

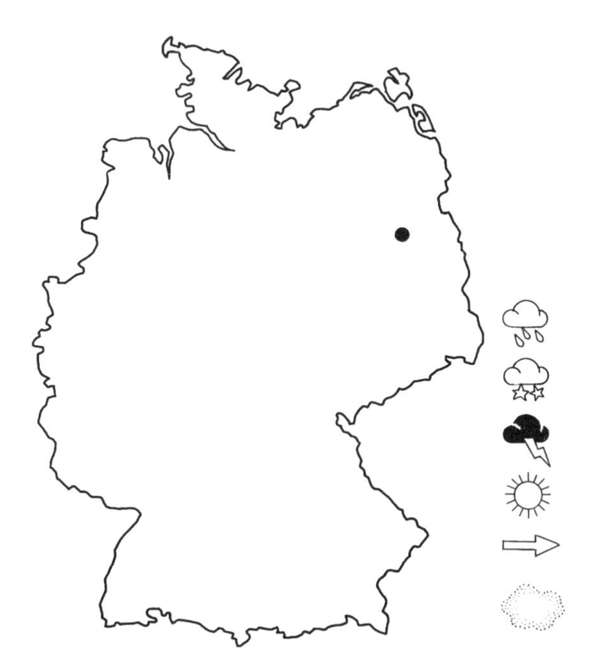

Aufgabe 9 Schule

Ein Schüler aus Forchheim erzählt von seiner Schule.

A pupil from Forchheim tells you about his school.

A Kreuze die richtigen Sätze an:

Put a cross in the box next to the correct sentences:

1 Der Junge geht auf eine Realschule. ☐

2 Die Schule ist in der Stadtmitte. ☐

3 Die Schule ist ganz neu. ☐

4 Es gibt keine Turnhalle. ☐

5 Er hat auch samstags Schule. ☐

6 Donnerstag ist sein Lieblingstag. ☐

7 Mathe ist sein Lieblingsfach. ☐

B Fülle jetzte diesen Stundenplan aus:

Now complete this timetable:

Aufgabe 10 Zu Hause

Gabriele erzählt von ihrem Haus.

Gabriele talks about her house.

1. Zeichne Gabrieles Haus in den Platz auf dem Bild:

Draw Gabriele's house into the space in the picture:

2. Kreuze an, welche Möbel Gabriele in ihrem Zimmer hat:

Tick the items of furniture which Gabriele has in her room:

ein Bett ☐

einen Sessel ☐

einen Eßtisch ☐

einen Schrank ☐

einen Nachttisch ☐

3. Was hat Gabriele noch in ihrem Zimmer?

What else does Gabriele have in her room?

4. Wie hilft Gabriele ihren Eltern? Was macht sie?

What does Gabriele do to help her parents?

Stunde	*Montag*	*Dienstag*	*Mittwoch*	*Donnerstag*	*Freitag*	*Sonnabend*
1						
2						
3						
4						
5						
6						

	Name	Taschengeld	verdienen	brauchen für	sparen für
1	Bettina				
2	Jens				
3	Holger				
4	Olaf				
5	Sigrid				
6	Claudia				

Aufgabe 11 Taschengeld

Sechs Jugendliche sprechen über Taschengeld. Höre zu und fülle dann die Tabelle aus.

Six teenagers are talking about pocket money. Listen carefully and then fill in the table above.

Aufgabe 12 Ausflüge

Die Tante deines deutschen Austauschpartners erzählt dir von einem Ausflug, den sie gestern mit ihrer Familie gemacht hat.

Your German exchange partner's aunt tells you about an outing which she went on yesterday with her family.

Später berichtest du, was dir die Tante gesagt hat. Fülle die Lücken im Text mit passenden deutschen Wörtern aus:

Later you re-tell what the aunt told you. Fill in the gaps of the text with suitable German words:

Die Tante und ihre ______________________

______________________ haben gestern einen Ausflug

gemacht. Sie sind zum ________________ gefahren.

Sie sind zuerst mit dem ________________ und dann

mit der ________________ gefahren. Der Zoo von

Frankfurt ist in der ________________. Sie haben

viele Tiere gesehen. Hansjörg interessiert sich für

________________ und ________________. Am

Nachmittag war das Wetter nicht so gut. Es hat

________________. Sie sind dann wieder

zurückgefahren. Um ________________________

________________ waren sie zu Hause.

Aufgabe 13 Auf dem Campingplatz

Du arbeitest während der Ferien auf einem Campingplatz. Du füllst die Anmeldeformulare aus, während dein Freund mit den Gästen spricht.

You are working on a campsite during the holidays. You fill in the registration forms while your friend talks to the guests.

Fülle die Formulare aus:

Fill in the forms:

1.

Name: ______________________

Aufenthalt: ____ *Tage* __________ *Woche(n)*

Personen: ______________________

Platz Nummer: ______________________

Zelt: ______________________

Wohnwagen: ______________________

Strom: ______________________

2.

Name: ______________________

Aufenthalt: ____ *Tage* __________ *Woche(n)*

Personen: ______________________

Platz Nummer: ______________________

Zelt: ______________________

Wohnwagen: ______________________

Strom: ______________________

3.

Name: ______

Aufenthalt: ____ *Tage* ______ *Woche(n)*

Personen: ______

Platz Nummer: ______

Zelt: ______

Wohnwagen: ______

Strom: ______

4.

Name: ______

Aufenthalt: ____ *Tage* ______ *Woche(n)*

Personen: ______

Platz Nummer: ______

Zelt: ______

Wohnwagen: ______

Strom: ______

Aufgabe 14 Man macht einen Termin aus

Hör zu, wie diese Leute einen Termin beim Arzt ausmachen. Heute ist Dienstag.

Listen to these people who are making appointments to see a doctor. It is Tuesday today.

Trage die Termine in den Terminkalender ein:

Enter the appointments into the diary:

MONTAG

DIENSTAG

MITTWOCH

DONNERSTAG

FREITAG

SONNABEND

STUNDE

Aufgabe 15 Im Sprechzimmer

Was fehlt diesen vier Patienten und was empfiehlt die Ärztin?

What is wrong with the four patients and what does the doctor recommend?

Sieh dir die Bilder an. Schreibe die richtigen Nummern (1–4) zu jedem Bild und darunter was die Ärztin empfiehlt.

Look at the pictures. Write the correct numbers (1–4) under each picture and what the doctor recommends.

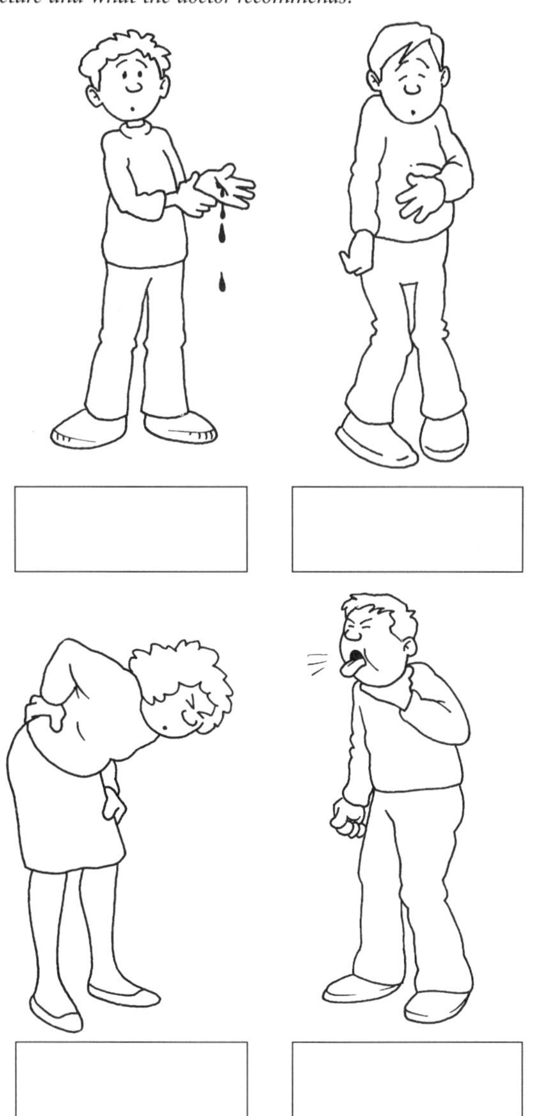

Aufgabe 16 In der Café-Konditorei

In einem Café hörst du zu, wie verschiedene Kunden Getränke und Kuchen bestellen.

In a café you overhear various customers ordering drinks and cakes.

Richtig oder Falsch? Schreibe R oder F in die Kästchen hinter den Sätzen:

True or False? Write R or F in the box after each sentence:

1 Die junge Frau bestellt eine Tasse Kaffee. ☐
Sie bestellt auch zwei Stück Erdbeerkuchen mit Sahne. ☐

2 Der Mann möchte ein Kännchen Tee mit Milch. ☐
Er bestellt auch ein Stück Schokoladenkuchen ohne Sahne. ☐

3 Die zwei Freunde bestellen zwei Glas Cola. ☐
Sie möchten auch zwei große Portionen Eis mit Sahne. ☐

4 Der Mann hätte gern eine Tasse Tee mit Milch. ☐
Er bestellt auch eine heiße Schokolade. ☐
Er möchte keinen Kuchen. ☐

Aufgabe 17 An der Imbißstube

Du wartest an einer Imbißstube in Deutschland auf einen Freund. Dabei hörst du wie verschiedene Kunden etwas zum Essen bestellen.

While you are waiting for a friend at a snack bar in Germany you overhear various customers order something to eat.

Schreibe auf, was diese Personen alles bestellt haben:

Write down what the people ordered (see top of page):

Nummer 1: ______________________________
____

Nummer 2: ______________________________
____

Nummer 3: ______________________________
____

Nummer 4: ______________________________
____

Nummer 5: ______________________________

Aufgabe 18 Im Restaurant

Es ist der erste Mai. Die Familie Bergmann, Mutter, Vater, Tochter, Sohn und Großmutter, machen einen Ausflug mit dem Auto. Sie fahren nach Boppard am Rhein, wo sie im Hotel 'Zum Schiff' zu Mittag essen.

It is the first of May. The Bergmann family, mother, father, daughter, son and grandmother, are on an excursion by car. They are travelling to Boppard on the Rhine, where they have lunch in the hotel 'Zum Schiff'.

Beantworte die Fragen:

Answer the questions:

Erster Teil

1 Was sagt der Kellner, wo die Familie sitzen kann?
2 Warum will Großmutter dort nicht sitzen?
3 Wo findet die Familie einen Tisch?

Zweiter und dritter Teil

Trage in die Tabelle ein, was die Leute bestellen:

Complete this table with the orders of the family members:

Person	Getränk	Vorspeise	Hauptgericht
Mutter			
Vater			
Sohn			
Tochter			
Großmutter			

Vierter Teil

Kreuze die richtige Antwort an:

Tick the correct answer:

1 Man wählt drei gemischte Eis mit Sahne. ☐
zwei gemischte Eis mit Sahne. ☐
drei gemischte Eis ohne Sahne. ☐

2 Die Familie hat drei Tassen Tee. ☐
drei Tassen Kaffee. ☐
zwei Tassen Kaffee. ☐

3 Der Vater bezahlt mit einem Hundertmarkschein. ☐
mit einer Kreditkarte. ☐
mit Kleingeld. ☐

Aufgabe 19 In der Bank

Du hörst verschiedene Dialoge in der Bank.

You hear various dialogues in a bank.

Wähle die richtige Antwort aus:

Choose the correct answer:

1 Der erste Kunde will
amerikanische Dollar umtauschen. ☐
französische Frankenumtauschen. ☐
Pfund Sterling umtauschen. ☐

2 Der zweite Kunde muß
seinen Fahrschein zeigen. ☐
seinen Ausweis zeigen. ☐
seine Kreditkarte zeigen. ☐

3 Der dritte Kunde möchte
900,— DM in Schilling umtauschen. ☐
90,— DM umtauschen. ☐
200,— DM umtauschen. ☐

4 Der dritte Kunde muß bis
zum Abend auf die Schilling warten. ☐
morgen auf die Schilling warten. ☐
zwölf Uhr auf die Schilling warten. ☐

5 Der vierte Kunde hat
schweizer Franken. ☐
französische Franken. ☐
kanadische Dollar. ☐

Aufgabe 20 Auf der Post

Du bist mit deiner Brieffreundin auf die Post in Erfurt gegangen. Dort hörst du verschiedene Gespräche am Postschalter.

You have gone to the post office in Erfurt with your penfriend. There you overhear various conversations at the counter.

Fülle jetzt diese Tabelle aus:

Now fill in the table:

Land/Stadt	Postkarte: DM	Brief: DM
England		
Spanien		
Südafrika		
Berlin		
Amerika		

Aufgabe 21 Im Bus

Du fährst mit deiner Brieffreundin mit dem Bus und hörst was die Leute zum Fahrer sagen.

You are travelling by bus with your penfriend and listen to what the people say to the driver.

Fülle die Tabelle aus:

Complete the table:

Nummer	Wieviele Personen	Richtung	Preis
1			
2			
3			
4			
5			

Aufgabe 22 Am Bahnhof

Du hörst diese Dialoge am Fahrkartenschalter der Bahn.

You hear these conversations at the railway ticket office.

Beantworte die Fragen:

Answer the questions:

Dialog 1

1 Wohin will die Frau fahren?
2 Wann fährt der Zug ab?
3 Von welchem Gleis fährt er ab?

Dialog 2

1 Was für eine Fahrkarte möchte der Mann?
2 Mit welchem Zug will er fahren?
3 Was kostet die Fahrkarte?

Dialog 3

1 Wohin möchte die junge Frau fahren?
2 Wann kommt der Zug an?
3 Muß sie umsteigen?

Dialog 4

1 Wann möchte der junge Mann nach Ulm fahren?
2 Möchte er in einem Nichtraucherabteil fahren?
3 Was für einen Platz möchte er?

Aufgabe 23 Mit dem Auto

Teil 1

Du machst einen Ausflug mit Claudia, der älteren Schwester deiner Brieffreundin. Ihr fahrt mit dem Auto. Zuerst muß Claudia zur Tankstelle fahren.

You are on an outing with Claudia, your penfriend's older sister. You are travelling by car. First, Claudia needs to stop at the petrol station.

Kreuze die richtigen Antworten an:

Tick the correct answers:

1 Claudia tankt normal. ☐
super. ☐
bleifrei. ☐
super bleifrei. ☐

2 Claudias Auto braucht noch Luft. ☐
Öl. ☐
Wasser. ☐
Gas. ☐

3 Die Getränke sind bei der Kasse. ☐
an der Toilette. ☐
am Eingang. ☐

Teil 2

Auf dem Weg zurück gibt es eine Panne. Claudia telefoniert mit der Werkstatt.

On the way home the car breaks down. Claudia phones a garage.

Kreuze die richtigen Antworten an:

Tick the correct answers:

4 Claudia telefoniert mit ihrem Vater. ☐
mit ihrem Freund. ☐
mit der Werkstatt. ☐
mit der Polizei. ☐

5 Sie ist auf der B45 in der Nähe eines Sees. ☐
eines Waldes. ☐
eines Dorfes. ☐
eines Berges. ☐

6 Die Bremse ist kaputt. ☐
Das Licht ist kaputt. ☐
Die Kupplung ist kaputt. ☐
Der Motor ist kaputt. ☐

Teil 3

Der Mechaniker kann das Auto nicht reparieren und bringt es zur Werkstatt.

The mechanic can't repair the car and tows it to the garage.

Kreuze die richtigen Antworten an:

Tick the correct answers:

7 Der Mechaniker kann das Auto
morgen reparieren. ☐
übermorgen reparieren. ☐
sofort reparieren. ☐
am Abend reparieren. ☐

8 Claudia fragt nach dem Weg zur Haltestelle. ☐
zum Bahnhof. ☐
zur Bank. ☐
zur U-Bahn Station. ☐

Aufgabe 24 Im Kino

Höre ein Gespräch zwischen einem Deutschen und seinem englischen Austauschpartner.

Listen to a conversation between a German and his English exchange partner.

Später schreibt der junge Engländer einen kurzen Bericht über den Abend für seinen Deutschlehrer. Fülle die Lücken aus:

Later the English boy writes a short report about the evening for his German teacher. Fill in the gaps of the text:

Erster Teil

Gestern abend war ich mit Jens zu Hause. Jens wollte zum ______________________ gehen, aber ich hatte keine Lust, weil ich nicht ______________________ kann. Dann hatte Jens die Idee, zum ______________________ zu gehen. Wir sind mit dem ________________ gefahren.

Zweiter Teil

Im Kino gibt es Plätze im ______________________ oder auf dem ____________________. Jens hat die Eintrittskarten gekauft. Es kostet nicht so viel, wenn man unter ____________________ Jahre ist. Jens hat auch zwei Tüten Chips und ______________________ __________ gekauft. Er hat ______________________ ______________________ bezahlt.

Aufgabe 25 Wie komme ich am Besten ...

Höre zu, wie verschiedene Leute nach dem Weg fragen.

Listen to various people asking the way.

Zeichne auf der Karte den Weg ein, den die Leute gehen müssen:

Draw the route which the four people need to take on the maps:

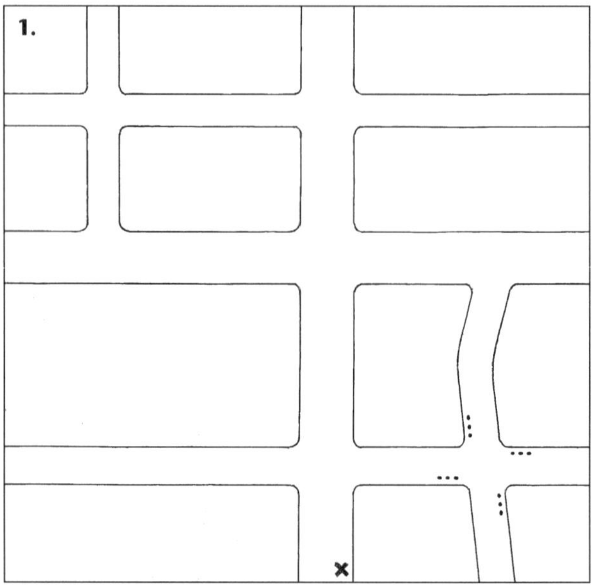

1.

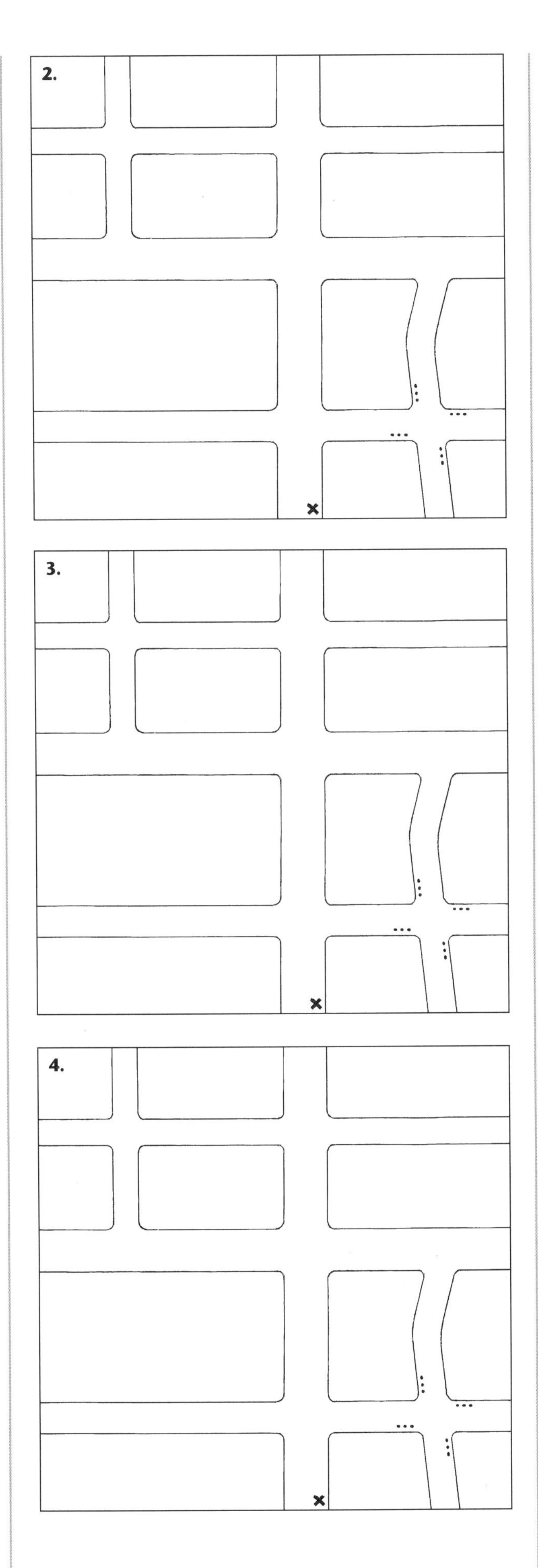

Aufgabe 26 Einkaufen – Obst und Gemüse

Du bist auf dem Markt in einer deutschen Stadt. Während du auf deinen Freund wartest, stehst du neben einem Marktstand und hörst was die Leute sagen.

You are in the market of a German town. While you are waiting for a friend, you are standing close to a market stall and overhear what the people are saying.

Fülle die Tabelle aus:

Fill in the table:

Nummer	Ware	Preis
1		
2		
3		
4		
5		

Aufgabe 27 Kleiderkauf

Erster Teil

Zwei Freundinnen, Bianca und Judith, fahren zusammen in die Stadt, um sich etwas Neues für die Sommerferien zu kaufen. Sie gehen zuerst in eine kleine Boutique.

Two friends, Bianca and Judith, are going into town together to buy new clothes for the summer holidays. First, they go into a boutique.

Beantworte die Fragen.

Answer the questions:

1 Wohin fahren Bianca und Judith?

2 Was wollen sie kaufen?

3 In was für ein Geschäft gehen sie zuerst?

Kreuze die richtige Antwort an:

Tick the correct answer:

4 Bianca probiert einen Rock an, aber er ist zu eng. ☐
kurz. ☐
lang. ☐
weit. ☐

Zweiter Teil

Bianca und Judith gehen dann zu einem großen Kaufhaus. In der Damenabteilung finden sie Röcke im Sonderangebot.

Bianca and Judith then go to a big department store. In the ladies' department they find skirts on special offer.

Kreuze die richtigen Antworten an:

Tick the correct answers:

5 Die Mädchen gehen in ein Kaufhaus. ☐
Parkhaus. ☐
Rathaus. ☐
Stadthaus. ☐

6 Bianca trägt Größe 83. ☐
38. ☐
36. ☐
48. ☐

7 Bianca möchte den braunen Rock anprobieren. ☐
dunkelblauen. ☐
gelben. ☐
schwarzen. ☐

8 Die Kasse ist neben dem Aufzug. ☐
Ausgang. ☐
Eingang. ☐
Fenster. ☐

Listening: answers

Aufgabe 1 Man stellt sich vor

Transcript

1 Ich heiße Silke Bayer B-A-Y-E-R. Ich bin 12 Jahre alt.

2 Tag, ich bin Max, Max Bertram B-E-R-T-R-A-M. Ich bin 16 Jahre alt.

3 Hallo, ich heiße Petra Roeder. Das schreibt man R-O-E-D-E-R. Ich bin 24.

4 Ich heiße Alexander Schulze, S-C-H-U-L-Z-E. Ich bin 13 Jahre alt.

5 Guten Tag, ich heiße Kirsten Wiesiol. Das schreibt man W-I-E-S-I-O-L. Ich bin 35 Jahre alt.

6 Mein Name ist Heiner Roth, R-O-T-H; mit T-H am Ende. Ich bin 65.

7 Darf ich mich vorstellen? Ich bin Dieter Fuhrmann. Soll ich das buchstabieren? F-U-H-R-M-A-N-N. Ich bin 47 Jahre alt.

8 Grüß Gott. Ich bin Susanne Killinger, K-I-L-L-I-N-G-E-R. Ich bin 18 Jahre alt.

9 Tag, ich heiße Peter Wagner, W-A-G-N-E-R, ja, hast du das? Ich bin 9 Jahre alt.

Answers

Nummer	Vorname	Familienname	Alter (Jahre)
1	Silke	Bayer	12
2	Max	Bertram	16
3	Petra	Roeder	24
4	Alexander	Schulze	13
5	Kirsten	Wiesiol	35
6	Heiner	Roth	65
7	Dieter	Fuhrmann	47
8	Susanne	Killinger	18
9	Peter	Wagner	9

Aufgabe 2 Telefonnummern

Transcript

1 - Hast du Telefon, Silke?
- Ja, meine Nummer ist 46 67 03.

2 - Und du, Max, hast du Telefon?
- Ja, das ist 4 33 18.

3 - Haben Sie Telefon, Frau Roeder?
- Ja, sie können mich unter 34 19 25 erreichen.

4 - Alexander, kann ich dich anrufen?
- Ja, meine Nummer ist 78 93 01.

5 - Frau Wiesiol, wie ist Ihre Telefonnummer, bitte?
- Meine Nummer ist: 51 29 56.

6 - Herr Roth, kann ich Sie telefonisch erreichen?
- Ja, meine Nummer im Büro ist 19 23 89.

7 - Kann ich Sie am Wochenende anrufen, Herr Fuhrmann?
- Ja, meine Nummer ist 8 22.

8 - Susanne, hast du Telefon?
- Ja, das ist 71 07 12.

9 - Peter, kannst du mir deine Telefonnummer sagen?
- Ja, die Nummer ist 89 40 35.

Answers

Nummer	Name	Telefonnummer
1	Silke	46 67 03
2	Max	4 33 18
3	Frau Roeder	34 19 25
4	Alexander	78 93 01
5	Frau Wiesiol	51 29 56
6	Herr Roth	19 23 89
7	Herr Fuhrmann	8 22
8	Susanne	71 07 12
9	Peter	89 40 35

Aufgabe 3 Wann bist du geboren?

Transcript

1 Silke — Ich bin am 28. Februar 1984 geboren.

2 Max — Ich bin am 16.6.1980 geboren.

3 Petra — Mein Geburtsdatum: Ich bin am 3. Dezember 1972 geboren.

4 Alexander — Ich bin am 2. Juli 1983 geboren.

5 Kirsten — Ich bin am 20. März 1961 geboren.

6 Heiner — Ich bin am 30. Oktober 1931 geboren.

7 Dieter — Ich bin am 4. Januar 1949 geboren.

8 Susanne — Ich bin am 31. Mai 1978 geboren.

9 Peter — Mein Geburtsdatum ist der 12. November 1987.

Answers

Nummer	Name	Geburtsdatum
1	Silke	28. Februar 1984
2	Max	16.6.1980
3	Petra	3. Dezember 1972

Nummer	Name	Geburtsdatum
4	Alexander	2. Juli 1983
5	Kirsten	20. März 1961
6	Heiner	30. Oktober 1931
7	Dieter	4. Januar 1949
8	Susanne	31. Mai 1978
9	Peter	12. November 1987

Aufgabe 4 Ich, Familie und Freunde

Transcript

Guten Tag. Ich heiße Max und bin 13 Jahre alt. Ich wohne mit meinen Eltern in Hanau, das ist in der Nähe von Offenbach. Ich habe zwei Geschwister: einen Bruder, Peter, und eine Schwester, Jutta. Mein Bruder ist 17 Jahre alt und geht noch in die Schule. Meine Schwester ist älter, sie arbeitet als Krankenschwester im Krankenhaus von Hanau. Mein Vater arbeitet in einem Büro. Meine Mutter ist Hausfrau. Wir haben zu Hause drei Tiere: einen Hund, eine Katze und einen Wellensittich. Meine Hobbys sind schwimmen, radfahren und lesen.

Hast du Geschwister? Wie alt sind sie? Was machen deine Eltern? Hast du Haustiere? Bitte erzähle doch ein bißchen von dir.

Answers:

NAME: Max

ALTER: 13 Jahre

WOHNORT: Hanau

GESCHWISTER: a) einen Bruder

b) eine Schwester

HAUSTIERE: Hund, Katze, Wellensittich

HOBBYS: schwimmen, radfahren, lesen

2 Answers to this will depend on your own circumstances.

Aufgabe 5 Freizeit

Transcript

Meine Hobbys sind schwimmen, radfahren und lesen. Ich lese Comics und Abenteuerromane. Ich habe schon mehr als hundert Bücher. Jeden Donnerstag gehe ich mit meinem Freund ins Schwimmbad. Ich fahre gern mit meinem Mountainbike in den Wald. Meine Schwester ist nicht sportlich. Sie musiziert gern. Sie spielt Klavier und Gitarre. Mein Bruder ist auch musikalisch. Er lernt seit vier Jahren Violine. Meine Mutter und mein Vater machen gern lange Wanderungen. Sie fahren dazu in die Berge. Mein Vater macht auch gern Gartenarbeit. Meine Mutter kann gut malen. Sie malt besonders gern Blumen und Tiere.

Was machst du in deiner Freizeit? Und deine Familie? Was sind ihre Hobbys?

Answers:

1 Comics und Abenteuerromane.
2 Jeden Donnerstag.
3 Klavier und Gitarre.
4 Er spielt Violine.
5 Wanderungen.
6 Gartenarbeit.
7 Sie malt Blumen und Tiere.

Aufgabe 6 Stadt

Transcript

Ich habe dir schon gesagt, daß ich in Hanau wohne. Hanau ist eine mittelgroße Stadt in der Nähe von Offenbach. Hanau ist eine Industriestadt. Es gibt hier viele Büros. In Hanau kann man gut einkaufen. Es gibt ein großes Einkaufszentrum in der Mitte der Stadt. Hanau hat einen Bahnhof. Man kann mit der S-Bahn schnell nach Offenbach und Frankfurt fahren. Meine Eltern fahren oft nach Frankfurt ins Theater oder in die Oper.

Answers

1 **F**
2 **R**
3 **R**
4 **F**
5 **F**
6 **R**

Aufgabe 7 Land

Transcript

Ich heiße Katja und wohne mit meinen Eltern und Geschwistern in Biberswald. Biberswald ist ein kleines Dorf in Bayern. In Biberswald gibt es nur zweihundert Personen. In unserem Dorf gibt es eine Kirche, eine kleine Schule, ein Dorfgasthaus und einen Laden. In diesem Laden kann man Lebensmittel und auch Souvenirs kaufen. Im Sommer kommen viele Touristen nach Biberswald. Sie besuchen die alte Kirche und machen Wanderungen. Man kann auch reiten und radfahren. Ich wohne gern auf dem Lande, weil ich Tiere gern habe. Zu Hause haben wir drei Hunde, zwei Ponys und ein paar Schafe. So viele Tiere kann man in der Stadt nicht haben. Auch ist es in Biberswald schön ruhig, es gibt wenig Autos und die Luft ist sauber.

Wir wohnen in einem alten Bauernhof. Vor dem Haus ist ein großer Garten mit Apfelbäumen. Links neben dem Haus ist ein kleiner Fluß und hinter dem Haus ist ein Wald. Rechts vom Haus ist die Landstraße und Felder. Ich wohne gern hier in Biberswald.

Answers:

A

1 Sie wohnt in Biberswald.
2 Es gibt nur zweihundert Personen.
3 Es gibt eine Schule, eine Kirche, ein Dorfgasthaus und einen Laden.
4 Sie besuchen die Kirche, wandern, reiten und fahren rad.
5 Sie hat drei Hunde, zwei Ponys und Schafe.

B Picture **C**.

Aufgabe 8 Wetter

Transcript

Das Wetter für heute, Sonntag den 15. Mai. In Norddeutschland gibt es am Vormittag noch vereinzelt Nebel. In Mitteldeutschland sonnig und warm. Temperaturen um 18 Grad. In Süddeutschland anfangs sonnig und warm, gegen Abend aber Regen und auch Gewitter. Im Westen Deutschlands bleibt es kühl mit Temperaturen um 10 Grad und Regen. Im Osten ist es windig mit leichten Regenschauern. Temperaturen zwischen 12 und 17 Grad. Das ist die Wettervorhersage. Im ersten Programm hören Sie jetzt die Sportnachrichten.

Answers

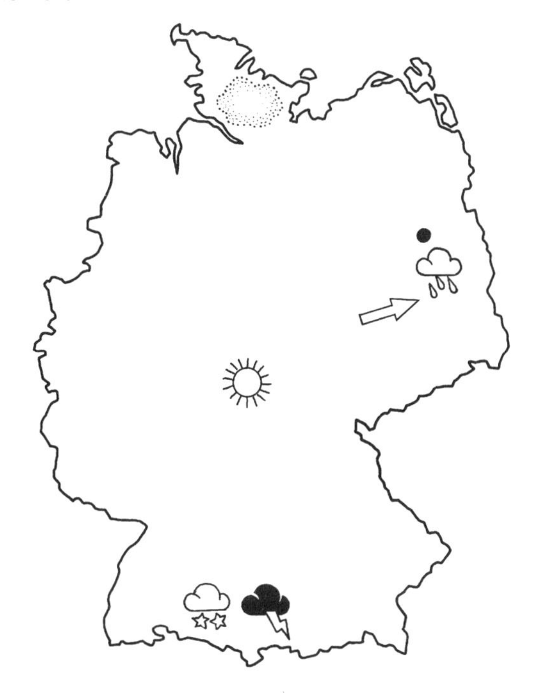

Aufgabe 9 Schule

Transcript

Ich gehe in die achte Klasse des Herdergymnasiums in Forchheim. Die Schule liegt in der Stadtmitte. Ich fahre mit dem Bus dorthin. Die Schule ist groß und alt. Es gibt etwa eintausend Schüler und Schülerinnen hier. Wir haben eine neue Turnhalle hinter der Schule. Es gibt auch einen Seitenbau mit den Labors für Biologie, Chemie und Physik. Mein Klassenzimmer ist im alten Teil der Schule im ersten Stock. Von den Fenstern kann man die Stadt sehen.

Ich habe von Montag bis Freitag Schule. Am Montag habe ich sechs Stunden: Mathe, Deutsch, Englisch, Erdkunde, Physik und Sport. Am Dienstag habe ich wieder sechs Stunden: eine Doppelstunde Kunst, dann Latein, Geschichte, Biologie und Deutsch. Mittwochs habe ich nur Englisch, Deutsch, Latein und Physik. Mittwoch ist mein Lieblingstag. Donnerstags habe ich Geschichte, Sport, Religion, Mathe und Englisch. Freitags habe ich noch einmal sechs Stunden: Mathe, Chemie, Erdkunde, Musik, Englisch und Werken. In der achten Klasse haben wir noch kein Französisch und keine Sozialkunde. Das kommt beides erst nächstes Jahr. Mein Lieblingsfach ist Mathe. Ich finde es nützlich. Deutsch macht mir keinen Spaß, weil ich immer schlechte Noten bekomme.

Answers

A

1 Der Junge geht auf eine Realschule. ☐
2 Die Schule ist in der Stadtmitte. ☒
3 Die Schule ist ganz neu. ☐
4 Es gibt keine Turnhalle. ☐
5 Er hat auch samstags Schule. ☐
6 Donnerstag ist sein Lieblingstag. ☐
7 Mathe ist sein Lieblingsfach. ☒

B See table at bottom of page.

Aufgabe 10 Zu Hause

Transcript

Meine Eltern und ich wohnen in einem modernen Haus. Es hat ein flaches Dach und ist ein Bungalow, das heißt es gibt nur ein Erdgeschoß. Ganz links ist die Garage. Daneben kommt die Haustür. Dann gibt es drei Fenster, ein kleines für das Badezimmer und zwei große Fenster für Küche und Eßzimmer. Die Schlafzimmer und das Wohnzimmer sind auf der anderen Seite, hinten im Haus.

Mein Zimmer ist sehr schön und groß, mit einem blauen Teppich und hellblauen Wänden. Die Möbel sind hellgrau: ein Bett, ein Schrank, ein Schreibtisch mit meinem Computer und ein Nachttisch. Ich habe auch ein altes Sofa von Großvater und einen Couchtisch. Der Blick von meinem Fenster ist wunderschön: direkt in den Garten auf Rasen und Schwimmbad.

Ich bin Einzelkind. Trotzdem muß ich zu Hause auch helfen. Ich spüle das Geschirr, decke den Tisch und bügle für die ganze Familie. Ich helfe meinen Eltern gerne, aber putzen tue ich nicht so gern.

Stunde	*Montag*	*Dienstag*	*Mittwoch*	*Donnerstag*	*Freitag*	*Sonnabend*
1	Mathe	Kunst	Englisch	Geschichte	Mathe	
2	Deutsch	Kunst	Deutsch	Sport	Chemie	
3	Englisch	Latein	Latein	Religion	Erdkunde	
4	Erdkunde	Geschichte	Physik	Mathe	Musik	
5	Physik	Biologie	–	Englisch	Englisch	
6	Sport	Deutsch	–	–	Werken	

Answers

1

2

ein Bett	☒
einen Sessel	☐
einen Eßtisch	☐
einen Schrank	☒
einen Nachttisch	☒

3 Sie hat einen Schreibtisch, einen Computer, ein Sofa und einen Couchtisch.

4 Sie spült das Geschirr, deckt den Tisch und bügelt.

Aufgabe 11 Taschengeld

Transcript

1 Bettina: Ich heiße Bettina. Ich bekomme 10,– DM Taschengeld pro Woche. Ich brauche es für Schreibwaren, Bonbons und Geschenke. Ich spare für einen Computer.

2 Jens: Tag, ich heiße Jens. Ich bin sechzehn Jahre alt. Ich bekomme kein Taschengeld, aber ich verdiene schon etwas. Ich arbeite jedes Wochenende in einem Supermarkt. Ich bekomme dafür 90,– DM. Ich spare für ein Auto. Auch brauche ich das Geld für Getränke, Musikkassetten und Ausgehen.

3 Holger: Ich heiße Holger. Ich bekomme 5,– DM Taschengeld pro Woche. Ich brauche es für Comics, Eislaufen und Spiele. Ich spare nichts.

4 Olaf: Ich bin Olaf. Ich habe Glück, denn ich bekomme viel Taschengeld, 30,– DM pro Woche. Ich brauche es für mein Mofa und für Kleidung. Ich interessiere mich sehr für Mode.

5 Sigrid: Ich heiße Sigrid Müller. Ich bekomme 15,– DM Taschengeld und ich verdiene auch 30,– DM. Ich trage Zeitungen aus. Ich spare mein Taschengeld für die Ferien. Ich möchte im Sommer nach Amerika fahren.

6 Claudia: Ich heiße Claudia. Ich bekomme kein Taschengeld, keinen Pfennig. Mein Vater ist arbeitslos. Deshalb ist unsere Familie jetzt arm.

	Name	Taschengeld	verdienen	brauchen für	sparen für
1	Bettina	DM 10,–	–	Schreibwaren Geschenke Computer	Bonbons
2	Jens	–	DM 90,–	Getränke Musikkassetten Ausgehen	Auto
3	Holger	DM 5,–	–	Comics Eislaufen Spiele	–
4	Olaf	DM 30,–	–	Mofa Kleidung	–
5	Sigrid	DM 15,–	DM 30,–	–	Ferien
6	Claudia	–	–	–	–

Aufgabe 12 Ausflüge

Transcript

Also, gestern sind wir alle, das heißt mein Mann und unsere zwei Kinder, zum Zoo gefahren. Ich meine den Zoo in Frankfurt. Wir sind schon um halb neun losgefahren. Zuvor habe ich noch in der Küche belegte Brote gemacht und ein richtig nettes Picknick zusammengestellt. Wir sind mit dem Auto bis nach Darmstadt gefahren. Dort haben wir in der Nähe des Ostbahnhofs geparkt und sind mit der Bahn weiter nach Frankfurt gefahren. Weißt du, mein Mann fährt nicht gerne mit dem Auto in die Stadtmitte von Frankfurt. Da gibt es viel zu viel Verkehr, und der Zoo liegt ja genau in der Stadtmitte. Ja, die Kinder haben viel Spaß gehabt.

Unser Hansjörg hat die Löwen und Tiger sehr gern, während sich Monika mehr für Reptilien interessiert. Wir haben im Zoo auf einer Wiese unser Picknick gegessen. Aber dann, am Nachmittag hat es plötzlich angefangen zu regnen. Das war nicht so gut. Wir wurden alle ganz naß. Na ja, später so gegen halb sechs waren wir wieder zu Hause. Ich glaube, Dir würde so ein Tag im Zoo sicher auch gefallen.

Answers

Die Tante und ihre **Familie (*or:* zwei Kinder und ihr Mann)** haben gestern einen Ausflug gemacht. Sie sind zum Zoo gefahren. Sie sind zuerst mit dem **Auto (*or:* Wagen)** und dann mit der **Bahn** gefahren. Der Zoo von Frankfurt ist in der **Stadtmitte**. Sie haben viele Tiere gesehen. Hansjörg interessiert sich für **Löwen** und **Tiger**. Am Nachmittag war das Wetter nicht so gut. Es hat **geregnet**. Sie sind dann wieder zurückgefahren. Um **halb sechs (*or:* fünf Uhr dreißig)** waren sie zu Hause.

Aufgabe 13 Auf dem Campingplatz

Transcript

1 – Entschuldigen Sie, haben Sie noch Platz frei?
– Ja, wieviele Personen sind Sie?
– Wir sind vier Personen.
– Haben Sie ein Zelt?
– Nein, wir haben einen Wohnwagen.
– Wie lange bleiben Sie?
– Zwei Nächte.
– Wie ist Ihr Name, bitte?
– Meyer, Alfred Meyer.
– Können Sie das bitte buchstabieren?
– M-E-Y-E-R.
– Danke schön. Nehmen Sie bitte Platz Nummer 17.

2 – Guten Tag. Wir möchten zwei Nächte bleiben, haben Sie noch Platz?
– Ja, wieviele sind Sie?
– Zwei Erwachsene und drei Kinder.
– Sind Sie mit dem Wohnwagen hier?
– Ja, wir haben einen Wohnwagen.
– Gut. Sie bekommen Platz Nummer 19.
– Könnten wir bitte einen Platz am See haben?
– Ja, das geht. Dann bekommen Sie Platz 23.
– Danke.
– Wie heißen Sie, bitte?
– Schmidt, S-C-H-M-I-D-T, Hans.
– Danke.

3 – Grüß Gott.
– Grüß Gott. Kann ich Ihnen helfen?
– Ja. Wir hätten gern einen Platz für eine Nacht.
– Gut. Das geht. Zelt oder Wohnwagen?
– Wir sind mit dem Zelt hier.
– Sind das nur Erwachsene?
– Ja, wir sind sechs Studenten, drei Jungen und drei Mädchen.
– OK. Das geht. Auf welchen Namen geht das?
– Bernd Töpfer. T-Ö-P-F-E-R.
– Danke. Sie bekommen Platz vier.

4 – Guten Tag. Haben Sie noch einen Platz für eine Woche?
– Für eine Woche. Leider nicht. Nur noch für drei Tage. Dann sind wir ausgebucht.
– Also, dann eben für drei Tage. Wir haben einen Wohnwagen und brauchen Strom.
– Ja, das geht. Wieviele Personen sind Sie?
– Wir sind nur zwei. Meine Frau und ich.
– Wie heißen Sie bitte?
– Berger. Eberhard Berger. B-E-R-G-E-R.
– Danke. Sie bekommen Platz Nummer 3, gleich hier um die Ecke, mit Strom.
– Danke schön. Wo sind denn die Duschen?
– Die sind gleich hier um die Ecke.
– Danke.

Answers

1.
Name: **MEYER**
Aufenthalt: **2** *Tage* ______ *Woche(n)*
Personen: **vier**
Platz Nummer: **17**
Zelt: ______
Wohnwagen: **X**
Strom: ______

2.
Name: **SCHMIDT**
Aufenthalt: **2** *Tage* ______ *Woche(n)*
Personen: **zwei Erwachsene, drei Kinder**
Platz Nummer: **23**
Zelt: ______
Wohnwagen: **X**
Strom: ______

3.
Name: **TÖPFER**
Aufenthalt: **1** *Tage* ______ *Woche(n)*
Personen: **6**
Platz Nummer: **4**
Zelt: **X**
Wohnwagen: ______
Strom: ______

4.

Name: BERGER

Aufenthalt: 3 *Tage* ____ *Woche(n)*

Personen: 2

Platz Nummer: 3

Zelt: ____

Wohnwagen: X

Strom: X

Aufgabe 14 Man macht einen Termin aus

Transcript

1 – Praxis Dr. Meyer, Guten Morgen.
– Guten Tag. Könnte ich einen Termin haben, bitte?
– Ja. Können Sie am Mittwoch um 15.00 Uhr kommen?
– Mittwoch um drei Uhr, ja das geht. Danke.
– Gut, wie ist ihr Name bitte?
– Franz Müller.
– Also, Herr Müller, ihr Termin ist am Mittwoch um 15.00 Uhr.

2 – Praxis Dr. Meyer, Guten Morgen.
– Hallo. Hier ist Schneider. Erika Schneider. Ich hätte gern einen Termin Donnerstagnachmittag. Geht das?
– Ja, Frau Schneider. Dr. Meyer hat am Donnerstag um halb vier, also um 15.30 Uhr, noch einen Termin frei.
– Danke, das paßt sehr gut. Auf Wiederhören.

3 – Praxis Dr. Meyer, bitte sehr.
– Guten Tag. Ich muß ganz dringend den Arzt sehen. Kann ich in einer Stunde kommen?
– Wie ist ihr Name, bitte?
– Mein Name? Becker. Doris Becker. Aber es ist für meine Tochter. Sie ist sehr krank. Hat hohes Fieber und rote Flecken.
– Also, Frau Becker, die Sprechstunde ist eigentlich erst um 16.00 Uhr, aber sie können schon um Viertel vor vier kommen. Früher geht es leider nicht.
– Vielen Dank. Wir kommen dann um Viertel vor vier.

4 – Praxis Dr. Meyer, wie kann ich Ihnen helfen?
– Guten Tag. Mein Name ist Karl Berger. Kann ich diese Woche noch den Arzt sehen? Es ist wegen meinem Rücken.
– Wie wäre es mit Freitag um 17.00 Uhr?
– Nein, das geht leider nicht. Könnte ich vormittags, so gegen halb neun kommen?
– Ja, paßt es am Freitag, um Viertel nach acht vormittags?
– Danke. Das geht. Dann kann ich vor der Arbeit kommen.

5 – Praxis Dr. Meyer. Was kann ich für Sie tun?
– Grüß Gott. Ich hätte gern einen Termin für eine Untersuchung.
– Ja. Geht es am Donnerstag um elf Uhr?
– Ja, das geht.
– Wie heißen Sie bitte?
– Brigitte Grün.
– Gut, Frau Grün. Ihr Termin ist am Donnerstag um elf Uhr.
– Danke. Auf Wiederhören.

Answers

MONTAG

DIENSTAG

15.45 Doris Becker

MITTWOCH

15.00 Franz Müller

DONNERSTAG

11.00 Frau Grün
15.30 Frau Erika Schneider

FREITAG

08.15 Karl Berger

SONNABEND

STUNDE

Aufgabe 15 Im Sprechzimmer

Transcript

1 – So, Herr Müller. Wo tut es denn weh?
– Ich habe schon seit vier Tagen Halsschmerzen und kann kaum schlucken. Ich habe auch Husten.
– Dann machen Sie mal bitte den Mund auf. Ja, das ist ganz rot. Ich gebe ihnen ein Rezept für Halstabletten. Die können Sie in der Apotheke holen.
– Danke, Frau Doktor.

2 – Guten Tag Frau Schmitt. Was kann ich für Sie tun?
– Es ist mein Rücken. Ich habe starke Rückenschmerzen.
– Ja, das tut mir leid. Am besten nehmen Sie Schmerztabletten, Aspirin. Sie sollten auch nichts Schweres tragen und sich ein bißchen ausruhen.
– Danke, Frau Doktor.

3 – Wie geht es Ihnen heute, Herr Schulze?
– Ach, Frau Doktor. Es geht schon besser. Das Fieber und die Kopfschmerzen sind weg. Aber ich habe jetzt Bauchschmerzen und auch Durchfall.
– So, so. Darf ich mal sehen. Tut es hier weh und hier?
– Ja, au, au. Ja, das tut sehr weh. Au.
– Sie haben eine schlimme Magenverstimmung. Ich

verschreibe Ihnen einen Saft. Den bekommen Sie in der Apotheke.
- Vielen Dank, Frau Doktor.

4 – Nun, Sven. Was hast du denn gemacht?
- Ich habe mich in die Hand geschnitten. Das war mit meinem Taschenmesser.
- Tja, du solltest halt vorsichtiger sein. Laß mal sehen. Ja, die Wunde ist tief. Ich werde dir die Hand verbinden. Dann geh zur Apotheke und hole dir eine Salbe. Ich gebe dir ein Rezept für Salbe. Deine Mutter kann dir sicher helfen, die jeden Tag drauf zu machen. Das wird dann schnell verheilen.
- Gut. Vielen Dank.

Answers

1 Herr Muller: Halstabletten

2 Frau Schmitt: Schmerztabletten, Aspirin

3 Herr Schulze: Saft

4 Sven: Salbe

Aufgabe 16 In der Café-Konditorei

Transcript

1 – Bitte schön. Haben Sie schon gewählt?
- Ja. Zwei Tassen Kaffee und zwei Stück Erdbeerkuchen mit Sahne.
- Sonst noch etwas?
- Nein danke, das war's.

2 – Was möchten Sie, bitte?
- Ein Kännchen Tee mit Milch und ein Stück Schokoladentorte.
- Mit Sahne?
- Nein danke. Ohne Sahne.

3 – Bitte schön?
- Zweimal Limonade. Ein Glas. Was für Eissorten haben Sie?
- Also wir haben Erdbeer, Vanille, Schokolade, Himbeer, Nuß und Mokka.
- Ein Nußeis bitte und ein Vanilleeis.
- Eine große oder kleine Portion?
- Kleine Portionen, bitte. Mit Sahne.
- Also, zwei Glas Limonade, ein kleines Nußeis und ein kleines Vanilleeis, beide mit Sahne. Kommt alles gleich.

4 – Herr Ober.
- Ja, bitte. Was wünschen Sie?
- Eine Tasse Tee mit Zitrone und eine heiße Schokolade.
- Möchten Sie auch Kuchen?
- Nein danke. Aber bringen Sie uns zwei Tüten Chips.

Answers

1	Die junge Frau bestellt eine Tasse Kaffee.	**F**
	Sie bestellt auch zwei Stück Erdbeerkuchen mit Sahne.	**R**
2	Der Mann möchte ein Kännchen Tee mit Milch.	**R**
	Er bestellt auch ein Stück Schokoladenkuchen ohne Sahne.	**R**
3	Die zwei Freunde bestellen zwei Glas Cola.	**F**
	Sie möchten auch zwei große Portionen Eis mit Sahne.	**F**
4	Der Mann hätte gern eine Tasse Tee mit Milch.	**F**
	Er bestellt auch eine heiße Schokolade.	**R**
	Er möchte keinen Kuchen.	**R**

Aufgabe 17 An der Imbißstube

Transcript

1 – Einmal Bockwurst.
- Mit Senf?
- Ja, mit Senf.
- 4,50 DM, bitte.

2 – Bitte schön?
- Zweimal Schaschlik und eine große Portion Pommes.
- Mit Ketchup?
- Nein, mit Mayonnaise, bitte.
- 18,25 DM, bitte.

3 – Eine Frikadelle und eine Bratwurst. Die Frikadelle mit Currysoße bitte.
- Das macht 8,90 DM bitte.

4 – Eine Dose Cola, bitte, und eine Currywurst.
- Die Wurst mit Brötchen oder mit Brot?
- Im Brötchen DM bitte.
- Das kommt auf 6,40 DM.

5 – Eine Bratwurst, bitte.
- Etwas dazu?
- Nein danke.
- 3,50 DM bitte.

Answers

1 Einmal Bockwurst mit Senf

2 Zweimal Schaschlik, 1 große Pommes Frites mit Mayonnaise

3 Eine Frikadelle mit Currysoße, 1 Bratwurst

4 Eine Cola, 1 Currywurst mit Brötchen

5 Eine Bratwurst

Aufgabe 18 Im Restaurant

Transcript

Erster Teil

Vater:	Guten Tag.
Kellner:	Guten Tag. Suchen Sie einen Tisch?
Vater:	Ja, einen Tisch für fünf bitte.
Kellner:	Wie wäre es mit draußen auf der Terrasse. Es gibt dort einen schönen großen Tisch unter den Bäumen.
Großmutter:	Ach nein, es ist mir ein bißchen zu kühl auf der Terrasse. Es ist ja noch nicht richtig Sommer.
Vater:	Du hast recht. Haben Sie einen Tisch am Fenster mit Blick auf den Rhein?
Kellner:	Ja, dort drüben. Ich hole noch einen extra Stuhl. Sie haben bestimmt alle genug Platz.
Vater:	Sicher, das geht. Danke.

Zweiter Teil

Mutter:	Die Speisekarte bitte.
Kellner:	Ja, kommt sofort. So, möchten Sie schon die Getränke bestellen?
Vater:	Ja, für die Kinder zweimal Limonade.
Tochter:	Nein, Vati. Ich hätte lieber eine Cola.
Vater:	Also, eine Limonade, eine Cola. Was möchtest du, Mutter?
Großmutter:	Ich würde schon gern ein Glas Weißwein trinken. Einen lieblichen bitte.
Vater:	Gut, also ein Glas Weißwein für meine Mutter. Und du, Inge?

Mutter: Ich nehme auch einen Wein.
Vater: Schön. Also zwei Glas Weißwein, und für mich ein alkoholfreies Bier bitte.
Kellner: Ja, ich glaube ich habe das alles notiert: eine Limo, eine Cola, zwei Glas Weißwein und ein alkoholfreies Bier.

Dritter Teil

Kellner: Sind Sie mit der Speisekarte fertig?
Mutter: Ja, wir haben gewählt? Was wollt ihr haben?
Tochter: Ich esse ja kein Fleisch mehr. Es ist immer schwer, was Vegetarisches zu finden. Also, ich nehme eine Gemüsesuppe und ein Omelette mit Pilzen und Käse. Dazu auch einen Salatteller.
Mutter: Gut. Und du, Sven?
Sohn: Ich esse gern ein Steak. Ich hätte gern das Pfeffersteak mit Pommes Frites und Salat.
Vater: Und du, Mutter? Was möchtest du?
Großmutter: Ich nehme auch eine Gemüsesuppe. Dann hätte ich gern Goulasch mit Nudeln und Erbsengemüse.
Mutter: Ja, und ich hätte gern die Forelle blau, mit Salzkartoffeln und Salat. Ja, das wäre alles.
Kellner: Gut. Einmal Omelette und Salatteller, zweimal Gemüsesuppe, einmal Pfeffersteak und einmal Forelle blau. Stimmt das so?
Vater: Ja, das stimmt. Nur ich habe noch nicht bestellt. Da kommt also noch ein Wiener Schnitzel mit Pommes Frites und Salat dazu. Als Vorspeise nehme ich eine Hühnerpastete.
Kellner: Danke. Ich habe alles notiert.

Vierter Teil

Kellner: Hat es ihnen geschmeckt?
Vater: Ja, danke. Es war ausgezeichnet?
Kellner: Möchten Sie einen Nachtisch oder einen Kaffee?
Vater: Ja, dreimal gemischtes Eis mit Sahne, einmal Obstsalat mit Sahne und ein Schokoladeneis ohne Sahne. Bringen Sie uns dann auch drei Tassen Kaffee.
Kellner: Danke schön.

(noise of dishes being brought and put down)

Vater: Herr Ober. Bitte zahlen.
Kellner: Ja, mein Herr. Ich bringe die Rechnung.
Vater: Nehmen Sie Kreditkarten?
Kellner: Das ist kein Problem. Einen Moment mal. So, unterschreiben Sie hier bitte.
Vater: Danke schön. Und das ist für Sie.
Kellner: Vielen Dank. Auf Wiedersehen.

Answers

Erster Teil

1 Auf der Terrasse.
2 Es ist zu kühl.
3 Am Fenster.

Zweiter und dritter Teil

See table at bottom of page.

Vierter Teil

1 Man wählt drei gemischte Eis mit Sahne.
2 Die Familie hat drei Tassen Kaffee.
3 Der Vater bezahlt mit einer Kreditkarte.

Aufgabe 19 In der Bank

Transcript

1 – Guten Tag. Ich möchte Geld wechseln.
– Ja, dann müssen Sie zu Schalter drei gehen.
– Guten Tag, ich habe fünfzig Pfund Sterling. Ich möchte sie wechseln.

Person	Getränk	Vorspeise	Hauptgericht
Mutter	Weißwein	–	Forelle blau Salzkartoffeln Salat
Vater	alkoholfreies Bier	Hühnerpastete	Wiener Schnitzel Pommes Frites Salat
Sohn	Limonade	–	Pfeffersteak Pommes Frites Salat
Tochter	Cola	Gemüsesuppe	Omelette mit Pilzen und Käse Salatteller
Großmutter	Weißwein	Gemüsesuppe	Goulasch Nudeln Erbsengemüse

- Ja, das geht.
- Wie steht das Pfund heute?
- 2,27 DM.
- Muß ich eine Gebühr zahlen?
- Ja, die Gebühr beträgt vier Mark. Gehen Sie bitte mit diesem Zettel zur Kasse. Dort bekommen Sie das Geld.
- Danke.

2 - Guten Morgen. Ich möchte gern einen Reisescheck einlösen.
- Ja. Haben Sie einen Ausweis dabei?
- Hier ist mein Paß.
- Gut. Unterschreiben Sie hier bitte, das Geld holen Sie sich an der Kasse.
- Danke schön.

3 - Grüß Gott. Könnte ich bitte österreichische Schilling haben?
- Ja, wieviel wollen Sie wechseln?
- Also, neunhundert Mark.
- Das tut mir leid. So viele Schilling habe ich heute nicht. Können Sie morgen wiederkommen? Ich kann das Geld dann für Sie bestellen.
- Ach, bis morgen warten. Das ist nicht so gut. Wir fahren morgen schon los nach Österreich. Wann macht denn die Bank auf?
- Wir sind ab neun Uhr geöffnet.
- Na, das geht.
- Die Schilling werden für Sie an der Kasse liegen.
- Vielen Dank.

4 - Guten Tag. Ich möchte dreißig schweizer Franken in D-Mark umtauschen.
- Ja. Kein Problem. So, hier ist Ihr Zettel. Nehmen Sie den Zettel mit zur Kasse.
- Danke schön.

Answers

1 Der erste Kunde will Pfund Sterling umtauschen.
2 Der zweite Kunde muß seinen Ausweis zeigen.
3 Der dritte Kunde möchte 900,–DM in Schilling umtauschen.
4 Der dritte Kunde muß bis morgen auf die Schilling warten.
5 Der vierte Kunde hat schweizer Franken.

Aufgabe 20 Auf der Post

Transcript

1 - Guten Tag. Was kostet ein Brief nach England, bitte?
- Eine Mark.
- Vier Briefmarken zu einer Mark, bitte.

2 - Ich möchte Postkarten nach Spanien schicken. Was kostet das?
- Eine Postkarte nach Spanien. Achtzig Pfennig.
- Drei Briefmarken zu achtzig Pfennig bitte.

3 - Eine Postkarte nach Südafrika bitte.
- Südafrika, das macht eine Mark zwanzig.
- Eine Briefmarke zu einer Mark zwanzig, bitte.

4 - Was kostet ein Brief nach Berlin?
- Ein Brief. Das macht eine Mark.
- Sechs Briefmarken zu einer Mark.

5 - Ein Brief nach Amerika, bitte.
- Ist das per Luftpost?
- Ja, Luftpost bitte.
- Das kostet dann eine Mark fünfzig.
- OK. Drei Briefmarken zu einer Mark fünfzig.

Answers

Land/Stadt	Postkarte: DM	Brief: DM
England	–	1,– DM
Spanien	80 Pf	–
Südafrika	1,20 DM	–
Berlin	–	1,– DM
Amerika	–	1, 50 DM

Aufgabe 21 Im Bus

Transcript

1 - Einmal zum Rathaus, bitte.
- Eine Mark.
- Kann ich am Rathaus aussteigen?
- Ja, der Bus hält genau vor dem Rathaus.

2 - Zweimal zum Schwimmbad, bitte.
- Da müssen Sie mit der Linie drei fahren. Dieser Bus fährt nur zum Bahnhof.
- Ach so. Danke.

3 - Ein Erwachsener, ein Kind zum Bahnhof bitte.
- Zwei Mark fünfzig bitte.
- Danke schön.

4 - Entschuldigen Sie, fahren Sie zum Flughafen.
- Nein, da fahren Sie am besten mit der U-Bahn.
- Danke.

5 - Zweimal zum Schloß, bitte.
- Seid ihr jünger als 14 Jahre?
- Nein. Ich bin sechzehn, aber meine Freundin ist dreizehn.
- Also, dann ist das ein Erwachsener und ein Kind, zwei Mark siebzig.

Answers:

Nummer	Wieviele Personen	Richtung	Preis
1	1	Rathaus	1,– DM
2	2	Schwimmbad	
3	1 Erwachsener 1 Kind	Bahnhof	2,50 DM
4	–	Flughafen	–
5	1 Erwachsener 1 Kind	Schloß	2,70 DM

Aufgabe 22 Am Bahnhof

Transcript

1 - Guten Tag. Wann fährt der nächste Zug nach Hameln?
- Um 13.45 Uhr. Sie haben gerade einen verpaßt.

- Einmal einfach nach Hameln, bitte.
- Zweiter Klasse?
- Ja, zweiter Klasse.
- 35,– DM bitte.
- Wo fährt er ab?
- Auf Gleis 9.
- Danke.

2
- Zweimal nach Hamburg, hin und zurück, bitte.
- Wollen Sie mit dem Inter-City fahren?
- Ja, bitte.
- Dann müssen Sie noch einen Zuschlag von zwölf Mark zahlen.
- In Ordnung.
- 68,— DM, bitte.

3
- Ich will am Donnerstagabend nach Genf fahren.
- Sie haben einen Zug um 19 Uhr.
- Wann kommt er in Genf an?
- Um 23.45 Uhr.
- Muß ich umsteigen?
- Nein, der Zug fährt durch.
- Danke.

4
- Ich fahre am Freitagvormittag nach Ulm. Könnte ich bitte einen Platz reservieren?
- Mit welchem Zug fahren Sie?
- Mit dem um 10.15 Uhr.
- Ja, das geht. Raucher oder Nichtraucherabteil?
- Raucherabteil, bitte.
- Möchten sie einen Fensterplatz, oder einen Seitengangplatz?
- Fensterplatz, bitte.
- Gut. Ihr Platz ist in Wagen M, Sitzplatz Nummer 29.

Answers

Dialog 1

1 Hameln

2 13.45 Uhr

3 Gleis 9

Dialog 2

1 Rückfahrkarte/hin und zurück

2 Inter-City

3 68,— DM

Dialog 3

1 Genf

2 23.45 Uhr

3 Nein

Dialog 4

1 Am Freitagvormittag

2 Nein

3 Fensterplatz

Aufgabe 23 Mit dem Auto

Teil 1

Transcript

- Volltanken, bitte.
- Super oder normal?
- Super bleifrei, bitte. Können Sie bitte auch den Luftdruck und das Öl kontrollieren?
- Also, die Luft ist in Ordnung, aber Sie brauchen einen halben Liter Öl.
- Gut. Danke. Kann ich hier Getränke kaufen?
- Ja, bei der Kasse.

Answers:

1 Claudia tankt super bleifrei.

2 Claudias Auto braucht noch Öl.

3 Die Getränke sind bei der Kasse.

Teil 2

Transcript

- Autohaus Schubert. Was kann ich für Sie tun?
- Guten Tag. Ich habe eine Panne. Können Sie einen Mechaniker schicken?
- Wo sind Sie denn?
- Ich bin auf der B45, am Ortsende von Höchst. Es gibt hier links eine Brücke und einen kleinen Wald.
- Ja, ich glaube, ich weiß wo Sie sind. Was ist denn los mit dem Wagen?
- Der Motor ist ganz heiß. Ich habe angehalten, aber jetzt startet das Auto nicht mehr.
- Was für einen Wagen haben Sie?
- Einen BMW 316.
- Bleiben Sie bitte am Wagen. Ich werde gleich einen Mechaniker schicken.

Answers:

4 Claudia telefoniert mit der Werkstatt.

5 Sie ist auf der B45 in der Nähe eines Waldes.

6 Der Motor ist kaputt.

Teil 3

Transcript

- Ja, mein Fräulein, da ist mehr kaputt als ich dachte.
- Ist es schlimm?
- Ja, der Motor ist ganz kaputt. Er hat kein Kühlwasser mehr.
- Wann können Sie es reparieren?
- Erst morgen, oder übermorgen. Ich habe sehr viel zu tun. Am besten lassen Sie den Wagen hier und fahren mit dem Zug nach Hause. Ich rufe Sie an, wenn ich mit dem Auto fertig bin.
- Hmm. Gut. So machen wir das. Wo ist denn der Bahnhof?
- Der ist ganz in der Nähe. Gehen Sie hier geradeaus bis zum Marktplatz. Der Bahnhof ist dann in der ersten Straße links.
- Danke schön.

Answers

7 Der Mechaniker kann das Auto übermorgen reparieren.

8 Claudia fragt nach dem Weg zum Bahnhof.

Aufgabe 24 Im Kino

Erster Teil

Transcript

- Was wollen wir heute Abend machen? Hast du Lust, in den Jugendklub zu gehen?
- Was macht man im Jugendklub?
- Ja, man kann Tischtennis spielen, andere Leute treffen. Heute ist dort eine Disco.

- Eine Disco. Ich kann nicht tanzen und mag Popmusik nicht so sehr.
- Ok, wollen wir ins Kino gehen?
- Gute Idee, was läuft denn?
- Also im Kino Rex gibt es *Ein Schweinchen namens Babe.* Hast du davon gehört?
- Ja, diesen Film gibt es in England auch. Er soll sehr komisch sein. Ist der Film in der Originalfassung?
- Nein, er ist auf deutsch, aber es gibt Untertitel. Also, machen wir uns auf den Weg. Nimm deine Jacke mit. Es kann später kalt werden.
- Gehen wir zu Fuß zum Kino?
- Nein, das würde zu lange dauern. Wir fahren mit dem Bus Linie 3. Der hält neben dem Kino.

Answers

Gesternabend war ich mit Jens zu Hause. Jens wollte zum ***Jugendklub*** gehen, aber ich hatte keine Lust, weil ich nicht ***tanzen*** kann. Dann hatte Jens die Idee, zum ***Kino*** zu gehen. Wir sind mit dem ***Bus (Linie 3)*** gefahren.

Zweiter Teil

Transcript

- Guten Abend. Zwei Eintrittskarten bitte.
- Seid ihr beide unter sechzehn?
- Ja, wir sind vierzehn Jahre alt.
- Gut, dann bezahlt ihr noch den Kinderpreis. Ab sechzehn muß man als Erwachsener zahlen. Welche Plätze möchtet ihr, Sperrsitz oder Balkon?
- Was ist denn billiger?
- Na, Balkon kostet mehr, sieben Mark für Kinder. Sperrsitz oder Parkett kostet nur vier Mark fünfzig.
- Also, zweimal Sperrsitz bitte.
- Möchtet ihr auch ein Programm?
- Nein Danke, aber geben Sie uns bitte zwei Tüten Chips und zwei Dosen Fanta.
- Das macht elf Mark dreißig bitte.
- Bitte sehr.
- Danke. Und drei Mark siebzig zurück. Viel Spaß.

Answers

Im Kino gibt es Plätze im ***Sperrsitz*** oder auf dem ***Balkon***. Jens hat die Eintrittskarten gekauft. Es kostet nicht so viel, wenn man unter ***sechzehn*** Jahre ist. Jens hat auch zwei Tüten Chips und zwei Dosen Fanta gekauft. Er hat ***11,30 DM (elf Mark dreißig)*** bezahlt.

Aufgabe 25 Wie komme ich am besten ...

Transcript

1
- Entschuldigung, wie komme ich am besten zum Bahnhof?
- Zum Bahnhof, hmm. Warten Sie mal. Also, gehen Sie hier geradeaus und nehmen Sie die zweite Straße links. Der Bahnhof ist auf der rechten Seite.
- Danke schön.
- Gern geschehen.

2
- Entschuldigen Sie bitte, ist hier in der Nähe ein Café?
- Ein Café. Ja, da ist eins am Schillerplatz.
- Wie komme ich zum Schillerplatz?
- Also das ist gar nicht weit. Gehen Sie hier rechts um die Ecke, dann geradeaus bis zur Ampel. Gehen Sie über die Ampel und das Café ist genau vor Ihnen.
- Vielen Dank.
- Bitte schön.

3
- Guten Tag. Können Sie mir sagen, wo das Museum ist?
- Natürlich. Es ist ein bißchen kompliziert. Am besten gehen Sie geradeaus. Dann nehmen Sie die dritte Straße links. Danach biegen Sie nach rechts ab.
- Ist es weit?
- Ungefähr anderthalb Kilometer.
- Na ja, das geht. Danke schön.
- Nichts zu danken.

4
- Grüß Gott. Können Sie mir bitte sagen, wie ich zum Rathaus komme?
- Ja, das kann ich. Das Rathaus ist ganz in der Nähe. Gehen Sie hier rechts und dann an der Ampel links. Das Rathaus ist auf der rechten Seite, gleich neben der Post.
- Danke.
- Bitte.

5
- Guten Tag. Wo ist denn hier die Galerie?
- Die Galerie. Hmm. Ich weiß auch nicht. Am besten Fragen Sie jemand anderen.
- OK. Danke.

Answers

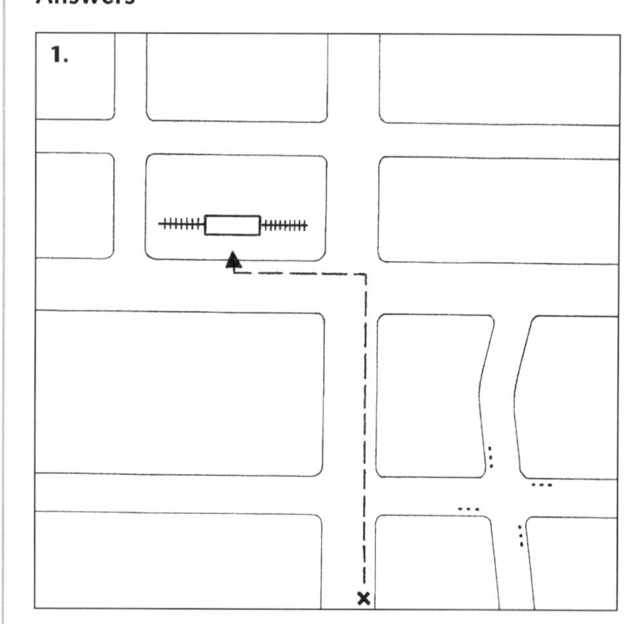

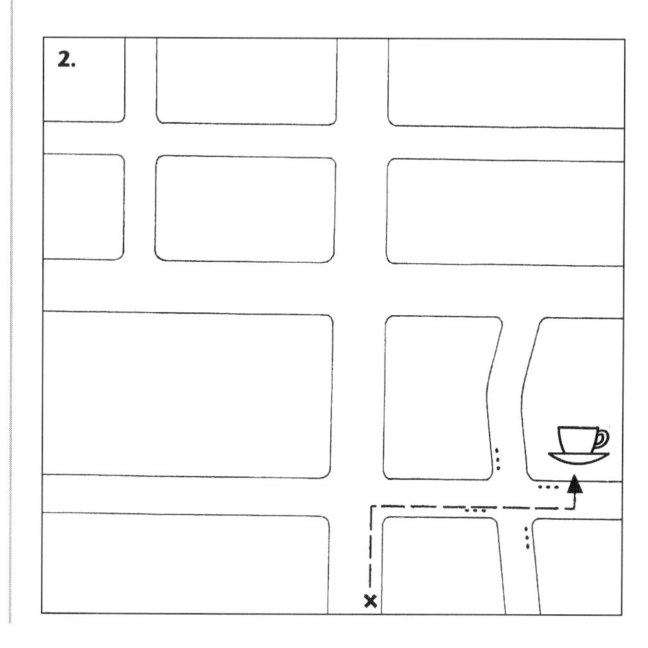

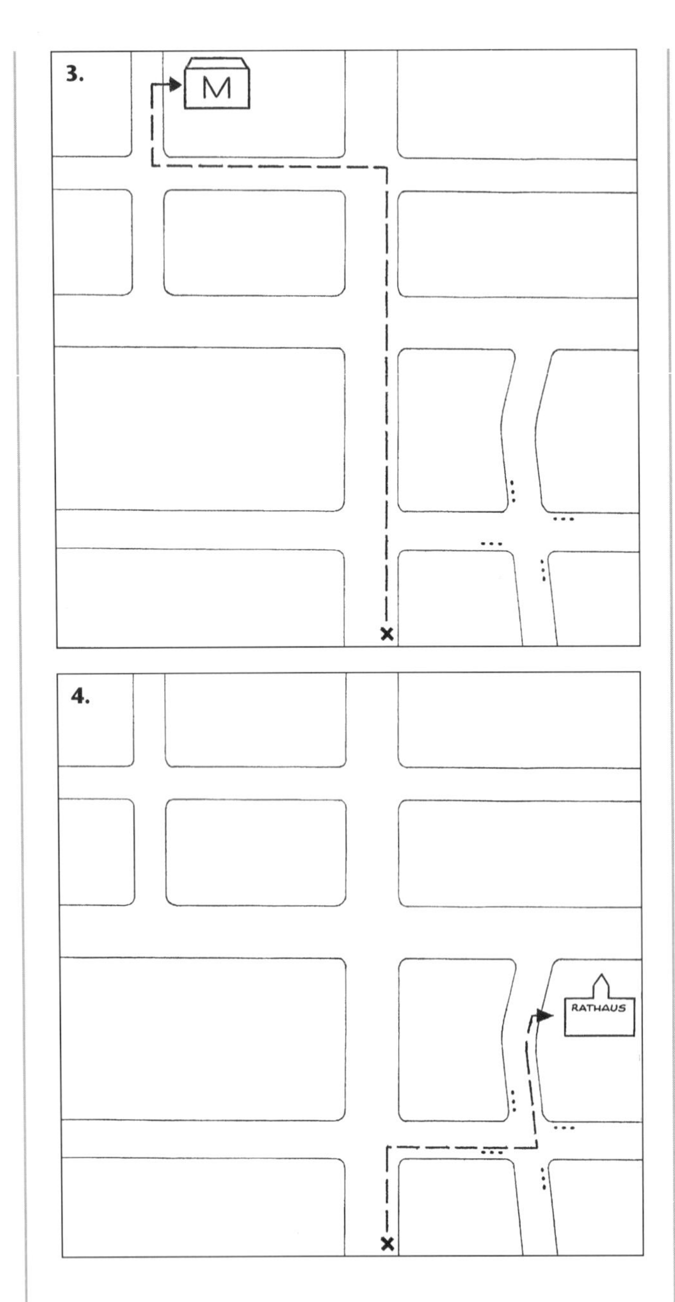

Aufgabe 26 Einkaufen – Obst und Gemüse

Transcript

1 – Was darf es sein?
– Ich möchte drei Äpfel, bitte.
– Sonst noch etwas?
– Ein Kilo Kartoffeln und ein Pfund Tomaten.
– Bitte sehr.
– Was kosten die Apfelsinen?
– Die Apfelsinen kosten 60 Pfennig das Stück.
– Geben Sie mir noch drei Apfelsinen. Das wäre es dann. Danke.
– Das macht alles zusammen 10,50 DM.
– Ich habe nur einen Hundertmarkschein? Können Sie 100 Mark wechseln?
– Ja, das geht. 89,50 DM zurück.

2 – Guten Tag. Haben Sie Birnen?
– Ja, drei Mark das Pfund.
– Also, zwei Pfund Birnen, bitte, und sechs Bananen.
– Sonst noch etwas?
– Nein danke, das war's.
– Das macht 9 DM, bitte.

3 – Morgen.
– Morgen.
– Ich hätte gern drei Kilo Kartoffeln und ein Kilo Karotten.
– Das ist alles?
– Ja.
– Das macht zusammen 7,20 DM.

4 – Grüß Gott.
– Grüß Gott, Herr Müller. Sie wünschen bitte?
– Ach, ein halbes Pfund Erdbeeren bitte und vier Zitronen, bitte.
– Sonst noch etwas?
– Ja, einen großen Blumenkohl bitte. Das ist dann alles.
– Danke, das kostet 15,00 DM.

5 – Ja, bitte?
– Ein Kilo grüne Bohnen und einen Kopfsalat.
– Sonst noch etwas?
– Ja, zwei Melonen und ein halbes Kilo Kirschen.
– Das wäre alles?
– Ja, das wäre alles.
– Danke. Das macht 17,50 DM alles zusammen.
– Ach, ich habe nur einen Fünfzigmarkschein.
– Na, das geht schon. So 32,50 DM zurück.

Answers

Nummer	Ware	Preis
1	3 Äpfel 1 Kilo Kartoffeln 1 Pfund Tomaten 3 Apfelsinen	10,50 DM
2	2 Pfund Birnen 6 Bananen	9,— DM
3	3 Kilo Kartoffeln 1 Kilo Karotten	7,20 DM
4	$^{1}/_{2}$ Pfund Erdbeeren, 4 Zitronen 1 großen Blumenkohl	15,00 DM
5	1 Kilo grüne Bohnen 1 Kopfsalat 2 Melonen $^{1}/_{2}$ Kilo Kirschen	17,50 DM

Aufgabe 27 Kleiderkauf

Erster Teil

Transcript

– Guten Tag, kann ich Ihnen helfen, meine Damen?
– Ja, wir möchten uns nur umsehen, bitte.
– Aber gerne, meine Damen.
– Du, Bianca, schau die Röcke dort. Die sehen echt dufte aus.

- Ja, du hast recht. Soll ich mal einen anprobieren.
- Na, warum nicht.
- Entschuldigen Sie, kann ich diesen Rock anprobieren bitte.
- Selbstverständlich. Die Kabinen sind dort drüben.
- Danke.

[*pause*]
- Und, Bianca. Paßt der Rock?
- Ich weiß nicht. Schau mal. Meinst du nicht, er ist ein bißchen zu lang?
- Nein, das finde ich nicht. Die Farbe steht dir sehr gut. Nur dürfte der Rock ein bißchen größer sein. Der hier ist etwas eng.
- Du hast recht. Entschuldigen Sie, haben Sie denselben Rock eine Nummer größer?
- Tut mir leid, dieser hier ist der letzte Rock. Wir haben ihn aber in braun.
- Schade, aber braun gefällt mir nicht. Danke für Ihre Hilfe.
- Auf Wiedersehen.
- Auf Wiedersehen.

Answers

1 In die Stadt

2 Kleider für die Ferien

3 In eine Boutique

4 Bianca probiert einen Rock an, aber er ist zu eng.

Zweiter Teil

Transcript

- Sieh dir das an. Alle diese Röcke im Sonderangebot. Nur 35,00 DM. Das ist wirklich preiswert.
- Ja, und meine Lieblingsfarbe ist auch dabei.
- Entschuldigen Sie, suchen Sie etwas Bestimmtes?
- Ja, ich suche einen Rock für mich.
- Welche Größe haben Sie?
- Größe 38, denke ich.
- Sehen wir mal, was wir in dieser Größe haben. So, also hier haben wir einen Rock in dunkelblau, in braun und einen in schwarz.
- Darf ich den schwarzen Rock anprobieren, bitte?

Etwas später:
- Ja, dieser Rock ist genau richtig. Den nehme ich. Wo muß ich bezahlen, bitte?
- Die Kasse ist dort hinten, neben dem Aufzug.
- Danke schön.

5 Die Mädchen gehen in ein Kaufhaus.

6 Bianca trägt Größe 38.

7 Bianca möchte den schwarzen Rock anprobieren.

8 Die Kasse ist neben dem Aufzug.

Reading: *questions*

Introduction

Reading tasks are perhaps one of the easiest in language learning. Usually you will be able to understand more than you are able to use actively.

When you face a reading passage, take the time to read it through once without immediately looking up words in a dictionary or glossary. Try to work out the general gist of the piece, what it is about. Then take a look at the questions and make sure you understand them. Next, read the text again and see where you will find the answers to the questions. Usually the questions on a passage follow the passage, so the first one will refer to the first paragraph and so on.

You will see that in this way you can manage most texts without a dictionary. Don't start looking up every single new word but just those which seem to be really necessary. When you use a dictionary take care which translation or meaning is given. Often a word can have several meanings, depending on the context. So don't assume the first one given is the correct one. Also watch out for adjectives used as nouns or verbs used as nouns.

Aufgabe 1 Im Bahnhof

Ordne die Schilder den richtigen Orten auf dem Plan zu.

Match the signs to the correct places on the plan at the bottom of the page.

1 Fahrkartenschalter ☐
2 Imbiß ☐
3 Gepäckschließfächer ☐
4 Gleis ☐
5 Toiletten ☐

Aufgabe 2 In der Stadt

Wo kann ich ... bekommen? Schreibe den richtigen Buchstaben in das Kästchen.

Where can I get ...? Write the correct letter in the box (see top of next page).

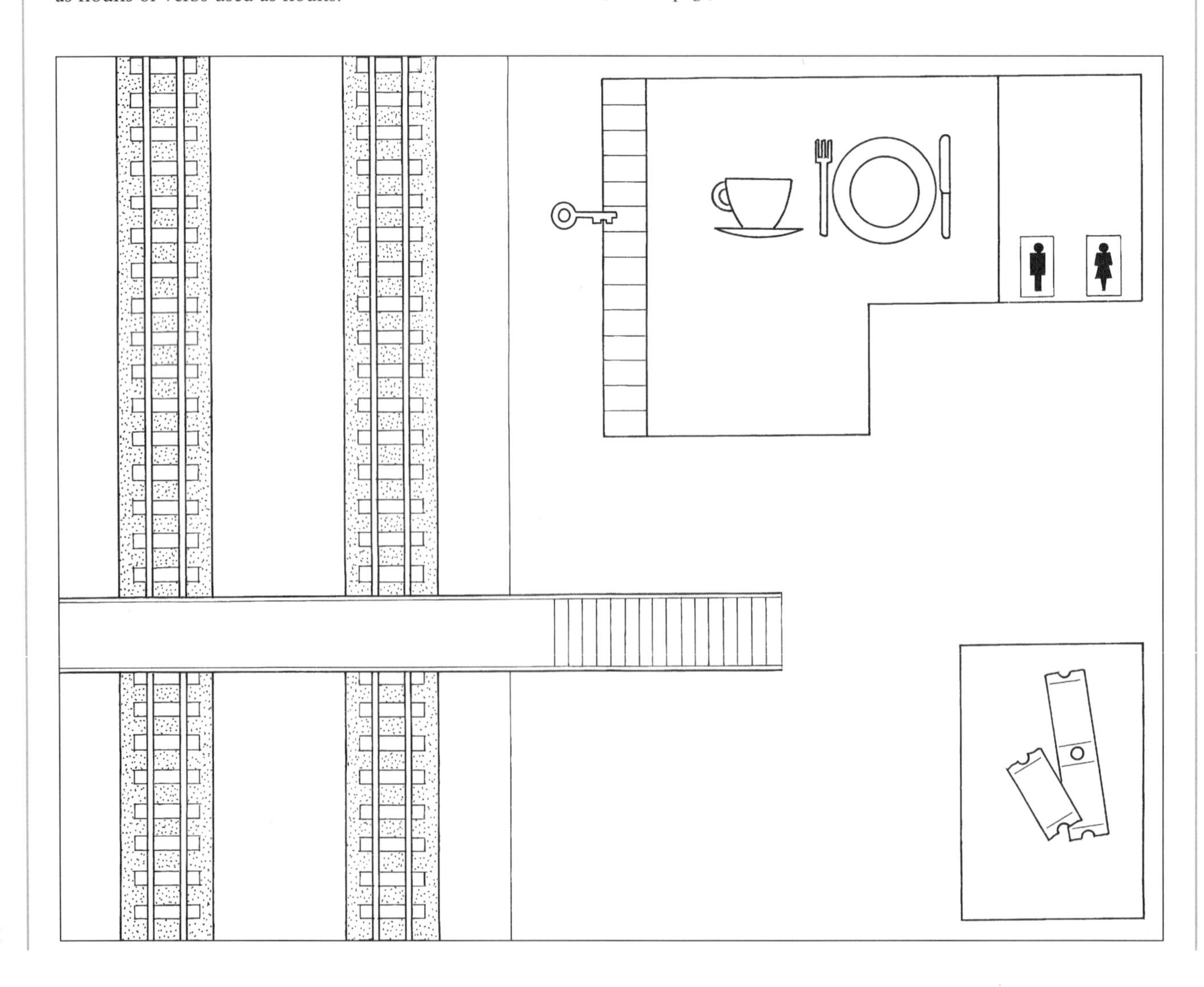

1 Kopfschmerztabletten ☐
2 Aufschnitt ☐
3 Brot ☐
4 Äpfel ☐
5 Taschenbuch ☐

Aufgabe 3 Ein Stadtplan

Welcher Buchstabe ist es?

Which letter is it?

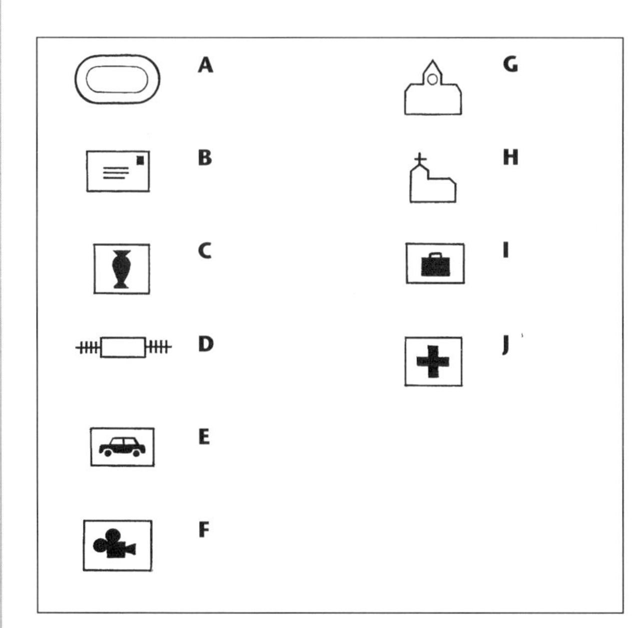

1 das Kino ☐
2 die Kirche ☐
3 der Bahnhof ☐
4 das Krankenhaus ☐
5 das Rathaus ☐
6 das Museum ☐
7 das Informationsbüro ☐
8 der Parkplatz ☐
9 die Post ☐
10 das Stadion ☐

Aufgabe 4 Man kocht Schokoladenpudding

Bringe die Anleitung in die richtige Reihenfolge.

Put the instructions into the right order.

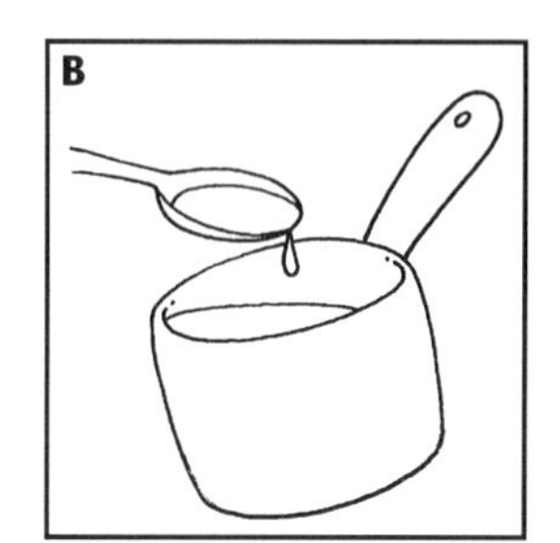

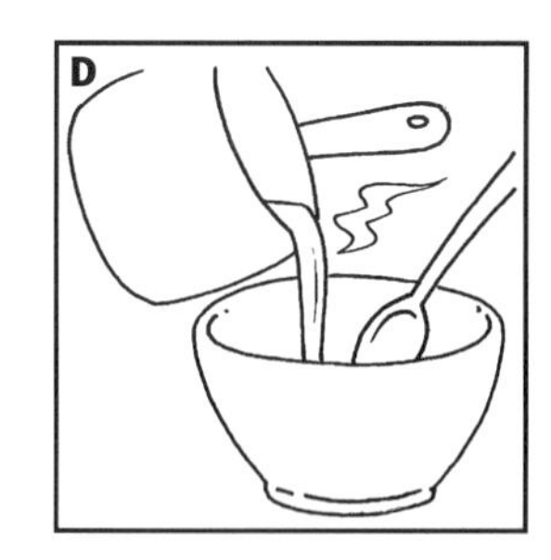

Anleitung

Die heiße Milch in die Schüssel geben. Rühren. ☐

Einen Liter Milch in einem Topf zum Kochen bringen. ☐

Das Puddingpulver mit dem Eßlöffel Milch in einer Schüssel anrühren. ☐

Einen Eßlöffel Milch aus dem Topf nehmen. ☐

Inhalt der Schüssel in den Topf zurückgeben. Kochen lassen. ☐

Aufgabe 5 Eine Speisekarte

Was hast du bestellt? Schreibe auf Englisch auf, welche drei Gänge du von der Speisekarte ausgesucht hast.

What did you order? Write in English the 3 courses you have chosen from the menu.

Vorspeisen

Tagessuppe	2,50 DM
Hühnersuppe	5,– DM
Nudelsuppe	5,50 DM
Hühnerpastete	6,– DM
Walddorf Salat	6,– DM

Hauptgerichte

Omelette mit Pilzen, Salzkartoffeln und Salat	9,50 DM
Wiener Schnitzel, Pommes Frites und Salat	12,– DM
Brathähnchen, Kartoffeln und Erbsengemüse	12,– DM
Pfeffersteak, Pommes Frites und Salat	15,– DM
Rindergoulasch mit Nudeln	15,– DM
Forelle blau, Kartoffeln, Erbsen und Karotten	16,– DM
Kalbsbraten, Knödel, Kohl	16,– DM

Nachspeisen

Obstsalat	2,50 DM
Vanillepudding	2,50 DM
Gemischtes Eis ohne Sahne	3,-- DM
mit Sahne	3,30 DM
Eisbecher mit Likör	5,-- DM

Getränke

Coca Cola 0,25 ℓ	2,– DM
Limonade 0,25 ℓ	2,– DM
Mineralwasser 0,2 ℓ	2,10 DM
Bier (hell) 0,2 ℓ	3,– DM
Bier (dunkel) 0,2 ℓ	3,– DM
Weißwein, Glas	4,– DM
Weißwein, Flasche	9,– DM

Aufgabe 6 Ein Stundenplan

Sieh dir den Stundenplan von Max an und beantworte die Fragen auf deutsch.

Look at Max's timetable and answer the questions in German.

Zeit	Montag	Dienstag	Mittwoch	Donnerstag	Freitag
7.45–8.30	Deutsch	Mathe	Englisch	Erdkunde	Biologie
8.35–9.20	Mathe	Englisch	Latein	Chemie	Kunst
9.35–10.20	Musik	Biologie	Sport	Physik	Kunst
10.25–11.10	Latein	Geschichte	Erdkunde	Biologie	Sport
11.20–12.05	Englisch	Chemie	Physik	Englisch	Sport

1 Wann beginnt die erste Stunde?
2 Wann hat Max Mathe?
3 Was hat Max in der dritten Stunde am Mittwoch?
4 Wieviele Fremdsprachen lernt Max?
5 Wieviele Stunden Englisch hat Max?

Aufgabe 7 Eine Telefonnotiz

Lies diese Notiz.

Read this message.

Martina hat um 5.00 Uhr angerufen.
Sie fragt: Willst du mit ihr heute abend Tennis spielen?
Wenn Ja – hole sie um 6.00 Uhr von zu Hause ab.
Wenn Nein – rufe sie vor 6.00 Uhr an. Sie möchte morgen zu Bettinas Party gehen.

Richtig oder Falsch?

True or false?

1 Martina hat um 6.00 Uhr angerufen. ☐
2 Martina will heute abend Tennis spielen. ☐
3 Martina will um 5.00 Uhr Tennis spielen. ☐
4 Du holst Martina von der Schule ab. ☐
5 Martina geht morgen zur Party. ☐

Aufgabe 8 Das Feriendorf Osterthal

Kreuze die richtige Antwort an.

Tick the correct answers.

Feriendorf Osterthal

- ideal für Ihre Ferien
- in der Nähe des Waldes
- eigenes Schwimmbad
- Tennisplätze
- Sauna und Solarium
- Reiten und Angeln möglich
- jedes Ferienhaus hat 4 bis 6 Betten, Küche mit Mikrowellenherd, Wohnzimmer mit Fernseher und Stereoanlage, WC und Dusche
- Restaurant im Feriendorf
- Frühstucksdienst: Nach Anruf bringt man das Frühstück zu Ihnen ins Ferienhaus.
- Preise von 45,– DM (Vorsaison) bis 73,– DM (Hauptsaison) pro Person und Nacht.
- Ermäßigung für Kinder
- Hunde erlaubt.

1 Das Feriendorf Osterthal ist in der Nähe
- des Strandes ☐
- des Waldes ☐
- des Schwimmbades ☐
- des Stadions ☐

2 Im Feriendorf Osterthal kann man
- reiten und angeln ☐
- wandern und skifahren ☐
- töpfern und musizieren ☐
- schwimmen und radfahren ☐

3 Jedes Ferienhaus hat
- ein Bad ☐
- eine Terrasse ☐
- ein Telefon ☐
- einen Fernseher ☐

4 Man bringt
- das Abendessen in das Ferienhaus. ☐
- den Kaffee ☐
- das Frühstück ☐
- das Mittagessen ☐

5 Es gibt eine Ermäßigung für
- Eltern ☐
- Familien ☐
- Hunde ☐
- Kinder ☐

Aufgabe 9 Im Freizeitpark

Lies die Broschüre mit Informationen über die Aktivitäten im Freizeitpark.

Read the brochure with information about the activities in the leisure park.

Tägliches Programm im Freizeitpark Lochmühle

von 9.00 Uhr bis 10.00 Uhr: Fütterung der Kleintiere, Schafe, Kaninchen, Ziegen.

ab 10.00 Uhr: Tennis und Federball .

von 11.00 Uhr: bis 12.00 Uhr Vorführung im Delphinarium (Delphine, Wale, Haie).

um 14.30 Uhr: Theater auf der Wiese.

von 14.00 Uhr bis 16.00 Uhr: Töpfern und Basteln in der Burg.

um 14.00 Uhr, 15.00 Uhr: und 16.00 Uhr: Wanderung durch den Naturpark.

Um wieviel Uhr kann man folgendes machen?

At what time can you do the following?

1 Um wieviel Uhr kann man Tiere sehen?
2 Um wieviel Uhr kann man Tennis spielen?
3 Um wieviel Uhr kann man spazierengehen?
4 Um wieviel Uhr kann man basteln?
5 Um wieviel Uhr kann man Theater sehen?

Lieber David,

vielen Dank für Deine Weihnachtskarte und den Brief. Ich hoffe, Du hast viele Geschenke bekommen. Hattest Du viel Spaß bei Deiner Großmutter?

Bei uns feiert man Weihnachten am Heiligen Abend, das heißt am 24. Dezember. Am Nachmittag sind alle Geschäfte geschlossen, Leute arbeiten nicht. Jeder ist zu Hause in der Familie. Wir gehen am Heilig Abend immer in die Kirche. Danach gibt es zu Hause die Geschenke. Im Wohnzimmer steht ein großer Weihnachtsbaum.

Am ersten Weihnachtsfeiertag kommen meine Großeltern zu uns. Wir essen eine Gans mit Knödeln und Rotkraut. Am Nachmittag gibt es immer Stollen und Sahne. Den Stollen backt meine Großmutter selbst. Sie kann sehr gut backen. Wie feierst Du Weihnachten?

Übermorgen ist Sylvester. Wir bleiben dann bis nach Mitternacht auf. Wir spielen Karten und hören Musik. Um Mitternacht läuten alle Glocken und viele Leute machen ein Feuerwerk. Das ist sehr laut aber auch lustig. Wir trinken Sekt und rufen: 'Prosit Neujahr.'

Der erste Januar ist Neujahr. Viele Familien gehen an diesem Tag in einem Restaurant essen.

So, ich muß jetzt noch schnell in Stadt, um etwas einzukaufen. Ich wünsche Dir alles Gute zum Neuen Jahr.

Viele Grüße auch an Deine Eltern,

Aufgabe 10 Weihnachten

Dein Brieffreund schreibt Dir einen Brief, in dem er über Weihnachten erzählt.

Your penfriend sends you a letter, in which he talks about Christmas.

Now answer these questions in English:

1. When do Germans celebrate Christmas?
2. What do Bernd and his family do before they open the presents?
3. What do they have in the living-room?
4. Who comes to visit on Christmas Day?
5. What food do the family eat?
6. What special thing do Germans do on New Year's Eve?
7. Where do a lot of families eat on New Year's Day?

Aufgabe 11 Ostern

Du erhälst einen Brief von deiner Brieffreundin, die dir etwas über Ostern schreibst.

You receive a letter from your penfriend, who tells you something about Easter.

Beantworte jetzt die Fragen:

Now answer the questions:

1. Welche Ferien hat Heike jetzt?
2. Wohin gehen Heike und ihre Familie am Ostersonntag?
3. Was suchen Heike und ihre Schwester später?
4. Wer hat diese Dinge versteckt?
5. Wie ist das Wetter?
6. Was tragen die Mädchen oft an diesem Tag?

Liebe Charlotte,

wie geht es Dir? Hast Du jetzt auch Ferien? Ich bin froh, daß wir zwei Wochen frei haben. Die letzten Wochen in der Schule waren sehr hektisch. Hast Du auch so viele Hausaufgaben und Klassenarbeiten?

Aber jetzt sind Osterferien – Gott sei Dank. Ostern ist in Deutschland nicht so ein großes Fest wie Weihnachten. Am Ostersonntag gehen wir natürlich erst in die Kirche. Später suchen meine Schwester und ich Ostereier. Das sind buntbemalte Hühnereier, die im Garten 'vom Osterhasen' versteckt wurden. Früher, als ich noch jünger war, glaubte ich an den Osterhasen. Es ist natürlich Vati, der die Eier versteckt. Auch gibt es Eier aus Schokolade.

Oft ist es an Ostern noch ziemlich kalt, aber man merkt doch, daß es bald Frühling und Sommer wird. Wenn die Sonne scheint, tragen wir unsere neuen Sommerkleider zum ersten Mal.

Was machst Du in den Osterferien? Ich freue mich schon auf Deinen Besuch im Mai.

Viele Grüße,

Aufgabe 12 Der Ausflug

Du liest einen Aufsatz, den dein deutscher Brieffreund für die Schule geschrieben hat.

You are reading an essay which your German penfriend has written for school.

Der Ausflug

Am ersten Mai haben meine Freunde, Bettina und Holger, und ich einen großen Ausflug gemacht. Wir haben uns mit unseren Fahrrädern um halb neun bei Bettina getroffen.

Zuerst sind wir nach Hüttenthal gefahren. Die Straße war klein und es gab nicht viele Autos. Das Wetter war schön, die Sonne hat geschienen und es gab keinen Wind.

Wir haben dann am See in Hüttenthal gehalten. Das Wasser im See war ganz kalt. Wir haben nicht gebadet.

Danach sind wir weiter nach Beerfelden gefahren. Die Straße war steil, immer bergauf. Das war hart. Aber nach einer Stunde waren wir da.

Später sind wir durch den Wald zu einem alten Schloß gefahren. Keiner wohnt in diesem Schloß. Es ist eine Ruine. Wir haben auf den Resten der dicken Mauern gespielt.

Plötzlich haben wir Donner gehört. Es hat angefangen zu regnen. Bettina hatte keinen Anorak, sie war ganz naß. Wir sind schnell nach Eberbach gefahren.

In Eberbach haben wir den Bahnhof gefunden. Wir sind in den Zug eingestiegen und nach Michelstadt gefahren. Eine halbe Stunde später waren wir wieder zu Hause. Meine Mutter hat uns heiße Schokolade und Suppe gemacht.

Numeriere die Bilder, so daß sie in der Reihenfolge der Geschichte stehen.

Number the pictures to put them in the correct order.

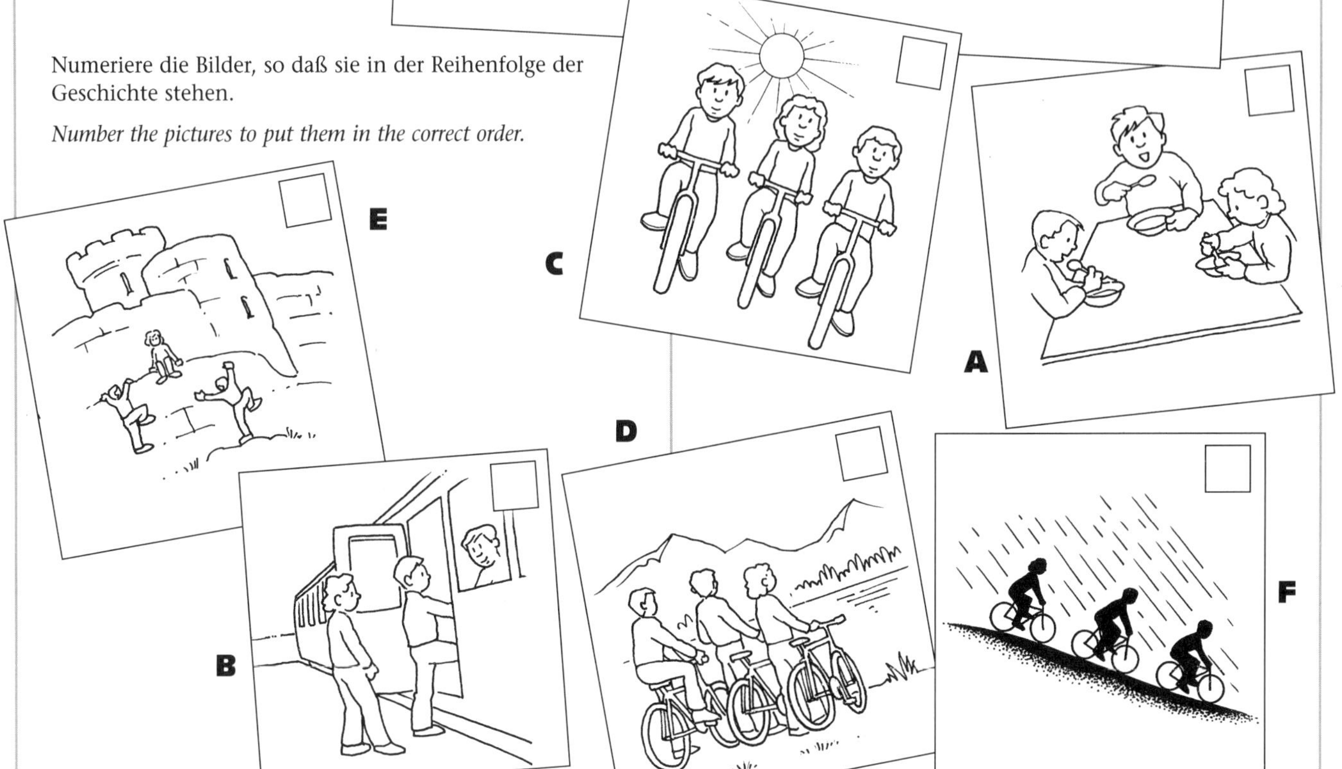

Aufgabe 13 Eine Reservierung

Lies diesen Brief.

Read this letter.

18 St Pauls Road
Northampton
NN12 7BD

den 19. April 1996

Hotel zur Sonne
Am Unterberg 13

D-64720 Michelstadt
Germany

Sehr geehrte Damen und Herren,

mit diesem Brief möchte ich eine Reservierung für die Zeit vom 15. bis zum 20. September machen.

Reservieren Sie bitte zwei Einzelzimmer und ein Doppelzimmer mit Halbpension.

Ich möchte gern in Michelstadt ein Auto mieten. Schicken Sie mir bitte eine Liste der Autoverleihfirmen und Preislisten.

Vielen Dank für Ihre Mühe,

mit freundlichen Grüßen

Jack Smith

Kreuze die Aussagen an, die richtig sind.

Tick the statements which are true.

Herr Smith	macht eine Reservierung	für zwei Nächte.	☐
		für vier Personen.	☐
	reserviert	zwei Doppelzimmer.	☐
		zwei Zimmer mit Dusche.	☐
		zwei Zimmer mit Frühstück.	☐
	möchte	ein Auto leihen.	☐
	möchte	eine Preisliste.	☐

Aufgabe14 Aus der Zeitung

Lies den Artikel und beantworte die Fragen auf englisch.

Read the article and answer the questions in English.

Teure Tierliebe

Düsseldorf, den 13. März

Eine alte Dame hatte gestern einen schweren Unfall in der Bahnhofstraße. Frau Hilde H.,78, Lehrerin, ist mit ihrem Auto zum Supermarkt gefahren. Unterwegs hat sie einen alten Hund gesehen, der allein über die Straße gelaufen ist. Hilde H. hat angehalten und das Tier in ihr Auto genommen. Kurz vor dem Bahnhof ist der Hund unruhig geworden und hat Hilde in ihre rechte Hand gebissen. Die alte Dame hat vor Schmerz geschrieen und war gegen zwei geparkte Wagen gefahren, der Wagen hat schließlich vor den Tischen des Bahnhofscafés angehalten. Der Sachschaden beträgt 22 000,— DM.

1. Where did the old lady have her accident?
2. What was her former job?
3. Which animal did she pick up?
4. What did the animal do, once it was in her car?
5. What did the lady hit with her car?
6. Where did her vehicle finally stop?

Reading: *answers*

Aufgabe 1 Im Bahnhof

Ordne die Schilder den richtigen Orten auf dem Plan zu.

Match the signs to the correct places on the plan.

1 Fahrkartenschalter **C**
2 Imbiß **B**
3 Gepäckschließfächer **E**
4 Gleis **A**
5 Toiletten **D**

Aufgabe 2 In der Stadt

1 Kopfschmerztabletten **F**
2 Aufschnitt **B**
3 Brot **A**
4 Äpfel **E**
5 Taschenbuch **C**

Aufgabe 3 Ein Stadtplan

Welcher Buchstabe ist es?

Which letter is it?

1 das Kino **F**
2 die Kirche **H**
3 der Bahnhof **D**
4 das Krankenhaus **J**
5 das Rathaus **G**
6 das Museum **C**
7 das Informationsbüro **I**
8 der Parkplatz **E**
9 die Post **B**
10 das Stadion **A**

Aufgabe 4 Man kocht Schokoladenpudding

Anleitung:

1 Einen Liter Milch in einem Topf zum Kochen bringen.
2 Einen Eßlöffel Milch aus dem Topf nehmen.
3 Das Puddingpulver mit dem Eßlöffel Milch in einer Schüssel anrühren.
4 Die heiße Milch in die Schüssel geben. Rühren.
5 Inhalt der Schüssel in den Topf zurückgeben. Kochen lassen.

Aufgabe 5 Eine Speisekarte

The answers to this will vary. Below is a translation of the menu to check your answers against.

Starters
soup of the day
chicken soup
noodle soup
chicken vol-au-vent
Waldorf salad

Main courses
omelette with mushrooms, potatoes and salad
Wiener schnitzel, chips, salad
roast chicken, potatoes, peas
pepper steak, chips, salad
beef goulash with noodles
trout, potatoes, peas and carrots
roast veal, dumplings, cabbage

Deserts
fruit salad
vanilla pudding
mixed ice without cream
with cream
knicker-bocker glory with liquor

Drinks
cola
lemonade
mineral water
beer (light)
beer (dark)
white wine (glass)

Aufgabe 6 Ein Stundenplan

1 Wann beginn die erste Stunde?
Um 7.45 Uhr

2 Wann hat Max Mathe?
Montag, in der zweiten Stunde.
Dienstag in der ersten Stunde.

3 Was hat Max in der dritten Stunde am Mittwoch?
Sport

4 Wieviele Fremdsprachen lernt Max?
Zwei

5 Wieviele Stunden Englisch hat Max?
Vier

Aufgabe 7 Eine Telefonnotiz

1 Martina hat um 6.00 Uhr angerufen. **F**
2 Martina will heute abend Tennis spielen. **R**
3 Martina will um 5.00 Uhr Tennis spielen. **F**
4 Du holst Martina von der Schule ab. **F**
5 Martina geht morgen zur Party. **R**

Aufgabe 8 Das Feriendorf Osterthal

1 Das Feriendorf Osterthal ist in der Nähe des Strandes ☐

des Waldes ☒
des Schwimmbades ☐
des Stadions ☐

2 Im Feriendorf Osterthal kann man
reiten und angeln ☒
wandern und skifahren ☐
töpfern und musizieren ☐
schwimmen und radfahren ☐

3 Jedes Ferienhaus hat
ein Bad ☐
eine Terrasse ☐
ein Telefon ☐
einen Fernseher ☒

4 Man bringt
das Abendessen in das Ferienhaus ☐
den Kaffee ☐
das Frühstück ☒
das Mittagessen ☐

5 Es gibt eine Ermäßigung für
Eltern ☐
Familien ☐
Hunde ☐
Kinder ☒

Aufgabe 9 Im Freizeitpark

1 Um wieviel Uhr kann man Tiere sehen?
Von 9.00 – 10.00 Uhr und 11.00 bis 12.00 Uhr

2 Um wieviel Uhr kann man Tennis spielen?
Ab 10.00 Uhr

3 Um wieviel Uhr kann man spazierengehen?
um 14.00, 15.00 und 16.00 Uhr

4 Um wieviel Uhr kann man basteln?
von 14.00 bis 16.00 Uhr

5 Um wieviel Uhr kann man Theater sehen?
um 14.30 Uhr

Aufgabe 10 Weihnachten

1 When do Germans celebrate Christmas?
On December 24th

2 What do Bernd and his family do before they open the presents?
Go to church

3 What do they have in the living-room?
A Christmas tree

4 Who comes to visit on Christmas Day?
The grandparents

5 What food do the family eat?
A goose and stollen

6 What special thing do Germans do on New Year's Eve?
They let off fireworks

7 Where do a lot of families eat on New Year's Day?
In a restaurant

Aufgabe 11 Ostern

1 Welche Ferien hat Heike jetzt?
Osterferien

2 Wohin gehen Heike und ihre Familie am Ostersonntag?
In die Kirche

3 Was suchen Heike und ihre Schwester später?
Ostereier

4 Wer hat diese Dinge versteckt?
Der Osterhase/ihr Vater

5 Wie ist das Wetter?
Es ist kalt

6 Was tragen die Mädchen oft an diesem Tag?
Neue Kleider

Aufgabe 12 Der Ausflug

Correct solution as here:.

A–1 Three children and their bikes by a lake.

B–2 Three children eating soup in a dining room.

C–3 Three children cycling in the sun.

D–4 The children climbing on the walls of an old castle.

E–5 The children cycling through the rain, downhill

F–6 The children catching the train back home.

Aufgabe 13 Eine Reservierung

Herr Smith

macht eine Reservierung	für zwei Nächte.	☐
	für vier Personen.	☒
reserviert	zwei Doppelzimmer.	☐
	zwei Zimmer mit Dusche.	☐
	zwei Zimmer mit Frühstück.	☐
möchte	ein Auto leihen.	☒
möchte	eine Preisliste.	☒

Aufgabe 14 Aus der Zeitung

1 Where did the old lady have her accident?
In Station Road.

2 What was her former job?
Teacher.

3 Which animal did she pick up ?
An old dog.

4 What did the animal do, once it was in her car?
Bit her right hand.

5 What did the lady hit with her car?
Two parked cars.

6 Where did her vehicle finally stop?
In front of the tables of the station café.

Speaking: *questions*

Introduction

Many people find this aspect of German the easiest, because you don't have to be quite so accurate when speaking as when writing. It is always more important to get the message across than to be grammatically exact. So don't be shy – speak out!

Remember to speak clearly. In German there are no silent endings. Every syllable of a word is pronounced. German vowel sounds are sometimes a bit tricky for British people to produce, especially the Umlauts ä, ö and ü. But don't give up, with practice you will improve, perhaps without even noticing it.

In this section you'll find a number of role-plays to do. Answers are given at the end of the section. The dialogues are recorded on the cassette. Use the pause or stop button on your cassette player to give you time to repeat the correct answers.

Situation 1 Wie komme ich am besten ... ?

Du bist in der Stadt und fragst nach dem Weg.

You are in town and ask the way.

Beispiel: Entschuldigung, wie komme ich am besten zum Rathaus?

1

2

3

4

5

6

7

8

9

POST

10

BANK

11

KAUFHAUS

Situation 2 Du beschreibst den Weg

Jetzt beschreibst du den Weg.

Now you describe the way.

1 Entschuldigung, wie komme ich zum Hallenbad?

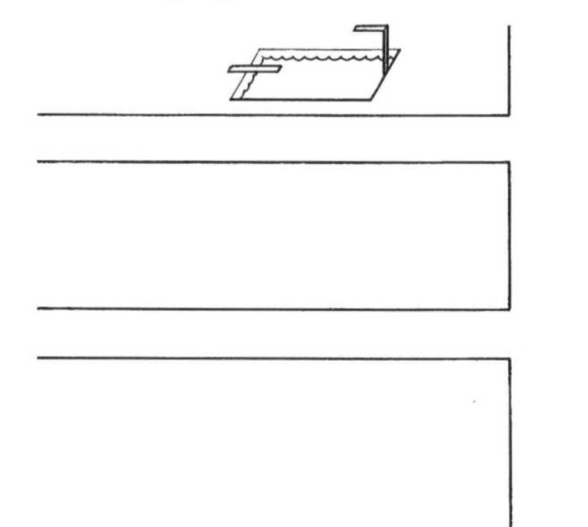

2 Entschuldigung, wie komme ich zum Dom?

3 Entschuldigung, wie komme ich am besten zum Hotel?

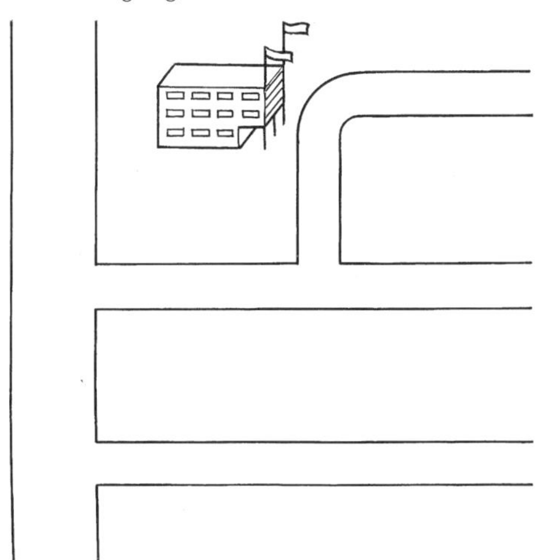

4 Entschuldigung, ist hier in der Nähe ein Briefkasten?

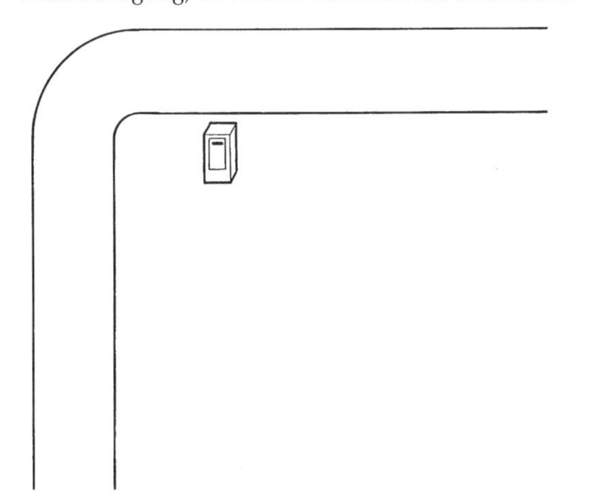

5 Entschuldigung, wie komme ich am besten zum Stadion?

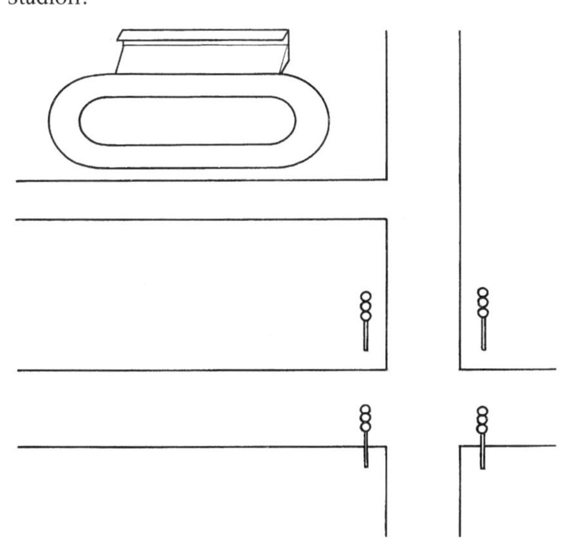

Situation 3 Was ist mit ihm los?

Schau dir diesen armen Jungen an. Kannst du sagen, was mit ihm los ist?

Look at this poor boy (at the top right-hand side of the page). Can you say what is wrong with him?

Situation 4 Wo tut es weh?

Kannst du sagen, wo es ihnen weh tut? Schau dir die Bilder an.

Look at the pictures. Can you say where it hurts?

1

2

3

4

5

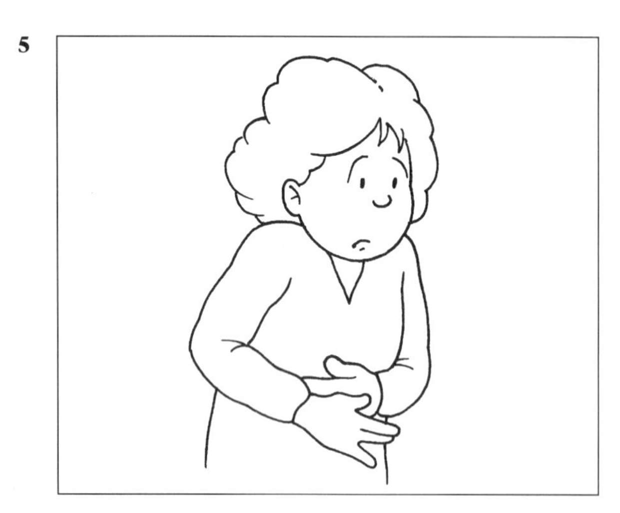

6

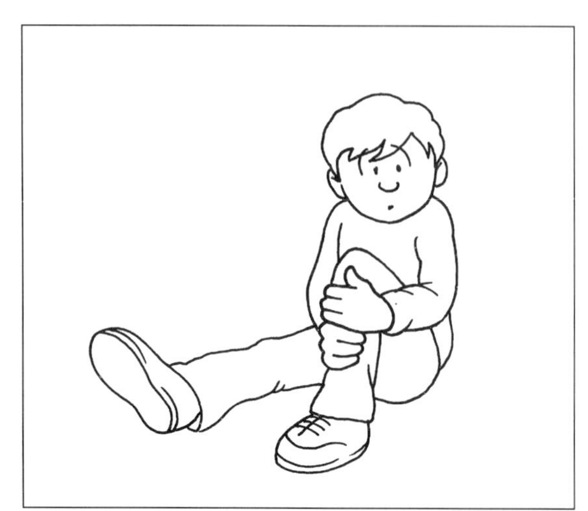

Situation 5 Du machst einen Termin aus

Du bist in Deutschland und möchtest einen Termin beim Zahnarzt. Was sagst du zur Sprechstundenhilfe?

You are in Germany and would like an appointment with the dentist. What do you say to the receptionist?

– Guten Tag. Praxis Dr. Meier. Kann ich Ihnen helfen?

– *Say you would like an appointment.*

– Paßt es Ihnen am nächsten Donnerstag?

– *Ask if they haven't got anything earlier.*

– Nein, früher geht es leider nicht.

– *Say that you will wait then.*

– Gut, also am Donnerstag um 15.00 Uhr.

– *Say thank you and good bye.*

Situation 6 Was bestellst du?

Du bist im Café und bestellst. Schau dir die Bilder an. Was sagst du?

You are in a café giving your order. Look at the pictures. What do you say?

1

2

3

4

5

Situation 7 Im Café

Ergänze den Dialog.
Complete the dialogue.

– Guten Tag, was wünschen Sie bitte?

– Ja, kommt sofort. ... Bitte sehr.

– Geht das zusammen oder getrennt?

– *Say you are paying together.*

– Gut, das macht 23,– DM, bitte.

– *Say you have only a 100,– DM note.*

– Das geht schon. So, bitte, 77,– DM zurück. Danke schön.

– *Say goodbye.*

Situation 8 An der Imbißstube

Bestelle Essen an der Imbißstube.

Order something to eat at the snack bar.

1 – Bitte sehr?
–

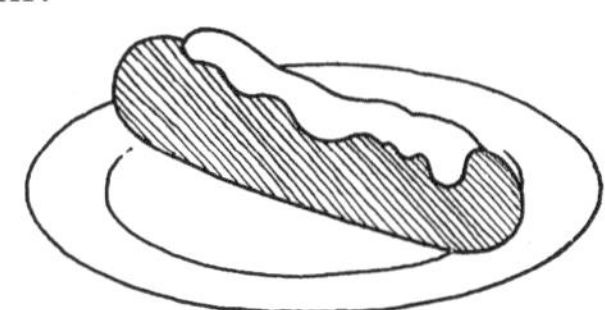

– Mit Senf?
–

– Das macht 4,— DM, bitte.

2 – Bitte sehr?
–

– Sonst noch etwas?
–

– 12,— DM, bitte.

3 – Was darf es sein?
–

– Eine große Portion?
–

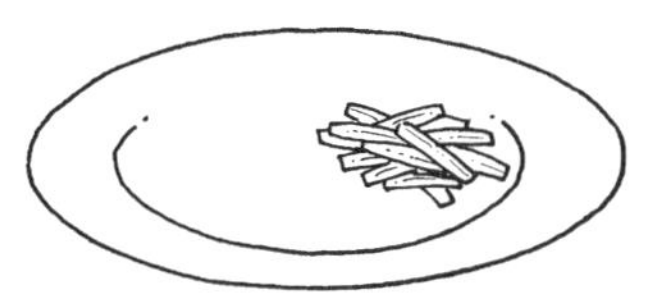

– Mit Ketchup?
–

– Und zu trinken?
–

– 8,— DM, bitte.

4 – Sie wünschen bitte?
–

– Ist das alles?
–

– Das macht 11,50 DM, bitte.

5 – Ja, bitte?
–

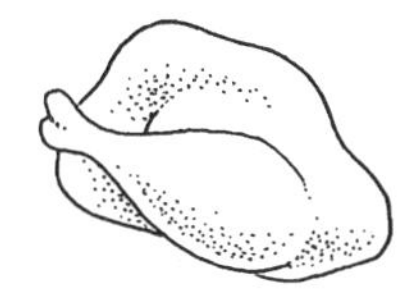

– Mit Pommes Frites?
–

– 6,— DM, bitte.

6 – Bitte sehr?

–

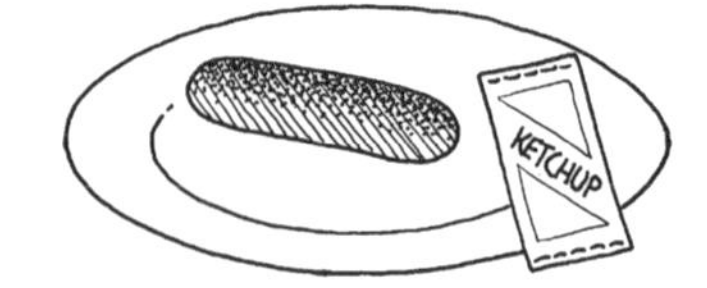

– Die Wurst mit Currysoße?

–

– Das macht dann 6,20 DM, bitte.

Situation 9 Im Restaurant

Schau dir die Speisekarte an. Dann beantworte die Fragen der Kellnerin. Suche die Speisen von der Karte aus.

Look at the menu. Then answer the waitress's questions. Choose dishes from the menu.

Menu

Vorspeisen

Tagessuppe	2,50 DM
Hühnersuppe	5,– DM
Nudelsuppe	5,50 DM
Hühnerpastete	6,– DM
Walldorf Salat	6,– DM

Hauptgerichte

Omelette mit Pilzen, Salzkartoffeln und Salat	9,50 DM
Wiener Schnitzel, Pommes Frites und Salat	12,– DM
Brathähnchen, Kartoffeln und Erbsengemüse	12,– DM
Pfeffersteak, Pommes Frites und Salat	15,– DM
Rindergoulasch mit Nudeln	15,– DM
Forelle blau, Kartoffeln, Erbsen und Karotten	16,– DM
Kalbsbraten, Knödel, Kohl	16,– DM

Nachspeisen

Obstsalat	2,50 DM
Vanillepudding	2,50 DM
Gemischtes Eis ohne Sahne	3,-- DM
mit Sahne	3,30 DM
Eisbecher mit Likör	5,-- DM

Getränke

Coca Cola 0,25 ℓ	2,– DM
Limonade 0,25 ℓ	2,– DM
Mineralwasser 0,2 ℓ	2,10 DM
Bier (hell) 0,2 ℓ	3,– DM
Bier (dunkel) 0,2 ℓ	3,– DM
Weißwein, Glas	4,– DM
Weißwein, Flasche	9,– DM

Die Kellnerin fragt:

– Haben Sie schon gewählt?

– ______________________________

– Was möchten Sie zu trinken?

– ______________________________

– Möchten Sie eine Vorspeise?

– ______________________________

– Was wünschen Sie als Hauptgericht?

– ______________________________

– Möchten Sie die Nachspeise schon jetzt bestellen?

– ______________________________

– Danke schön. Es kommt sofort.

Situation 10 Einkaufen am Markt

Du gehst auf dem Wochenmarkt einkaufen. Was sagst du?

You are shopping in the market. What do you say?

1 – Guten Tag, was darf es sein?

–

– Sonst noch etwas?

–

– Also, das macht 6,– DM zusammen.

2 – Guten Morgen. Sie wünschen, bitte?

–

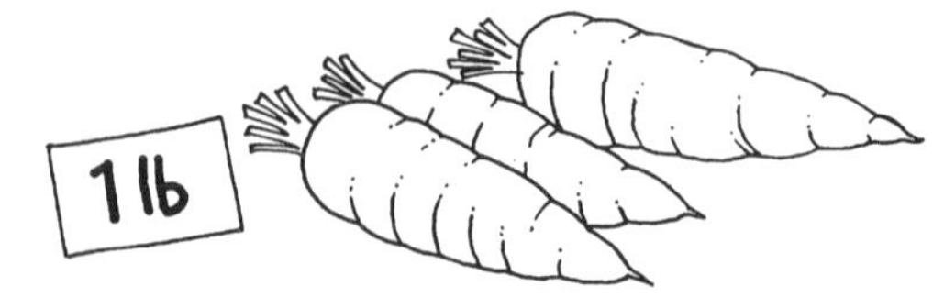

– Das wäre alles?

–

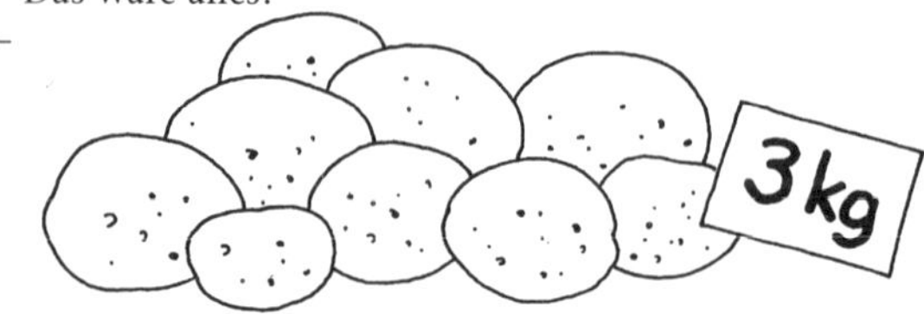

– Das macht 4,– DM, bitte.

3 – Guten Tag. Was möchten Sie, bitte?

–

– Sonst noch etwas?

–

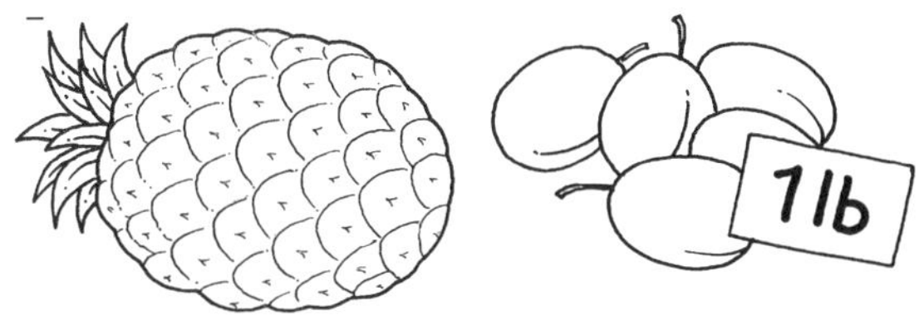

– Danke. Das macht dann 9,20 DM, bitte.

4 – Grüß Gott. Was darf es sein?

–

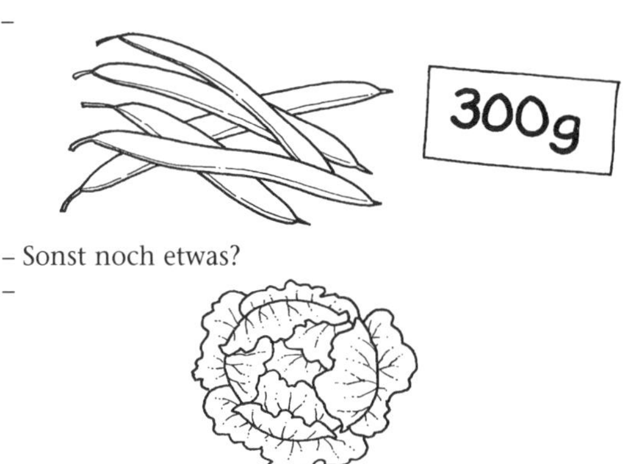

– Sonst noch etwas?

–

– So, das kostet 5,— DM

Situation 11 Reiseandenken

Du suchst ein Geschenk für deine Schwester. Der Verkäufer zeigt dir ein Buch, aber es ist zu teuer. Du hast nur 15,– DM. Der Verkäufer zeigt dir dann eine Trachtenpuppe. Deine Schwester mag so etwas nicht. Zum Schluß zeigt er dir einen grünen Schal. Du möchtest den Schal, aber in rot. Du bittest den Verkäufer, das als Geschenk einzupacken.

You are looking for a present for your sister. The assistant shows you a book, but it is too expensive. You have only 15,– DM. The assistant then shows you a doll in traditional costume. Your sister doesn't like that sort of thing. In the end, he shows you a green scarf. You would like the scarf, but in red. Finally, you ask the assistant to wrap it as a present.

– Guten Tag. Suchen Sie etwas Bestimmtes?

– You want a present for your sister.

– Wie wäre es mit einem Buch? Das hier kostet nur 20,– DM.

– It is too expensive.

– Oder schauen Sie hier, eine Trachtenpuppe.

– Your sister doesn't like dolls.

– Vielleicht einen Schal. Dieser kostet nur 10,– DM. Er ist sehr schön.

– You would like a scarf, but in red.

– Kein Problem. Wir haben ihn auch in rot.

– Ask him to wrap it as a present.

– Natürlich. Kommen Sie bitte mit zur Kasse.

Situation 12 Deine Brieffreundin kauft einen Rock

Du kaufst mit deiner Brieffreundin in einem Kaufhaus ein. Du hilfst ihr, einen Rock zu finden.

You are shopping in a department store with your penfriend. You are helping her to find a skirt.

– Tell her to look over there. There are skirts on special offer.

– Oh ja, diese Röcke sind einfach toll.

– Ask her if she wants to try one on.

– Ja, das ist eine gute Idee. Ich nehme diesen schwarzen hier.

[Nach ein paar Minuten]

Was meinst du? Paßt er mir?

– You say it is a bit tight.

– Du hast recht. Ich nehme ihn in der nächsten Größe.

– You tell her that this skirt really suits her.

– Danke. Ich nehme ihn.

Situation 13 Du kaufst einen Pullover

Du suchst einen Pullover für dich.

You are looking for a jumper for yourself.

– Ask the shop assistant if they have any jumpers on special offer.

– Ja, wir haben diese hier. Sie kosten nur 35,— DM.

– Say you would like to try one on.

– Aber gerne. Welche Größe haben Sie?

– Say you need size 34.

– In dieser Größe haben wir einen in dunkelblau.

– Say you'd like one in dark green.

– Kein Problem. Hier ist derselbe Pullover in dunkelgrün.

– Ask if you can try it on.

– Die Umkleidekabinen sind dort drüben.

– Say the jumper fits. Ask where you pay.

– Die Kasse ist gleich neben dem Ausgang.

Situation 14 Auf der Bank

Du bist auf der Bank.

You are at the bank.

1 – Guten Tag.

– Say you'd like to change £50.

– Kein Problem.

– Ask what the exchange rate is.

– Sie bekommen 2,25 DM für ein Pfund.

– Ask if there is a commission.

– Ja, Sie müssen eine Kommission von 5,— DM zahlen.

2 *– Say you would like to cash a traveller's cheque.*

– Ist das für amerikanische Dollar?

– Say no, pounds sterling.

– Gut, wieviel möchten Sie wechseln?

– Say £100.

– Haben Sie einen Ausweis dabei?

– Say you have got your passport.

– Ja, das geht. Unterschreiben Sie bitte hier.

3 *– Say you would like to change 130,— DM.*

– Welche Währung* möchten Sie?

– Say you'd like Austrian Schillings.

– So, gehen Sie mit diesem Zettel zur Kasse.

(*=currency)

Situation 15 In der Post

Du bist in der Post und kaufst Briefmarken.

You are in the post office buying stamps.

1 – Bitte sehr?

–

– 1,— DM

–

– 3,— DM bitte.

2 –

– 80 Pfennige.

–

– 4,— DM, bitte.

3 –

– 80 Pfennig und 1,— DM.

–

– 2,60 DM.

4 –

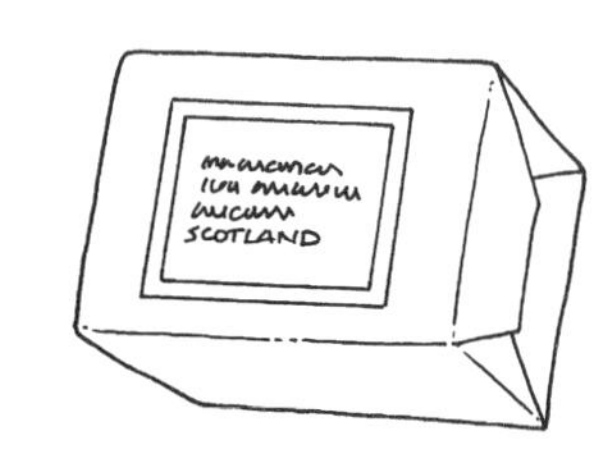

– Das müssen wir wiegen. Also, 1,5 kg, das macht 9,– DM.

–

– 1,– DM.

–

– Das kommt dann auf 10,– DM zusammen.

5 –

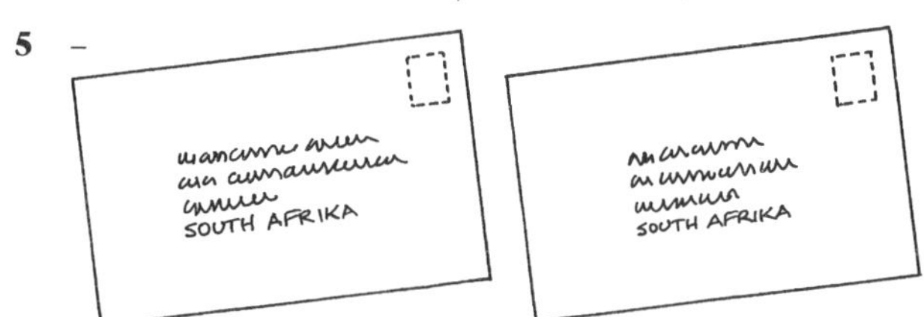

– Nach Südafrika. Also das sind 1,20 DM.

–

– Das macht 2,40 DM, bitte.

Situation 16 Mit dem Bus

Du fährst mit dem Bus in einer deutschen Stadt. Was sagst du zum Fahrer?

You are travelling by bus in a German town. What do you say to the driver?

1

2

3

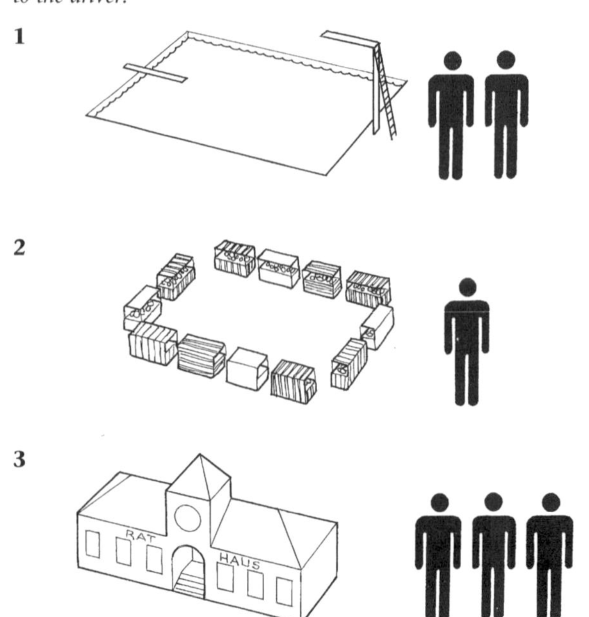

4

5

6

7

8

9

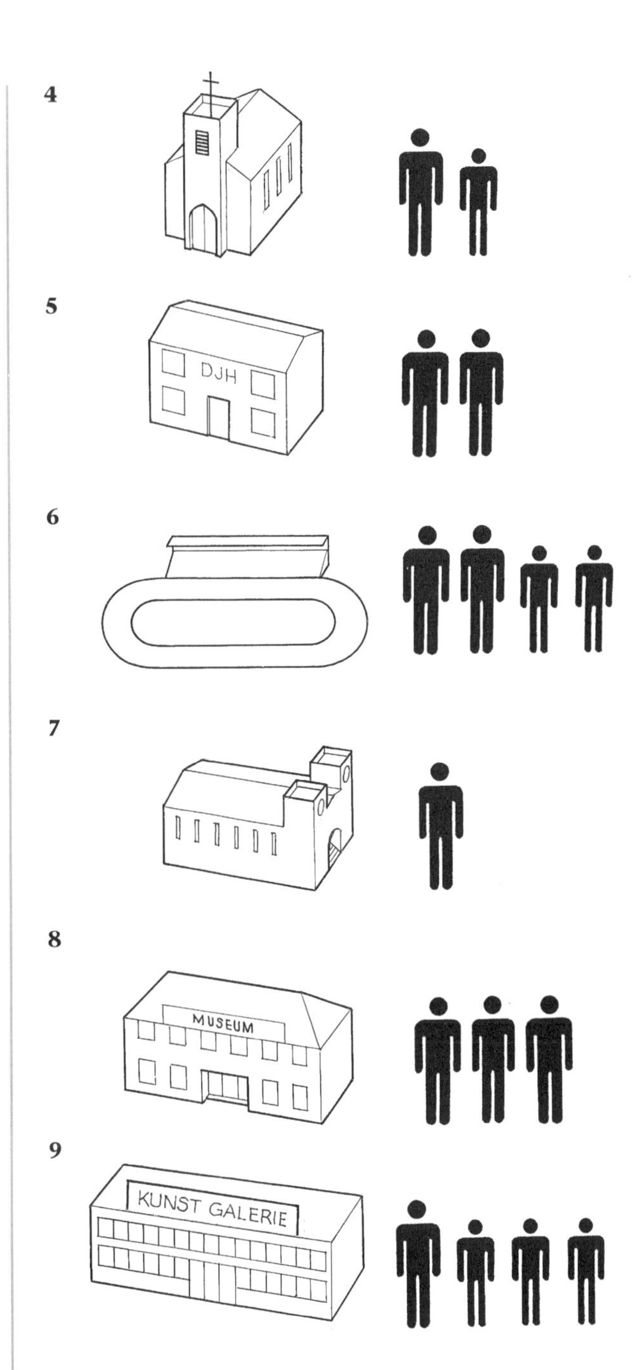

Situation 17 Mit der Bahn

Du bist am Fahrkartenschalter.

You are at the ticket office.

1 – *Ask when the next train to Bonn leaves.*
- Um 15.45 Uhr.
- *Ask where it leaves from.*
- Von Gleis 3.
- *Ask when it will arrive in Bonn.*
- Er kommt um 17.05 Uhr an.

2 – *Say you want to travel to Bochum on Thursday morning. Is there a train?*
- Ja, sie haben einen Zug um 10.15 Uhr.
- *Ask when it will arrive in Bochum.*
- Um 12. 25 Uhr.
- *Ask what platform.*
- Gleis 5a.
- *Ask if you have to change.*
- Nein, der Zug fährt durch.

3 – *Say you'd like a return ticket to Dortmund.*
- Erster Klasse?
- *Say no, second class.*
- 25,– DM bitte.
- *Ask what time the train leaves.*
- Der nächste Zug ist um 10.35 Uhr.
- *Ask what time it will arrive in Dortmund.*
- Um 12.45 Uhr.

4 – *Say you'd like to reserve a seat.*
- Für welchen Zug ist das?
- *For the train at 12.15 on Tuesday to Bremen.*
- Raucher oder Nichtraucherabteil?
- *Say you'd like a non-smoking compartment.*
- Fensterplatz, Mittelplatz oder Seitengangplatz?
- *Say you'd like a window seat.*
- Ja, das geht. Sie haben Platz Nummer B12.

5 – *Say you'd like two single tickets to Bremerhaven.*
- Das macht 20,– DM.
- *Ask if the train goes direct.*
- Nein, sie müssen in Bremen umsteigen.

6 – *Say you'd like two returns to Hameln, one adult and one child.*
- 46,– DM, bitte.
- *Ask when the next train leaves.*
- Um 20.40 Uhr, Gleis drei.

Situation 18 Im Kino

Du gehst mit einem Freund in Deutschland ins Kino.

You are going to the cinema in Germany with a friend.

1 – Guten Abend.
- *Say you'd like two tickets for the film.*
- Wo möchten Sie sitzen?
- *Say on the balcony.*
- Das kostet dann 16,– DM.
- *Ask when the film finishes.*
- So gegen 22.00 Uhr.

2 – Guten Abend.
- *Ask if the film tonight has subtitles.*
- Nein, er ist im englischen Originalton.
- *Ask for three tickets near the screen.*
- Das macht 18,– DM, bitte.
- *Ask when the film starts.*
- In einer halben Stunde.

3 – Guten Abend.
- *Say you'd like two tickets, one adult, one child.*
- Das kostet 15,— DM.
- *Ask if the film is in English.*
- Nein, er ist auf deutsch synchronisiert.
- *Say that doesn't matter.*

Situation 19 Im Theater

Du gehst mit einem Freund in Deutschland ins Theater.

You are going to the theatre in Germany with a friend.

– Guten Tag.

– *Say you'd like four tickets for the performance on Tuesday.*

– Wo wollen Sie sitzen.

– *Ask for seats near the front.*

– Wir haben noch vier Plätze in Reihe neun. Geht das?

– *Say yes, that's fine.*

– Das kostet dann 75,— DM.

– *Ask if you can pay by credit card.*

– Ja, natürlich. Kein Problem.

Speaking: *answers*

Situation 1 Wie komme ich am besten ... ?

1 *Entschuldigung, wie komme ich am besten zum Rathaus?*
2 *Wie komme ich am besten zum Museum?*
3 *Wie komme ich am besten zum Fluß?*
4 *Wie komme ich am besten zum Park?*
5 *Wie komme ich am besten zur Kirche?*
6 *Wie komme ich am besten zum Parkhaus?*
7 *Wie komme ich am besten zur Jugendherberge?*
8 *Wie komme ich am besten zum Café?*
9 *Wie komme ich am besten zur Post (zum Postamt)?*
10 *Wie komme ich am besten zur Bank?*
11 *Wie komme ich am besten zum Kaufhaus?*

Situation 2 Du beschreibst den Weg

1 *Gehen Sie geradeaus und nehmen Sie die zweite Straße links.*
2 *Gehen Sie geradeaus. Der Dom ist auf der rechten Seite.*
3 *Gehen Sie hier geradeaus und nehmen Sie die erste Straße rechts. Dann gehen Sie nach links. Das Hotel ist auf der linken Seite.*
4 *Gehen Sie hier um die Ecke.*
5 *Gehen Sie hier geradeaus. Gehen Sie bis zur Ampel. An der Ampel geradeaus, dann nehmen Sie die erste Straße links.*

Situation 3 Was ist mit ihm los?

Er hat sich das Bein gebrochen. Er hat sich in die Hand geschnitten. Er hat die Hand verstaucht. Er hat Bauchschmerzen. Er hat Fieber.

Situation 4 Wo tut es weh?

1 *Er hat Kopfschmerzen.*
2 *Sie hat Halsschmerzen.*
3 *Er hat Zahnschmerzen.*
4 *Das Kind hat Ohrenschmerzen.*
5 *Ihr ist übel.*
6 *Sein Bein tut weh.*

Situation 5 Du machst einen Termin aus

– Guten Tag. Praxis Dr. Meier. Kann ich Ihnen helfen?
– *Ich möchte einen Termin haben.*
– Paßt es Ihnen am nächsten Donnerstag?
– *Geht es nicht früher?*
– Nein, früher geht es leider nicht.
– *Gut, dann warte ich.*
– Gut, also am Donnerstag um 15.00 Uhr.
– *Vielen Dank. Auf Wiederhören.*

Situation 6 Was bestellst du?

1 *Zwei Tassen Kaffee und zwei Stück Apfelkuchen.*
2 *Ein Kännchen Tee und zwei Stück Schokoladentorte.*
3 *Zwei Glas Limonade, ein Eis, eine Tüte Chips.*
4 *Eine Tasse Schokolade, eine Tasse Tee mit Milch, ein Stück Erdbeerkuchen.*
5 *Ein Kännchen Kaffee, eine Tasse Tee mit Zitrone, ein Glas Cola, ein Stück Käsekuchen, ein Stück Torte, ein Eis.*

Situation 7 Im Café

– Guten Tag, was wünschen Sie bitte?
– *Zwei Tassen Kaffee, ein Kännchen Tee mit Milch, zwei Eis, ein Stück Käsekuchen.*
– Ja, kommt sofort. ... Bitte sehr.
– *Zahlen bitte.*
– Geht das zusammen oder getrennt?
– *Zusammen bitte.*
– Gut, das macht 23,– DM, bitte.
– *Ich habe nur einen Hundertmarkschein.*
– Das geht schon. So, bitte, 77,– DM zurück. Danke schön.
– *Auf Wiedersehen.*

Situation 8 An der Imbißstube

1 – Bitte sehr?
– *Eine Bockwurst, bitte.*
– Mit Senf?
– *Ja, bitte.*
– Das macht 4,– DM, bitte.

2 – Bitte sehr?
– *Zweimal Schaschlik, zwei Dosen Cola.*
– Sonst noch etwas?
– *Nein danke.*
– 12,– DM, bitte.

3 – Was darf es sein?
– *Eine kleine Portion Pommes Frites, zweimal Bratwurst.*
– Eine große Portion?
– *Nein, eine kleine Portion.*
– Mit Ketchup?
– *Nein, mit Mayonnaise.*
– Und zu trinken?
– *Nichts, danke.*
– 8,– DM, bitte.

4 – Sie wünschen bitte?
– *Zweimal Frikadelle, eine Dose Cola, eine Bockwurst.*
– Ist das alles?
– *Ja, das ist alles.*
– Das macht 11,50 DM, bitte.

5 - Ja, bitte?
- *Ein halbes Hähnchen.*
- Mit Pommes Frites?
- *Nein, mit Brötchen.*
- 6,- DM, bitte.

6 - Bitte sehr?
- *Zwei Dosen Limonade, eine Bratwurst mit Soße.*
- Die Wurst mit Currysoße?
- *Ja, mit Currysoße.*
- Das macht dann 6,20 DM, bitte.

Situation 9 Im Restaurant

Answers for this will vary. Possible answers are:

- Haben Sie schon gewählt?
- *Ja.*
- Was möchten Sie zu trinken?
- *Mineralwasser.*
- Möchten Sie eine Vorspeise?
- *Nudelsuppe.*
- Was wünschen Sie als Hauptgericht?
- *Pfeffersteak.*
- Möchten Sie die Nachspeise schon jetzt bestellen?
- *Ein gemischtes Eis, bitte.*
- Danke schön. Es kommt sofort.

Situation 10 Einkaufen am Markt

1 - Guten Tag, was darf es sein?
- *Ein Kilo Äpfel.*
- Sonst noch etwas?
- *Drei Bananen und ein Pfund Erdbeeren.*
- Also, das macht 6,- DM zusammen.

2 - Guten Morgen. Sie wünschen, bitte?
- *Ein Pfund Karotten, bitte.*
- Das wäre alles?
- *Nein, drei Kilo Kartoffeln.*
- Das macht 4,- DM, bitte.

3 - Guten Tag. Was möchten Sie, bitte?
- *Ein halbes Pfund Birnen.*
- Sonst noch etwas?
- *Ja, eine Ananas, ein Pfund Pflaumen.*
- Danke. Das macht dann 9,20 DM, bitte.

4 - Grüß Gott. Was darf es sein?
- *300 Gramm grüne Bohnen, bitte.*
- Sonst noch etwas?
- *Einen Kohl, bitte.*
- So, das kostet 5,— DM

Situation 11 Reiseandenken

- Guten Tag. Suchen Sie etwas Bestimmtes?
- *Ja, ich suche ein Geschenk für meine Schwester.*
- Wie wäre es mit einem Buch? Das hier kostet nur 20,- DM.
- *Nein, das ist zu teuer.*
- Oder schauen Sie hier, eine Trachtenpuppe.
- *Nein, meine Schwester mag das nicht.*
- Vielleicht einen Schal. Dieser kostet nur 10,— DM. Er ist sehr schön.
- *Haben Sie den Schal auch in rot?*
- Kein Problem. Wir haben ihn auch in rot.
- *Können Sie den Schal als Geschenk einpacken?*
- Natürlich. Kommen Sie bitte mit zur Kasse.

Situation 12 Deine Brieffreundin kauft einen Rock

- *Schau dort! Da sind Röcke im Sonderangebot.*
- Oh ja, diese Röcke sind einfach toll.
- *Möchtest Du einen anprobieren?*
- Ja, das ist eine gute Idee. Ich nehme diesen schwarzen hier.

[Nach ein paar Minuten]

- Was meinst du? Paßt er mir?
- *Er ist ein bißchen eng.*
- Du hast recht. Ich nehme ihn in der nächsten Größe.
- *Dieser Rock paßt dir wirklich sehr gut.*
- Danke. Ich nehme ihn.

Situation 13 Du kaufst einen Pullover

- *Haben Sie Pullover im Sonderangebot?*
- Ja, wir haben diese hier. Sie kosten nur 35,- DM.
- *Ich möchte einen Pullover anprobieren.*
- Aber gerne. Welche Größe haben Sie?
- *Ich habe Größe 34.*
- In dieser Größe haben wir einen in dunkelblau.
- *Ich möchte denselben Pullover in dunkelgrün.*
- Kein Problem. Hier ist derselbe Pullover in dunkelgrün.
- *Kann ich den Pullover anprobieren?*
- Die Umkleidekabinen sind dort drüben.
- *Der Pullover paßt. Wo muß ich bezahlen?*
- Die Kasse ist gleich neben dem Ausgang.

Situation 14 Auf der Bank

1 - Guten Tag.
- *Ich möchte fünfzig Pfund wechseln.*
- Kein Problem.
- *Wie steht der Kurs heute?*
- Sie bekommen 2,25 DM für ein Pfund.
- *Muß ich eine Kommission bezahlen?*
- Ja, Sie müssen eine Kommission von 5,- DM zahlen.

2 - *Ich möchte einen Reisescheck einlösen.*
- Ist das für amerikanische Dollar?
- *Nein, das ist für Pfund Sterling.*
- Gut, wieviel möchten Sie wechseln?
- *Einhundert Pfund.*
- Haben Sie einen Ausweis dabei?
- *Ja, ich habe meinen Reisepaß hier.*
- Ja, das geht. Unterschreiben Sie bitte hier.

3 - *Ich möchte einhundertdreißig Mark wechseln.*
- Welche Währung möchten Sie?

- *Ich hätte gern österreichische Schilling.*
- So, gehen Sie mit diesem Zettel zur Kasse.

Situation 15 In der Post

1 - Bitte sehr?
- *Was kostet ein Brief nach England?*
- 1,- DM
- *Drei Briefmarken zu einer Mark bitte.*
- 3,- DM bitte.

2 - *Was kostet eine Postkarte nach Irland, bitte?*
- 80 Pfennige.
- *Fünf Briefmarken zu achtzig Pfennig, bitte.*
- 4,- DM, bitte.

3 - *Was kosten eine Postkarte und ein Brief nach Wales?*
- 80 Pfennig und 1,- DM.
- *Eine Briefmarke zu einer Mark, und zwei zu achtzig Pfennig.*
- 2,60 DM.

4 - *Was kostet ein Paket nach Schottland?*
- Das müssen wir wiegen. Also, 1,5 kg, das macht 9,- DM.
- *Und was kostet ein Brief nach Schottland?*
- 1,- DM.
- *Eine Briefmarke zu einer Mark.*
- Das kommt dann auf 10,— DM zusammen.

5 - *Was kosten zwei Briefe nach Südafrika?*
- Nach Südafrika. Also das sind 1,20 DM.
- *Zwei Briefmarken zu einer Mark zwanzig, bitte.*
- Das macht 2,40 DM, bitte.

Situation 16 Mit dem Bus

1 *Zweimal zum Schwimmbad.*
2 *Einmal zum Markt.*
3 *Dreimal zum Rathaus.*
4 *Ein Erwachsener, ein Kind zur Kirche.*
5 *Zweimal zur Jugendherberge.*
6 *Zwei Erwachsene, zwei Kinder zum Stadion.*
7 *Einmal zum Dom.*
8 *Dreimal zum Museum.*
9 *Ein Erwachsener, drei Kinder zur Galerie.*

Situation 17 Mit der Bahn

1 - *Wann fährt der nächste Zug nach Bonn?*
- Um 15.45 Uhr.
- *Wo fährt er ab?*
- Von Gleis 3.
- *Wann kommt er in Bonn an?*
- Er kommt um 17.05 Uhr an.

2 - *Ich will am Donnerstagvormittag nach Bochum fahren. Wann fährt ein Zug?*
- Ja, sie haben einen Zug um 10.15 Uhr.
- *Wann kommt der Zug in Bochum an?*
- Er kommt um 12.25 Uhr an.
- *Wo fährt er ab?*
- Gleis 5a.
- *Muß ich umsteigen?*
- Nein, der Zug fährt durch.

3 - *Ich möchte eine Rückfahrkarte nach Dortmund.*
- Erster Klasse?
- *Nein, zweiter Klasse.*
- 25,— DM bitte.
- *Wann fährt der Zug ab?*
- Der nächste Zug ist um 10.35 Uhr.
- *Wann kommt der Zug in Dortmund an?*
- Um 12.45 Uhr.

4 - *Ich möchte einen Platz reservieren.*
- Für welchen Zug ist das?
- *Für den Zug um 12.15 Uhr am Dienstag nach Bremen.*
- Raucher oder Nichtraucherabteil?
- *Nichtraucherabteil, bitte.*
- Fensterplatz, Mittelplatz oder Seitengangplatz?
- *Einen Fensterplatz, bitte.*
- Ja, das geht. Sie haben Platz Nummer B12.

5 - *Zweimal einfach nach Bremerhaven, bitte.*
- Das macht 20,- DM.
- *Fährt der Zug durch?*
- Nein, sie müssen in Bremen umsteigen.

6 - *Zweimal nach Hameln, hin und zurück, ein Erwachsener und ein Kind.*
- 46,- DM, bitte.
- *Wann fährt der nächste Zug?*
- Um 20.40 Uhr, Gleis drei.

Situation 18 Im Kino

1 - Guten Abend.
- *Zwei Eintrittskarten für den Film, bitte.*
- Wo möchten Sie sitzen?
- *Auf dem Balkon.*
- Das kostet dann 16,— DM
- *Wann endet der Film?*
- So gegen 22.00 Uhr.

2 - Guten Abend.
- *Hat der Film Untertitel?*
- Nein, er ist im englischen Originalton.
- *Drei Plätze in der Nähe der Leinwand.*
- Das macht 18,- DM, bitte.
- *Wann beginnt der Film?*
- In einer halben Stunde.

3 - Guten Abend.
- *Zwei Eintrittskarten, ein Erwachsener, ein Kind, bitte.*
- Das kostet 15,- DM.
- *Ist der Film in Englisch?*
- Nein, er ist auf deutsch synchronisiert.
- *Das macht nichts.*

Situation 19 Im Theater

– Guten Tag.

– Ich hätte gern vier Karten für die Vorstellung am Dienstag.

– Wo wollen Sie sitzen?

– Ich möchte Plätze vorne.

– Wir haben noch vier Plätze in Reihe neun. Geht das?

– Ja, das geht.

– Das kostet dann 75,– DM.

– Kann ich mit Kreditkarte zahlen?

– Ja, natürlich. Kein Problem.

Writing: *questions*

Introduction

You will be asked to do a variety of writing tasks for your homework, apart from simply copying vocabulary or exercise sentences.

When you do written work in German there are a number of points to watch out for:

- Remember to use capital letters at the beginning (see grammar section for capital letters and Nouns).
- When you have finished a piece of written work, check your verb endings (see grammar section for Verbs).
- You need to watch out that adjectives agree with the noun they refer to (see grammar section for Adjectives).

Writing letters

Often you will be asked to write letters or postcards.

Letters to friends

A letter to a penfriend will begin with *Lieber* if it is addressed to a boy and with *Liebe* if it is for a girl. *Liebe* is also used when you write to two or more people.

Your letter will start with a lower case letter, except for names or nouns.

Example:

Liebe Helga,
wie geht es Dir? ...

In a letter the words *Du, Dir, Dich, Dein* always start with a capital letter.

You can finish a letter to a penfriend with one of the following phrases:

mit freundlichen Grüßen	*yours sincerely*
bis bald	*see you soon*
schreib bald	*write soon*
Tschüß	*cheerio*

Then you write *Dein* if you are a boy or *Deine* if you are a girl and sign your name.

Formal business letters

If you write to an information office, campsite, etc. you begin your letter with the more formal:

Sehr geehrte Damen und Herren,

You will use the formal *Sie* to mean you. *Sie, Ihr, Ihnen* always start with a capital letter.

Your formal letter always ends with

mit freundlichen Grüßen	*yours sincerely*
mit bestem Gruß	*Best wishes*

You then sign your name. You don't put *Dein/Deine*.

Aufgabe 1 Mein Familienstammbaum

Fülle den folgenden Familienstammbaum für dich aus:

Complete your family tree in German:

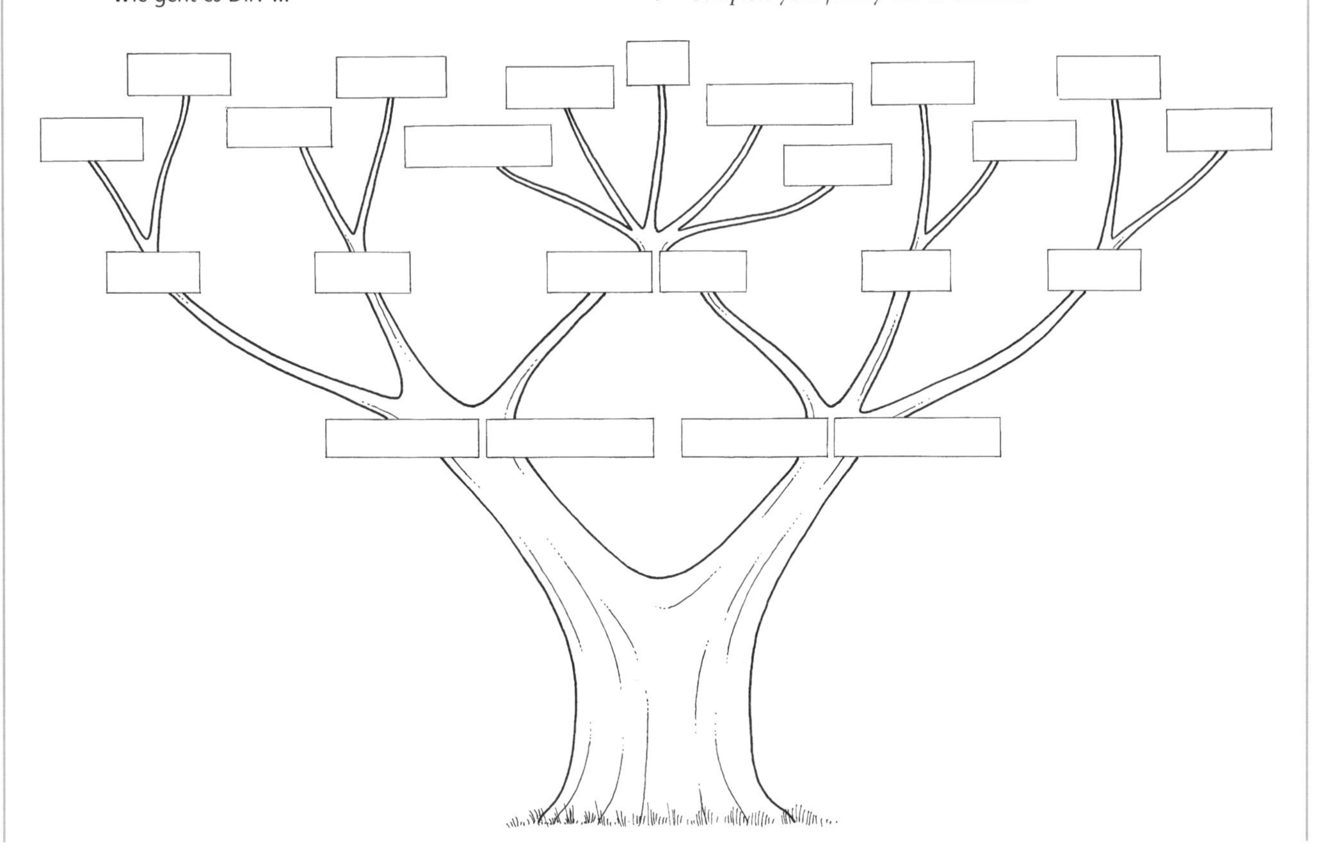

Aufgabe 2 Davids Brief

1 A Schreibe den Brief ab, indem du die Bilder durch Worte ersetzt:

Copy out the letter, inserting the correct words for the pictures:

Lieber Joachim,

ich bin dein neuer englischer Brieffreund. Ich heiße David Longburn und bin 13 Jahre alt. Ich wohne in Basingstoke, das ist in . Wir haben ein  **.**

Ich habe zwei 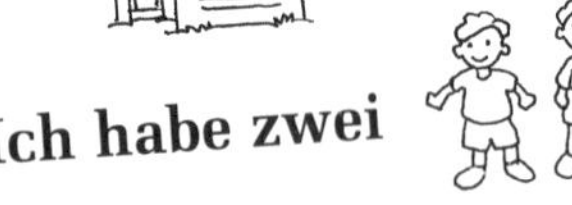 **und eine**  **. Meine Schwester ist älter, sie ist schon 22 Jahre alt. Wir haben einen**  **und einen**  **.**

Meine Hobbys sind  **und**  **. Ich bin in der achten Klasse in einer Gesamtschule. Es gibt immer viele Hausaufgaben.**

Morgen ist Samstag, und ich gehe mit meinem Vater zum 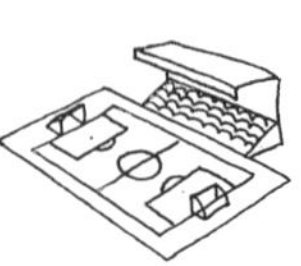 **. Wir werden ein Fußballspiel sehen. Ich bin Fan von Manchester United.**

Schreib bitte bald,

Dein

David

2 Schreibe jetzt diesen Brief noch einmal, aber jetzt so, daß er für dich stimmt.

Write out this letter again, but now with information which is true for you.

(For vocabulary and phrases see also the sections on Ich, Familie, Freunde; Freizeit *and* Das Familienleben *on pages 109, 113 and 121).*

Aufgabe 3 zu Hause

Schau dir dieses Bild von einem Haus an. Schreibe die Namen der Zimmer in die richtigen Kästchen.

Look at the picture of a house. Write the names of the rooms into the correct boxes.

Aufgabe 4 Im Zimmer eines Teenagers

Teste dich selbst. Schreibe so viele Wörter wie möglich hinter die Linien, die zu den Möbeln führen. Vergiß nicht die richtige Form des Artikels (der, die, das).

Test yourself. Label as many pieces of furniture as possible. Don't forget the correct gender (der, die, das).

Aufgabe 5 Freizeit

Schreibe diesen Brief ab, indem du die Bilder mit den richtigen Wörtern ersetzt:

Copy out the letter, replacing the pictures with the correct words:

Liebe Maria,

vielen Dank für Deinen Brief und die zwei Fotos von deiner Lieblingsgruppe. Ich höre auch gern Popmusik.

Heute schreibe ich Dir über meine Hobbys. Ich spiele seit drei Jahren  **. Ich übe fast jeden Tag. Donnerstags gehe ich zur Turnhalle, wo ich**  **treibe. Am Freitag gehe ich zur** 

.

Meine Schwester sammelt 

. Ihr zweites Hobby ist  **. Meine Eltern**  **gern. Ich mag das nicht.**

Schreib bald wieder,

Deine Sabrina

Aufgabe 6 Was machen sie?

A Schreibe die deutschen Wörter neben die Bilder:

Write the German words next to the pictures:

1 ______________________________

2 ______________________________

3 ______________________________

4 ______________________________

5 ______________________________

6 ______________________________

7 ______________________________

8 ______________________________

9 ______________________________

10 KINO ______________________________

B Schreibe jetzt Sätze für jedes Bild. Beginne mit 'Ich ...'.

Now write a sentence for each picture. Begin with 'Ich ...'.

____

____

____

____

____

____

____

____

____

____

Aufgabe 7 Ein Stadtplan

Schreibe die Namen der Gebäude unter die Symbole im Stadtplan, damit dein Brieffreund/deine Brieffreundin besser den Weg findet:

Write the names of the buildings under the symbols in the town plan so that your penfriend can find his/her way better:

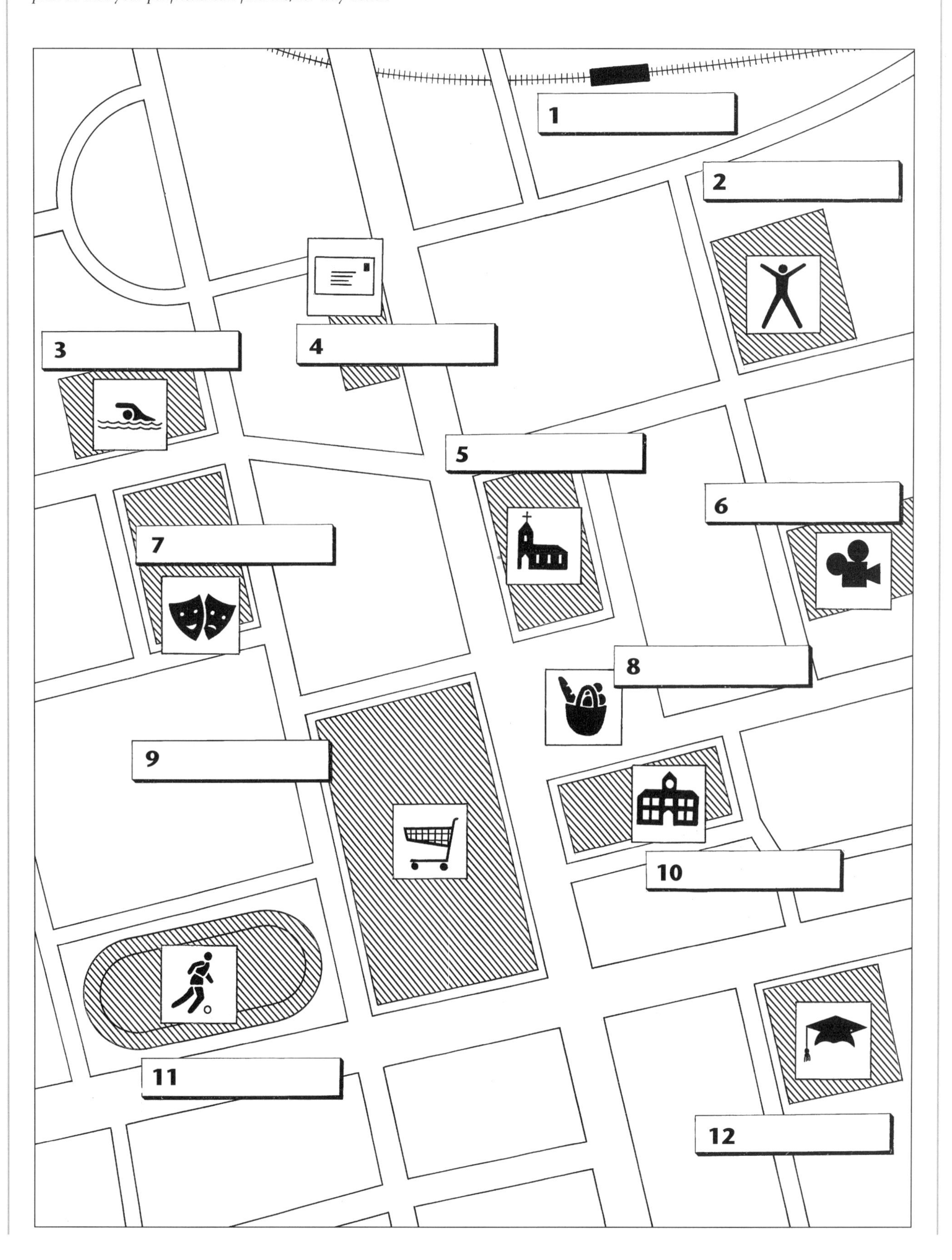

Aufgabe 8 Die Wetterkarte

Schau dir die Wetterkarte an und dann ergänze die Sätze:

Look at the weather map opposite and then complete the sentences:

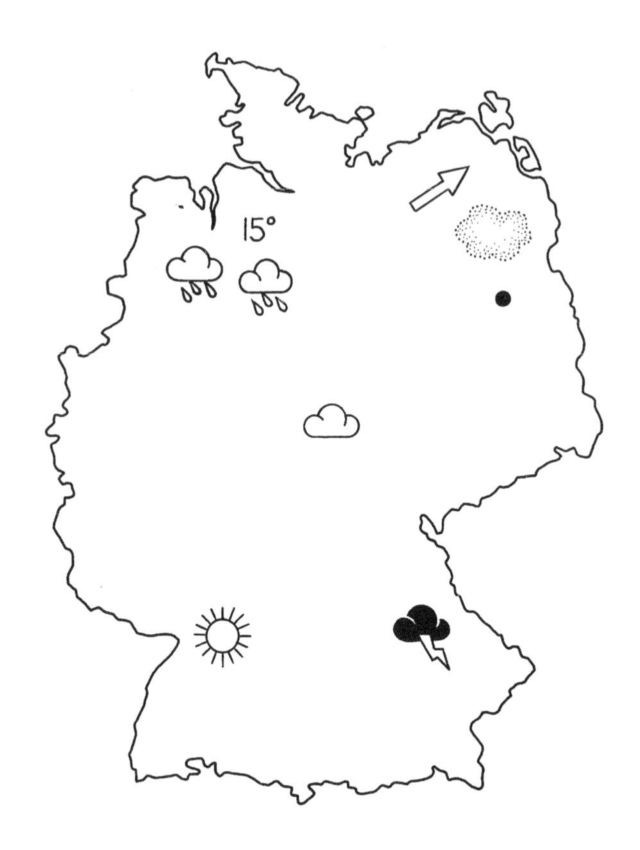

1. Im Nordwesten ______________________,

   Temperaturen um 15 Grad.

2. ______________________ im Nordosten.

3. In Mitteldeutschland ist es ______________________.

4. Der Südwesten Deutschlands ist ______________________.

5. Im Südosten wird es ______________________ geben.

Aufgabe 9 Mein Stundenplan

Schreibe deinen Stundenplan auf deutsch in das Formular:

Write your timetable in German on this blank.

Zeit	Montag	Dienstag	Mittwoch	Donnerstag	Freitag

Aufgabe 10 Einkaufen

1 Du gehst auf dem Markt einkaufen. Schreibe eine Liste mit zehn Obst und Gemüsesorten, die du dort kaufen willst.

You are going shopping in the market. Write a list with ten items of fruit and vegetable which you want to buy there.

2 Schreibe jetzt eine Einkaufsliste für zehn Lebensmittel, die dir dein Brieffreund im Supermarkt kaufen soll.

Now write a shopping list for ten items of food which your German penfriend is to buy for you in a supermarket.

3 Deine Brieffreundin möchte für dich einkaufen gehen. Du schreibst eine Liste mit fünf Geschäften und fünf Dingen, die sie kaufen soll.

Your penfriend wants to go shopping for you. You write a list with five shops and five items which she is to buy.

Aufgabe 11
Eine Packliste

Dein deutscher Brieffreund wird mit dir nach Schottland fahren. Schreib ihm eine Liste von zehn Sachen, die er in seinen Rucksack packen soll.

Your German penfriend is coming to Scotland with you. Write a list for him of ten items which he needs to pack in his rucksack.

Aufgabe 12 Postkarten

Schau dir diese Postkarten an, dann ergänze die Postkarten unten.

Look at these postcards, then fill in the blanks in the ones on *page 96*

Hallo,
viele Grüße aus Schottland.
Das Wetter ist schrecklich: nur Regen.
Gestern waren wir in Edinburgh im Kino. Morgen wollen wir wandern.
Bis nächste Woche,
Dein George.

Liebe Tante Inge,
wir senden Dir viele Grüße aus
Irland. Das Essen hier schmeckt
sehr gut. Es gibt jeden Tag Fisch.
Hast Du einen schönen Urlaub
in Bayern gehabt?
In einer Woche kommen wir wieder
nach Hause,
Deine Ursula.

Lieber Ulrich,
hier in Wales ist es sehr
schön. Die Sonne scheint. Gestern
haben wir einen alten Bauernhof
besucht. Heute abend gehen wir
im Restaurant essen.
Viele Grüße Dein Matthias.

Fülle die Lücken in diesen Postkarten aus:

Fill in the gaps in these postcards:

1

Lieber ______________

Viele ______________ aus ______________ . Das Wetter ist

______________ . Die ______________ scheint. Heute

abend gehen wir ____________________________ .

Bis ______________ Woche,

Dein ______________

2

Hallo,

______________ Grüße Cornwall. Gestern waren wir im

______________ . Heute gehen wir ______________ .

Wir war Dein ______________ in Frankreich.

Wir kommen nächste ______________ nach

______________ zurück.

Dein Peter und Familie

Aufgabe 13 Reservierungen für die Jugendherberge

Sieh dir den folgenden Brief an eine Jugendherberge an.

Look at the following letter to a youth hostel.

Lieber Herbergsvater,

ich habe vor, im kommenden Juli nach Deutschland zu fahren. Haben Sie vom 13. bis zum 15. Juli noch Platz frei? Wir sind drei Jungen und zwei Mädchen.
Können wir in der Jugendherberge Frühstück und Mittagessen haben?
Bitte bestätigen Sie die Reservierung. Vielen Dank im voraus,

mit freundlichen Grüßen

Schreibe die folgenden Briefe ab, indem Du die Lücken mit passenden Wörten ausfüllst.

Copy out the following letters, filling in the gaps.

1

Lieber ____________________,

ich habe vor, im kommenden [MAY] nach

Deutschland zu fahren. Haben Sie vom [MAY 21 22 23 24 25] noch

Platz frei. Wir sind .

Können wir in der Jugendherberge leihen?

Bitte bestätigen Sie die Reservierung. Vielen Dank im

voraus,

mit freundlichen Grüßen

2

L_______________ Herbergsvater,

wir haben vor, im [calendar: OCTOBER] nach Deutschland zu fahren

Haben Sie vom [calendar: OCTOBER 3 4 5 6] . Wir sind [two figures] .

Können wir in der Jugendherberge Abendessen

bekommen? Bitte bestätigen Sie die_______________.

Vielen Dank im _______________,

mit _______________ Grüßen

Aufgabe 14
Hotelreservierungen

Schau dir diesen Brief an ein Hotel an. Fülle dann die Lücken im zweiten Brief aus. Die Anfangsbuchstaben der Wörter sind jeweils gegeben.

Look at the letter to a hotel. Then fill in the gaps in the second letter. The first letter of each word is given.

Sehr geehrte Damen und Herren,

ich möchte ein Doppelzimmer mit Dusche und ein Einzelzimmer mit Bad reservieren. Das ist für die Zeit vom 15. bis zum 21. Juni. Haben die Zimmer Telefon und Fernsehen? Können wir im Hotel Abendessen bekommen? Bitte bestätigen Sie die Reservierung und schicken Sie uns eine Preisliste. Vielen Dank für Ihre Hilfe,

mit freundlichen Grüßen

Sehr geehrte D________________ und

H________________,

ich möchte zwei E________________ mit Bad und zwei

D________________ mit D________________ vom 15.

bis zum 25. September reservieren. Haben Sie dann noch Platz

frei?

Können wir im Hotel A________________ bekommen?

Bitte b________________ Sie die R________________

und schicken Sie uns einen Hotelprospekt. Vielen Dank für Ihre

H________________,

mit f________________ Grüßen

Aufgabe 15 Ein Reservierungsbrief

Deine Nachbarin möchte in Deutschland Urlaub machen. Du schreibst für sie einen Brief an ein Hotel in Freiburg.

Your neighbour would like to go on holiday in Germany. You write a letter for her to a hotel in Freiburg.

Include the following points:

- Ask for a double room with shower and a single room with bath, from 11th until 18th June.
- Ask if there is TV and telephone in the room.
- Ask the hotel to confirm the booking.

Writing: answers

Many writing tasks have a wide range of possible answers. The answers given here are correct. However, there are often many other possible solutions. For some exercises no answers are given for obvious reasons.

Aufgabe 1 Mein Familienstammbaum

Answers for this will depend on individual circumstances.

Aufgabe 2 Davids Brief

1

Lieber Joachim,

ich bin dein neuer englischer Brieffreund. Ich heiße David Longburn und bin 13 Jahre alt. Ich wohne in Basingstoke, das ist in **Südengland**. Wir haben ein **Haus**.

Ich habe zwei **Brüder** und eine **Schwester**. Meine Schwester ist älter, sie ist schon 22 Jahre alt. Wir haben einen **Hund** und einen **Wellensittich**.

Meine Hobbys sind **lesen** und **radfahren**. Ich bin in der achten Klasse in einer Gesamtschule. Es gibt immer viele Hausaufgaben.

Morgen ist Samstag, und ich gehe mit meinem Vater zum **Stadion**. Wir werden ein Fußballspiel sehen. Ich bin Fan von Manchester United.

Schreib bitte bald,

Dein
David

2 Answers for this will depend on individual circumstances

Aufgabe 3 zu Hause

1 der Speicher
2 das Bad
3 das Schlafzimmer
4 die Küche
5 der Eßraum *or* das Eßzimmer
6 das Wohnzimmer
7 der Parkplatz
8 der Keller

Aufgabe 4 Im Zimmer eines Teenagers

1 der Kleiderschrank
2 die Tür
3 das Bett
4 das Sofa
5 der Teppich
6 der Couchtisch
7 das Fernsehen
8 der Stuhl
9 der Schreibtisch
10 der Computer
11 das Radio
12 das Regal
13 das Fenster

Aufgabe 5 Freizeit

Liebe Maria,

vielen Dank für Deinen Brief und die zwei Fotos von deiner Lieblingsgruppe. Ich höre auch gern Popmusik.

Heute schreibe ich Dir über meine Hobbys. Ich spiele seit drei Jahren **Klavier**. Ich übe fast jeden Tag. Donnerstags gehe ich zur Turnhalle, wo ich **Gymnastik** treibe. Am Freitag gehe ich zur **Disco**.

Meine Schwester sammelt **Briefmarken**. Ihr zweites Hobby ist **radfahren**. Meine Eltern **wandern** gern. Ich mag das nicht.

Schreib bald wieder,

Deine Sabrina

Aufgabe 6 Was machen sie?

A

1 schwimmen
2 reiten
3 tanzen
4 Fußball spielen
5 Gitarre spielen
6 lesen
7 im Garten arbeiten
8 Freunde treffen
9 kochen
10 ins Kino gehen

B

1 Ich schwimme.
2 Ich reite.
3 Ich tanze.
4 Ich spiele Fußball.
5 Ich spiele Gitarre.
6 Ich lese.

7 Ich arbeite im Garten.

8 Ich treffe Freunde.

9 Ich koche.

10 Ich gehe ins Kino.

Aufgabe 7 Ein Stadtplan

1 der Bahnhof

2 das Freizeitzentrum

3 das Schwimmbad

4 das Postamt

5 die Kirche

6 das Kino

7 das Theater

8 der Markt

9 das Einkaufszentrum

10 das Rathaus

11 das Stadion

12 die Schule

Aufgabe 8 Die Wetterkarte

1 Im Nordwesten **Regen**, Temperaturen um 15 Grad.

2 **Nebel und Wind** im Nordosten.

3 In Mitteldeutschland ist es **bedeckt**.

4 Der Südwesten Deutschlands ist **sonnig**.

5 Im Südosten wird es **Gewitter** geben.

Aufgabe 9 Mein Stundenplan

Answers for this will depend on individual circumstances

Aufgabe 10 Einkaufen

1 Possible answers include:
Äpfel, Birnen, Orangen, Ananas, Erdbeeren, Karotten, Bohnen, Kartoffeln, Salat, Kohl

2 Possible answers include:
Milch, Müsli, Joghurt, Käse, Limonade, Brot, Butter, Wurst, Kuchen, Eis

3 Possible answers include:

Bäckerei	10 Brötchen
Metzgerei	100 Gramm Aufschnitt
Buchhandlung	Zeitung
Post	3 Briefmarken
Kaufhaus	1 Strumpfhose

Aufgabe 11 Eine Packliste

Possible answers include:
Pullover, Hose, Hemd, Socken, Regenmantel, Mütze, Schal, Badehose, Handtuch, Schuhe

Aufgabe 12 Postkarten

Possible answers:

1 Liebe + **girl's name**
Viele **Grüße** aus **+ name of place**. Das Wetter ist **sonnig/gut/schlecht**. Die Sonne **scheint**. Heute abend gehen wir **ins Kino/zum Theater/in die Disco**.
Bis **nächste** Woche,
Dein **+ boy's name**

2 Hallo,
Viele Grüße **aus** Cornwall. Gestern waren wir im **Schwimmbad/Kino/Theater**. Heute gehen wir **reiten/rudern/kegeln**.
Wie war Dein **Urlaub** in Frankreich.
Wir kommen nächste **Woche** nach **Hause/or: name of town** zurück.
Dein Peter und Familie

Aufgabe 13 Reservierungen für die Jugendherberge

1

Lieber **Herbergsvater**,

ich habe vor, im kommenden **Mai** nach Deutschland zu fahren. Haben Sie vom **22. bis zum 25. Mai** noch Platz frei. Wir sind **zwei Jungen und ein Mädchen**.

Können wir in der Jugendherberge **Bettwäsche** leihen?

Bitte bestätigen Sie die Reservierung. Vielen Dank im voraus,

mit freundlichen Grüßen

2

L**ieber** Herbergsvater,

wir haben vor, im **kommenden Oktober** nach Deutschland zu fahren.

Haben Sie vom **3. bis zum 6. Oktober noch Platz frei**?

Wir sind **zwei Mädchen**.

Können wir in der Jugendherberge Abendessen bekommen? Bitte bestätigen Sie die

Reservierung. Vielen Dank im **Voraus**,

mit **freundlichen** Grüßen

Aufgabe 14 Hotelreservierungen

Sehr geehrte D**amen** und H**erren**,

ich möchte zwei E**inzelzimmer** mit Bad und zwei D**oppelzimmer** mit **Dusche** vom 15. bis zum 25. September reservieren. Haben Sie dann noch Platz frei?

Können wir im Hotel A**bendessen** bekommen?

Bitte b**estätigen** Sie die Reservierung und schicken Sie uns einen Hotelprospekt. Vielen Dank für Ihre H**ilfe**,

mit f**reundlichen** Grüßen

Aufgabe 15 Ein Reservierungsbrief

Your letter should be something like this:

Sehr geehrte Damen und Herren,

ich möchte ein Doppelzimmer mit Dusche und ein Einzelzimmer mit Bad vom 11. bis zum 18. Juni reservieren. Haben Sie dann noch Platz frei?

Gibt es ein Telefon und Fernseher im Zimmer?

Bitte bestätigen Sie die Reservierung. Vielen Dank für Ihre Hilfe.

Mit freundlichen Grüßen

Section four

Vocabulary Introduction

The **topics** to be covered are arranged in three **Areas of Experience**, **A**, **B** and **C** respectively. Each of these can in turn be broken down into three headings.

- **Area of Experience A** is called **Everyday activities**, and includes:
  - classroom language
  - home and school life
  - food, health, and fitness
- **Area of Experience B** is called **Personal and social life**, and includes:
  - yourself, your family, and your personal relationships
  - your free time and social activities
  - holidays and special occasions
- **Area of Experience C** is called **The world around us** and includes:
  - your home town and local area
  - the natural and man-made environment
  - people, places, and customs

The vocabulary in this book has not been arranged in the same order as the Areas of Experience listed above. Instead, we have used our teaching experience to put vocabulary in the order in which you might expect to come across it in Key Stage 3 by the end of Year 9. If you are learning German as a second language it is possible you might not cover all the ground by the end of Year 9, depending on when you started learning German.

The chart on the next page will tell you, at a glance, the order in which the vocabulary topics are arranged in this book and where you can find them.

Topic		AoE
Allgemeines (pp. 108–9)	Grüße (p. 108) Glückwunsche (p. 108) Fragewörter (p. 108) Präpositionen (pp. 108–9) Farben (p. 109)	
Ich, Familie, Freunde (pp. 109–11)	Personalien (p. 109) Adresse (p. 109) Haustiere (p. 110) Familienmitglieder (p. 110) Berufe (p. 111)	B
In der Klasse (pp. 111–13)	Im Klassenzimmer (p. 111) Der Lehrer/die Lehrerin sagt: (p. 112) Der Schüler/die Schülerin sagt: (p. 113) Das Alphabet (p. 113) Zeichensetzung (p. 113)	A
Freizeit (pp. 113–16)	Hobbys (p. 113) Sport (p. 113) Musik (p. 114) Informatik (p. 115) Andere Hobbys (p. 115)	A
Stadt (p. 116)	In der Stadt (p. 116)	C
Wie komme ich am besten...? (pp. 116–17)	Wegbeschreibung (p. 116)	C
Land (pp. 117–18)		C
Wetter (p. 118)		C
Schule (pp. 118–20)	In der Schule (p. 118) Das Personal (p. 118) Fächer (p. 118) Gebäude (p. 119) Schulverben (p. 119)	A
Gesund heit und Fitneß (pp. 120–1)	Körperteile (p. 120) Beim Arzt, beim Zahnarzt (p. 120) Apotheke (pp. 120–1)	A
Das Familienleben (pp. 121–3)	Wohnung (p. 121) Zimmer (p. 121) Teile des Gebäudes (p. 121) Badezimmer (p. 121) Schlafzimmer (p. 121) Wohnzimmer (pp. 121–2) Eßzimmer (p. 122) Küche (p. 122) Garten (p. 122)	A
Der Alltag (pp. 123)		A
Taschengeld (pp. 123–4)		B
im der Café in der Konditorei (p. 124)	Getränke (p. 124)	A
an der Imbißstube (p. 124)		A
im Restaurant (pp. 124–5)	Vorspeisen (p. 124) Hauptgerichte (p. 124) Nachspeisen (p. 124)	A
Einkaufen (pp. 125–6)	Kleiderkauf (p. 125) Im Lebensmittelgeschäft (p. 125) Fleisch (p. 125) Gemüse (pp. 125–6) Obst (p. 126) Getränke und snacks (p. 126) Reiseandenken (p. 126)	C
Bank und Post (p. 127)	Bank (p. 127) Post (p. 127)	C
Bus, Bahn und Auto (pp. 127–8)	Transportmittel (p. 127) mit der Bahn (pp. 127–8) mit dem Bus (p. 128) mit dem Flugzeug (p. 128) die Überfahrt (p. 128)	C
Ausflüge (pp. 128–9)	Ausgehen (p. 00) im Kino, im Theater (p. 129)	B
Feiertage (p. 130)		B
Ferien (pp. 130–2)	Camping (pp. 130–1) Jugendherberge (p. 131) Hotel (pp. 131–2) am Meer (p. 132) auf dem Land (p. 132)	B
Die Medien (pp. 133–4)	Medien (p. 133) Geräte (p. 133) im Kino (p. 133) im Fernsehen, im Radio (p. 133) Sendungen (p. 133) Bücher (pp. 133–4)	A

Checklist of language tasks

This list follows the order of topics in the Vocabulary topic section (see chart on page 103).

Tick off each thing you learn how to do as you go through your course.

There is a second box provided to help you with your revision.

		Learnt	Revised
Allgemeines			
I can	greet people		
	make sociable noises		
	give good wishes		
	give my opinion		
I know	the question words		
	my German prepositions		
	the colours		
Ich, Familie, Freunde			
I can give my	age		
	name		
	date of birth		
	address		
	phone number		
I can say	where I come from		
I can talk about	my pets		
	my family		
I know	the names of jobs and professions		
In der Klasse			
I know	classroom objects		
I understand	classroom commands		
I can	make classroom requests in German		
	spell out loud using the German alphabet		
	use the German words for punctuation		
Freizeit			
I can talk about	hobbies		
	sport		
	music		
	information technology		
	other hobbies		
Die Stadt			
I know	the names of places in town		
I can	describe the town/village I live in		

		Learnt	Revised
Wie komme ich am besten... ?			
I can	ask for directions		
	understand directions		
	give directions		
Das Land			
I know	the names of features of the countryside		
I can	give my opinion of living in the country		
Weather			
I can	understand simple weather forecasts		
	discuss the weather		
Schule			
I know	the names of different types of school		
I can discuss	holidays, terms, timetable and staff		
I know	the names of school subjects		
I can	describe the building		
I know	useful 'school' verbs		
I can discuss	school routine		
Gesundheit und Fitneß			
I know	parts of the body		
I can survive	at the doctor's		
	at the dentist's		
	at the chemist's		
Das Familienleben			
I can describe	housing		
	rooms		
	parts of buildings		
	the contents of the bathroom		
	the contents of the bedroom		
	the contents of the living room		
	the contents of the dining room		
	the contents of the kitchen		
	the garden		
I can	describe family activities		
	offer to help		
Der Alltag			
I can	describe morning and evening routines		

		Learnt	Revised
Das Taschengeld			
I can	talk about coins and notes		
	say how much pocket money I get		
	say what I spend it on		
	say what I am saving up for		
Im Café, in der Konditorei			
I know	the names of drinks		
	the names of foods		
I can	order what I want		
An der Imbißstube			
I know	the names of drinks		
	the names of foods		
I can	order what I want		
Im Restaurant			
I know	the names of drinks		
	the names of foods		
I can	order what I want		
Einkaufen			
I know	the names of shops and departments in shops		
I know	the names of clothing items		
	the names of materials		
I can	buy clothes		
I know	the names of meats		
	the names of vegetables		
	the names of fruits		
I can	buy meat, fruit and vegetables		
I know	the names of drinks and snacks		
	the names of souvenirs		
I can	buy drinks, snacks and souvenirs		
Bank und Post			
I know	money vocabulary		
I can	change money		
I know	post office vocabulary		
I can survive	in the post office		
Bus, Bahn und Auto			
I know	the names of means of transport		
	railway vocabulary		
I can	buy tickets		

		Learnt	Revised
Bus, Bahn und Auto			
	enquire about trains		
I know	bus vocabulary		
I can	enquire about buses		
I know	plane vocabulary		
I can	buy tickets		
	enquire about planes		
I can	discuss Channel crossings		
Ausflüge			
I can	talk about going out for the evening		
	discuss sport, cinema, theatre, youth club		
	invite someone out		
	make excuses		
	agree		
	make arrangements		
	ask about price and times		
	buy tickets		
	say what I did yesterday evening		
Feiertage			
I know	the names of holidays and festivals		
I can	discuss how they are celebrated		
Die Ferien			
I can	discuss holiday plans		
	obtain tourist information		
I know	camping vocabulary		
	youth hostel vocabulary		
I can	survive in a youth hostel		
I know	hotel vocabulary		
I can	survive in a hotel		
I know	seaside vocabulary		
	country holiday vocabulary		
I can	discuss what I did on holiday		
	give my opinion		
Die Medien			
I know	the names of the media		
	the names of media equipment		
	the types of film		
I can	discuss a cinema visit		
I know	the types of TV programme		
I can	discuss viewing habits		

		Learnt	Revised
Die Medien			
	give my opinion		
	ask permission to watch TV		
	ask permission to listen to the radio		
I know	the types of books and magazines		
I can	discuss reading habits		

Vocabulary topics

Key:

*	verb takes *sein* in the perfect tense
ausgehen	separable verb: **bold** part separates

Allgemeines — General

Grüße — Greetings

Guten Morgen!	Good morning!
Guten Tag!	Good day, hello, good afternoon!
Guten Abend!	Good evening!
Gute Nacht!	Good night!
Grüß Gott!	Good day (in South Germany)!
Auf Wiedersehen!	Goodbye!
Tschüß!	Cheerio!
Bis bald!	See you soon!
Bis dann!	See you later!
Bis morgen!	See you tomorrow!
Wie geht's?	How are you?
Danke, gut.	Fine, thanks.
Darf ich dir meinen Freund Klaus vorstellen?	May I introduce my friend Klaus
Es freut mich, dich kennenzulernen.	I am pleased to meet you.
bitte	please
danke	thank you
Entschuldigen Sie	excuse me, sorry
Entschuldigung	excuse me, sorry

Redewendungen — Fillers

ja, natürlich	yes, of course
einverstanden	agreed
Das ist sehr freundlich.	That is very kind.
Ich glaube/denke	I think
Ich glaube nicht	I don't think
vielleicht	perhaps
Das macht nichts	It doesn't matter
Das ist mir egal	I don't mind
Wie schade!	What a pity
Viel Spaß!	Enjoy yourself

Glückwünsche — Best wishes

Herzlichen Glückwunsch zum Geburtstag!	Happy Birthday!
Frohe Weihnachten!	Happy Christmas!
Alles Gute im neuen Jahr!	Happy New Year!
Viel Glück!	Good luck!
Gute Reise!	Have a good journey!
Frohe Ostern!	Happy Easter!
Alles Gute!	Best wishes/All the best!

Meinungen — Opinions

Ich mag	I like
Ich liebe	I adore
Ich mag ... nicht.	I don't like ...
Ich hasse	I hate
Das ist interessant	That is interesting
Das ist langweilig	That is boring
Ich finde ...	I think

Fragewörter — Question words

darf ich ...	may I ...
gibt es	is there, are there
um wieviel Uhr	at what time
wann	when
warum	why
was	what
welcher, welche, welches	which
wer	who
wie	how
wie viele	how many
wieviel	how much
wo	where
wohin	where to

Präpositionen — Prepositions

These have been given with their most common meanings. Check them also in the grammar section.

an	at
auf	on
aus	from
bei	at the house of
für	for

gegenüber	opposite
hinter	behind
in	in
in der Nähe von	near
mit	with
nach	after
neben	next to
ohne	without
über	over
unter	under
von	from
vor	in front of, before
zu	to
zwischen	between

Die Farben — Colours

blau	blue
braun	brown
dunkel...	dark ...
dunkelblau	dark blue
dunkelgrün	dark green
gelb	yellow
grau	grey
grün	green
hell...	light ...
hellblau	light blue
hellgrün	light green
kastanienbraun	chestnut brown
marineblau	navy blue
rosa	pink
rot	red
schwarz	black
weiß	white

Ich, Familie, Freunde — Myself, family, friends

Personalien — Personal details

das Alter	age
der Ausweis (e)	identity card
die Dame (n)	lady
die Eltern (pl)	parents
der Familienname (n)	surname
die Frau (en)	Mrs, Ms, woman
das Fräulein (-)	Miss, young girl
der Geburtstag (e)	birthday
der Geburtsort (e)	place of birth
die Geschwister (pl)	brothers and sisters
der Herr (en)	Mr, Sir, gentleman
der Monat (e)	month
der Name (n)	name
der Reisepaß (-pässe)	passport
das Sternzeichen (-)	star sign
Wassermann	Aquarius
Fische	Pisces
Widder	Aries
Stier	Taurus
Zwilling	Gemini
Krebs	Cancer
Löwe	Leo
Jungfrau	Virgo
Waage	Libra
Skorpion	Scorpio
Schütze	Sagittarius
Steinbock	Capricorn
die Unterschrift (en)	signature
der Vorname (n)	first name, christian name

buchstabieren	to spell
heißen	to be called
schreiben	to write
unterschreiben	to sign
wohnen	to live

Phrases

Fragen — Questions

Wie heißt du?	What's your name?
Wie alt bist du?	How old are you?
Wo wohnst du?	Where do you live?
Wann ist dein Geburtstag?	When is your birthday?
In welchem Jahr bist du geboren?	In which year were you born?
Welche Nationalität hast du?	Which nationality are you?
Woher kommst du?	Where do you come from?

Antworten — Answers

Ich heiße Petra Meier.	My name is Petra Meier.
Ich heiße Petra mit Vornamen und Meier mit Familienname.	My first name is Petra and Meier is my surname.
Ich bin zwölf Jahre alt.	I am twelve years old.
Ich wohne in Dortmund.	I live in Dortmund.
Mein Geburtstag ist der 14. Juni.	My birthday is the 14th June.
Ich bin 1983 geboren.	I was born in 1983.
Ich bin Engländer(in)	I am English
Schotte/in	Scottish
Waliser(in)	Welsh
Ire/in	Irish
Brite/in	British
Ich komme aus Bournemouth in Südengland.	I come from Bournemouth in the South of England.

Die Adresse — Address

die Adresse (n)	address
die Allee (n)	avenue
die Anschrift (en)	address
der Bezirk (e)	district
das Dorf (Dörfer)	village

die	Gasse (n)	alley, lane
das	Land (Länder)	country
der	Platz (Plätze)	square, place
das	Postfach (-fächer)	PO box
die	Postleitzahl (en)	postcode
die	Sackgasse (n)	cul-de-sac
die	Stadt (Städte)	town
der	Stadtteil (e)	district, part of a town
die	Straße (n)	street, road
die	Telefonnummer (n)	telephone number
der	Weg (e)	way, road, path

Beispiele deutscher Anschriften

Herrn
Holger Stender
Mathildenstraße 11

64285 Darmstadt

Frau
Anneliese Maier
Am Heuberg 12

64720 Michelstadt
Germany

Haustiere / Pets

der	Fisch (e)	fish
der	Hamster (-)	hamster
der	Hund (e)	dog
der	Kanarienvogel (-vögel)	canary
die	Katze (n)	cat
die	Maus (Mäuse)	mouse
das	Meerschweinchen (-)	guinea-pig
das	Pferd (e)	horse
das	Pony (Ponys)	pony
die	Ratte (n)	rat
die	Schildkröte (n)	tortoise
die	Schlange (n)	snake
der	Wellensittich (e)	budgie
	anschmiegsam	affectionate
	bissig	liable to bite
	bösartig	vicious
	gehorsam	obedient
	groß	big
	klein	small
	zierlich	dainty, delicate
	ausmisten	to muck out
	bürsten	to brush
	füttern	to feed
	saubermachen	to clean
	spazierenführen	to take for a walk

Phrases

Ich habe einen Hund. Er ist ziemlich groß und braun.	I have a dog. He is fairly big and brown.
Er ist ein Labrador.	It is a labrador.
Ich führe meinen Hund jeden Tag spazieren.	I take my dog for a walk every day.
Meine Katze ist sehr anschmiegsam.	My cat is very affectionate
Mein Bruder hat Fische. Er muß sie füttern und das Aquarium einmal in der Woche saubermachen.	My brother has fish. He has to feed them and once a week he has to clean out the aquarium.
Ich habe keine Haustiere.	I haven't got any pets.
Ich bin allergisch gegen Hunde und Katzen.	I am allergic to dogs and cats.

Familienmitglieder / Family members

das	Baby (s)	baby
der/die	Bekannte (n)	friend/acquaintance
der	Brieffreund (e)	penfriend (male)
die	Brieffreundin (nen)	penfriend (female)
der	Bruder (Brüder)	brother
der	Cousin (s)	cousin (male)
die	Eltern (pl)	parents
der	Enkel (n)	grandson
die	Enkelin (nen)	granddaughter
der/die	Erwachsene (n)	adult
die	Familie (n)	family
die	Frau (en)	woman/wife
der	Freund (e)	friend (male)
die	Freundin (nen)	friend (female)
die	Großeltern (pl)	grandparents
die	Großmutter (-mütter)	grandmother
der	Großvater (-väter)	grandfather
der/die	Heranwachsende (n)	adolescent
der	Junge (n)	boy
das	Kind (er)	child
die	Kusine (n)	cousin (female)
das	Mädchen (-)	girl
der	Mann (Männer)	man, husband
die	Mutter (Mütter)	mother
die	Mutti (s)	mummy
die	Oma (s)	grannny
der	Onkel (s)	uncle
der	Opa (s)	grandad
der	Papi	daddy
die	Schwester (n)	sister
der	Sohn (Söhne)	son
der	Stiefbruder (-brüder)	half-brother, stepbrother
die	Stiefmutter (-mütter)	stepmother
die	Stiefschwester (n)	half-sister, stepsister
der	Stiefvater (-väter)	stepfather
die	Tante (n)	aunt
die	Tochter (Töchter)	daughter
der	Vater (Väter)	father

der Vati	daddy
der/die Verlobte (n)	fiancé(e)
der/die Verwandte (n)	relative
geschieden	divorced
verheiratet	married
verlobt	engaged
verwitwet	widowed
sich gut/schlecht verstehen mit	to get on well/badly with
gut/schlecht auskommen mit	to get on well/badly with
sich streiten	to argue
sich vertragen	to get on
mögen	to like
Krach haben mit	to have an argument with
mein Stammbaum	my family tree

Phrases

Hast du Geschwister?	Have you got any brothers or sisters?
Ja, ich habe einen Bruder/eine Schwester.	Yes, I have got a brother/sister.
Ja, ich habe zwei Brüder/zwei Schwestern.	Yes, I have got two brothers/sisters.
Nein, ich bin Einzelkind.	No, I am an only child.
Hast du viele Verwandte?	Have you got lots of relatives?
Ja, ich habe eine Tante, Mary, und zwei Onkeln, Keith und John.	Yes, I have one aunt, Mary, and two uncles, Keith and John.
Wie verstehst du dich mit deinen Verwandten?	How do you get on with your relatives?
Ich komme mit meinen Kusinen/Cousins gut aus aber ich kann meinen Onkel John nicht leiden.	I get on well with my cousins, but I can't stand my uncle John.

Berufe — Jobs

der Angestellte (n)	office worker
der Arbeiter (-)	worker (unskilled)
der Arzt/die Ärztin	doctor
der Direktor/die Direktorin	manager
der Elektriker/die Elektrikerin	electrician
der Fahrer/die Fahrerin	driver
der Frisör/die Friseuse	hairdresser
der Geschäftsmann/die Geschäftsfrau	businessman/woman (self-employed)
der Industriekaufmann/die Industriekauffrau	businessman/woman
der Ingenieur	engineer
der Krankenpfleger	nurse (male)
die Krankenschwester	nurse (female)
der Lehrer/die Lehrerin	teacher
der Maurer/die Maurerin	bricklayer/builder
der Mechaniker/die Mechanikerin	mechanic
der Polizist/die Polizistin	police officer
der Postbeamte/die Postbeamtin	post office worker
die Putzfrau	cleaner
die Sekretärin	secretary
der Verkäufer/die Verkäuferin	sales assistant
der Vertreter/die Vertreterin	sales representative
angestellt	employed
arbeitslos	unemployed
halbtags	part-time
stundenweise	hourly
arbeiten	to work

Phrases

Mein Bruder arbeitet bei Siemens.	My brother works for Siemens.
Meine Mutter arbeitet stundenweise in einer Apotheke.	My mother works on an hourly basis for a chemist.
Mein Vater ist seit zwei Jahren arbeitslos.	My father has been unemployed for two years.

In der Klasse — In class

Im Klassenzimmer — In the classroom

die Antwort (en)	answer
das Beispiel (e)	example
das Bild (er)	picture
der Bleistift (e)	pencil
der Boden (Böden)	floor
das Buch (Bücher)	textbook/book
der Buntstift (e)	coloured pencil
der Computer (-)	computer
die Decke (n)	ceiling
der Fehler (-)	mistake
das Fenster (-)	window
der Filzstift (e)	felt-tip
die Frage (n)	question
der Füller (-)	ink pen
die Hausaufgabe (n)	homework
das Heft (e)	exercise book
der Hocker (-)	stool
die Kassette (en)	cassette
der Kassettenrekorder (-)	cassette recorder
die Kreide (n)	chalk
der Kuli (s)	biro
das Lineal (e)	ruler
das Mäppchen (-)	pencil case
der Marker (-)	marker pen
die Note (n)	mark, grade
das Papier	paper
das Poster (-)	poster
das Problem (e)	problem
der Projektor (en)	projector
der Radiergummi (s)	rubber

das Regal (e)	shelf
der Satz (Sätze)	sentence
der Schrank (Schränke)	cupboard
der Schreibtisch (e)	desk
der Schüler (-)	pupil (male)
die Schülerin (nen)	pupil (female)
der Stuhl (Stühle)	chair
die Stunde (n)	lesson
der Stundenplan (-pläne)	timetable
die Tafel (n)	blackboard
der Tisch (e)	table
die Tür (en)	door
die Uniform (en)	uniform
die Unterrichtsstunde (n)	lesson
die Wand (Wände)	wall
das Waschbecken (-)	sink
das Zeugnis (se)	school report
abschreiben	to copy
auswendig lernen	to learn by heart
lernen	to learn
schreiben	to write
üben	to practise
verbessern	to correct
wiederholen	to repeat
zuhören	to listen

Phrases

Der Lehrer/die Lehrerin sagt:	**The teacher says:**
Kommt herein!	Come in.
Setzt Euch!	Sit down.
Ruhe, bitte!	Be quiet, please.
Seid bitte still!	Don't talk, please.
Mach die Tür/das Fenster zu!	Shut the door/the window.
Ich stelle jetzt die Anwesenheit fest.	I'm now going to call the register.
Wer fehlt?	Who is absent?
Nehmt eure Hefte heraus!	Take your excercise books out.
Nehmt euer Deutschbuch heraus!	Get out your German textbook.
Schlagt bitte Seite 43 auf!	Please turn to page 43.
Lest den Text!	Read the text.
Sucht ... im Wörterbuch/ im Wortschatz.	Look up ... in the dictionary/in the vocabulary.
Hört (der Kassette) zu!	Listen (to the cassette).
Wiederholt!	Repeat.
Noch einmal, alle zusammen.	Once more, all of you together!
Beantwortet die Fragen!	Answer the questions.
Schreibt das auf!	Write it down.
Macht euch Notizen!	Take notes.
Seit wann lernst du Deutsch?	How long have you been learning German?
Schaut an die Tafel!	Look at the blackboard.
Schreibt das Datum (auf die linke Seite).	Write the date (on the left).
Schreibt den Titel!	Write the title.
Unterstreicht den Titel!	Underline the title.
Numeriert die Antworten von eins bis fünf!	Number the answers from 1 to 5.
Verbessert eure Antworten!	Correct your answers.
Buchstabiere das Wort 'Haus'.	Spell the word 'Haus'.
Kreuzt das richtige Kästchen an.	Tick the correct box.
Richtig oder Falsch?	True or false?
Wählt die richtige Antwort.	Choose the correct answer
Das ist richtig.	That's correct.
Macht eure Bücher zu!	Close your books.
Reicht die Hefte an Mark weiter.	Pass your exercise books to Mark.
Mark, bringe die Hefte zu mir ins Lehrerzimmer.	Mark, bring the books to me in the staffroom.
Wähle eine Karte aus, Sam.	Sam, choose a card.
Wählt einen Partner.	Choose a partner.
Arbeitet in einer Gruppe zu zweit/zu dritt.	Work in a group of two/three.
Arbeitet mit eurem Partner	Work with your partner.
Bereitet einen Dialog vor.	Prepare a dialogue.
Übt diesen Dialog.	Practise this dialogue.
Schreibt die Hausaufgaben auf.	Write your homework down.
Das ist für Freitag.	It is for Friday.
Lernt die Vokabeln.	Learn the vocabulary.
Das macht ihr bitte bis morgen.	Please do this for tomorrow.
Das ist für einen Test am Montag.	It is for a test on Monday.
Versteht ihr das?	Do you understand this?
Ist alles klar?	Is it all clear?
Beeile dich!	Hurry up.
Räumt eure Sachen weg.	Put your things away.
Steht auf!	Stand up.
Stellt die Stühle auf/unter den Tisch.	Put the chairs on/under the table.
Komm bitte morgen um 9 Uhr zu mir ins Lehrerzimmer.	Come and see me tomorrow at 9 a.m. in the staffroom.
Der Lehrer/die Lehrerin korrigiert:	The teacher marks:
Du hast achtzehn von zwanzig Punkten.	You've got eighteen out of twenty.
Du hast nur vier von zwanzig.	You have only got four out of twenty.
ausgezeichnet	excellent
sehr gut	very good
gut	good

befriedigend	satisfactory
ungenügend	insufficient
guter Versuch	good attempt

Der Schüler/die Schülerin sagt:	**The pupil says:**
Ich lerne seit zwei Jahren Deutsch.	I have been learning. German for two years.
Ich verstehe (nicht).	I (don't) understand.
Ich weiß nicht.	I don't know.
Ich habe eine gute/schlechte Note.	I got a good/bad mark.
Sprichst du/Sprechen Sie Deutsch?	Do you speak German?
Ich habe mein Buch/Heft/ Mäppchen vergessen.	I have forgotten my book/exercise book/pencil-case.
Ich brauche ein neues Heft.	I need a new exercise book.
Mein Heft ist voll.	My exercise book is full up.
Entschuldigen Sie, bitte, ...	Please Miss/Sir ...
Auf welcher Seite sind wir?	Which page are we on?
Wie sagt man 'felt-tip' auf deutsch?	How do you say 'felt-tip' in German?
Wie schreibt man 'Hund'?	How do you spell 'Hund'?
Wie spricht man das aus?	How do you pronounce it?
In welches Heft schreiben wir das?	Which exercise book shall we do this in?
Darf ich das Fenster aufmachen?	May I open the window?
Darf ich austreten?	May I leave the room?
Darf ich meinen Bleistift spitzen?	May I sharpen my pencil?
Ich bin in der sechsten/ siebten/achten Klasse.	I am in year six/seven/eight.

Das Alphabet — Alphabet

(approximate English sound equivalents are given here)

a	ah
b	bay
c	say
d	day
e	eh?
f	eff
g	gay
h	ha!
i	ee
j	yacht
k	car
l	ell
m	emm
n	enn
o	oh!
p	pay
q	coo
r	air
s	ess
t	tay
u	ooo!
v	fow (like foul)
w	vay
x	ekks
y	upsilon
z	tsed
ß	ess tsed or scharfes ess
ä	ah Umlaut
ö	oh Umlaut
ü	ooo Umlaut

Zeichensetzung — Punctuation

der	Absatz (Absätze)	paragraph
die	Anführungstriche	speech marks
der	Bindestrich	hyphen
das	Fragezeichen	question mark
das	Komma	comma
der	Punkt	full stop
der	Satz (Sätze)	sentence
	großschreiben	to write with a capital letter
	kleinschreiben	to write with a lower case (small) letter

Freizeit — Free time

Hobbys — Hobbies

der	Abend (e)	evening
die	Ferien (plural only)	holidays
die	Freizeit	free time, leisure time
die	Jugend	youth, young people
der	Jugendclub (s)	youth club
der/die	Jugendliche (n)	youngster
das	Jugendzentrum (-zentren)	youth centre
der	Nachmittag (e)	afternoon
das	Training	training
der	Verein (e)	club
das	Wochenende (n)	weekend

Der Sport (die Sportarten) — Sport (s)

der	Fußball	football
die	Gymnastik	gymnastics
die	Leichtathletik	athletics
das	Kricket	cricket
der	Kricketspieler (-)	cricket player
die	Mannschaft (en)	team
das	Mitglied (er)	member
das	Reiten	riding
das	Schwimmbad (-bäder)	swimming pool
das	Schwimmen	swimming
das	Spiel	game, match
das	Stadion (Stadien)	stadium

das Tennis	tennis
der Tennisplatz (-plätze)	tennis court
das Turnen	gymnastics
die Turnhalle (n)	gym
der Wassersport	watersports
der Wintersport	winter sport
angeln	to fish
baden	to swim/bathe
gewinnen	to win
radfahren*	to cycle
reiten*	to ride
Rollschuh laufen*	to roller-skate
Schlittschuh laufen*	to ice-skate
schwimmen	to swim
segeln	to sail
skifahren*	to ski
skilaufen*	to ski
spazierengehen*	to go for a walk
spielen	to play
Sport treiben	to do sport
trainieren	to train
verlieren	to lose
windsurfen	to windsurf

Phrases

Was machst du in der Freizeit?	What do you do in your free time?
Ich bin Mitglied im Sportverein.	I am a member of the sports club.
Ich spiele Fußball in der A-Mannschaft.	I play football in the A-team.
Ich gehe jeden Dienstag zum Training.	I go to training every Tuesday.
Am Samstag haben wir ein Spiel.	We have a match on Saturday.
Letzte Woche haben wir drei zu null gewonnen.	Last week we won three–nil.
Welche Sportarten magst du?	Which sports do you like?
Ich spiele gern Tennis im Sommer, und im Winter fahre ich Ski.	I like playing tennis in summer, and I go skiing in winter.
Ich treibe nicht gern Sport.	I don't like doing sport.
Ich sehe gern Leichtathletik im Fernsehen.	I like watching athletics on TV.
Bist du Mitglied in einem Verein?	Are you a member of a club?
Wann spielst du Kricket?	When do you play cricket?
Ich spiele zweimal in der Woche, montags und donnerstags.	I play twice a week, on Mondays and Thursdays.
Ich schwimme gern im Hallenbad.	I like swimming in the indoor pool.
Was kostet der Eintritt für einen Schüler/eine Schülerin?	How much is the entrance fee for a pupil?
Was sind die Öffnungszeiten des Schwimmbads?	What are the opening times of the swimming pool?
Ist das Schwimmbad am Sonntag geöffnet?	Is the pool open on Sundays?
Ich hätte gern eine Eintrittskarte für ein Kind und zwei Erwachsene.	I'd like a ticket for a child and two adults.
Wie lange ist die Badezeit?	How long is a swimming session?

Die Musik — Music

die Blockflöte (n)	recorder
das Cello (s)	cello
der Chor (Chöre)	choir
die Compact Disc/CD	CD
die Flöte/die Querflöte (n)	flute
die Geige (n)	violin
die Gitarre (n)	guitar
die Gruppe (n)	group
der Hit (s)	hit song
das Instrument (e)	instrument
die Klarinette (n)	clarinet
das Klavier (e)	piano
das Konzert (e)	concert
die Lieblingsgruppe (n)	favourite group
der Lieblingssänger (-)	favourite singer
das Lied (er)	song
die klassische Musik	classical music
das Orchester (-)	orchestra
der Plattenspieler (-)	record player
die Popmusik	pop music
das Radio (s)	radio
der Sänger (-)	singer (male)
die Sängerin (nen)	singer (female)
der Schlager (-)	hit song (in German)
das Schlagzeug	drum kit
die Trompete (n)	trumpet
die Volksmusik	folk music
der Walkman™	walkman™
hören	to listen to
singen	to sing
spielen	to play
üben	to practise

Phrases

Spielst du ein Instrument?	Do you play an instrument?
Ja, ich spiele Klavier.	Yes, I play the piano.
Wie lange spielst du schon Klavier?	How long have you been playing the piano?
Ich spiele seit drei Jahren.	I have been playing for three years.
Wie oft übst du?	How often do you practise?
Ich übe jeden Tag eine Stunde.	I practise every day for an hour.

Ich spiele kein Instrument aber ich singe in einem Chor in der Schule.	I don´t play an instrument but I sing in the school choir.
Interessierst du dich für Musik?	Are you interested in music?
Ja, Musik ist sehr wichtig für mich.	Yes, music is very important to me.
Welche Musik magst du am liebsten?	What is your favourite music?
Ich höre gern Popmusik.	I like listening to pop music.
Hast du einen Lieblingssänger/eine Lieblingsgruppe?	Do you have a favourite singer/group?
Mein Lieblingssänger ist xyz, und abc ist meine Lieblingsgruppe.	My favourite singer is xyz and abc is my favourite group.
Abc sind spitze/einfach Klasse.	Abc are great.
Nein, ich habe keine Lieblingsgruppe.	No, I haven't got a favourite group.
Ich höre alle englische Gruppen gern.	I like listening to all English groups.
Ich kann DEF nicht ausstehen.	I can't stand DEF.
Gehst du oft in ein Konzert?	Do you often go to concerts?
Nein, aber letzte Woche bin ich zu einem Konzert von GHI gegangen.	No, but last week I went to a concert by GHI.
Die Stimmung war toll.	The atmosphere was great.
Ich habe viele Kassetten aber nur wenige CDs.	I have lots of cassettes but only a few CDs.
Schallplatten und CDs sind sehr teuer.	Records and CDs are very expensive.

Die Informatik / IT

Die Informatik	IT
der Bildschirm (e)	screen
der Computer (-)	computer
das Computerspiel (e)	computer game
der Computervirus (-viren)	computer virus
die Datei	file, data base
die Diskette	disk
der Drucker (-)	printer
die Maus	mouse
der Monitor (e)	monitor
das Tabellenprogramm	spreadsheet
die Tastatur (en)	keyboard
die Textverarbeitung	word processing
das Videospiel (e)	video game
editieren	to edit
bearbeiten	to edit
faxen	to fax
formatieren	to format
laden	to load
löschen	to delete
speichern	to save

Andere Hobbys / Other hobbies

Andere Hobbys	Other hobbies
der Bierdeckel (-)	beer mat
die Briefmarke (n)	stamp
das Fernsehen	TV
der Film (e)	film
der Fotoapparat (e)	camera
die Geschichte (n)	history
das Gesellschaftsspiel (e)	board game
die Handarbeit (en)	needlework
das Kreuzworträtsel (-)	crossword
der Modelbau	making models
das Pferd (e)	horse
der Roman (e)	novel
die Sammlung (en)	collection
die Videokamera (s)	video-camera, camrecorder
anfangen	to begin
ausgehen*	to go out
basteln	to do DIY
ein Schloß besichtigen	to visit a stately home
bezahlen	to pay
einkaufen	to shop
fernsehen	to watch TV
finden	to find
fotografieren	to take photos
in die Stadt gehen*	to go into town
häkeln	to crochet
hören	to listen to
lesen	to read
einen Einkaufsbummel machen	to go round the shops
einen Schaufensterbummel machen	to go window shopping
malen	to paint (a picture)
nähen	to sew
reisen*	to travel
sammeln	to collect
spazierengehen*	to go for walks
Karten spielen	to play cards
Schach spielen	to play chess
stricken	to knit
tanzen	to dance
sich mit Freunden treffen	to meet friends
wandern*	to hike
zeichnen	to draw

Phrases

Sammelst du etwas?	Do you collect anything?
Ich sammle Frösche. Ich habe schon hundert.	I collect frogs. I have got one hundred already.
Welche Bücher liest du?	What type of books do you read?
Ich lese Abenteuerromane.	I read adventure novels.

Ich spiele Schach.	I play chess.
Ich spiele gern Gesellschaftsspiele.	I like playing board games.
Ich höre gern Radio.	I like listening to the radio.
Was sind die Hobbys deiner Familie?	What are the hobbies of your family?
Mein Bruder singt im Schulchor, meine Schwester ist Mitglied einer Laienspielgruppe, meine Mutter macht Volkstanz, und mein Vater wandert gern.	My brother sings in the school choir, my sister is a member of an amateur theatre group, my mother does folk dancing and my father likes hiking.
Ich besichtige gern alte Schlösser.	I like visiting stately homes.

Die Stadt / Town

In der Stadt / In town

der Bahnhof (-höfe)	railway station
die Bibliothek (en)	library
der Busbahnhof (-höfe)	bus station
der Dom (Dome)	cathedral
das Einkaufszentrum (-zentren)	shopping centre
die Fabrik (en)	factory
der Flughafen (-häfen)	airport
die Fußgängerzone (n)	pedestrian precinct
die Haltestelle (n)	bus stop
das Hotel (s)	hotel
die Industriestadt (-städte)	industrial town
das Informationsbüro	tourist information office
das Kaufhaus (-häuser)	department store
das Kino (s)	cinema
die Kirche (n)	church
das Krankenhaus (-häuser)	hospital
der Markt (Märkte)	market
das Museum (Museen)	museum
das Parkhaus (-häuser)	multi-story car park
die Post	post office
das Rathaus	town hall
das Reisebüro (s)	travel agency
das Stadion (Stadien)	stadium
die Stadt (Städte)	town
die Tankstelle (n)	filling station
das Theater (-)	theatre
das Verkehrsamt	tourist information office
die öffentlichen Verkehrsmittel (pl)	public transport
der Vorort (e)	suburb
alt	old
gepflegt	tidy
groß	big, large
historisch	historical
klein	small
laut	noisy, loud
modern	modern
ruhig	quiet
sauber	clean
schmutzig	dirty
verschmutzt	polluted
bauen	to build
einkaufen gehen*	to go shopping
Freunde treffen	to meet friends
renovieren	to renovate
restaurieren	to restore
spazierengehen*	to go for walks
wohnen	to live

Phrases

Wo wohnst du?	Where do you live?
Ich wohne in Northampton, in Mittelengland.	I live in Northampton, in the Midlands.
Ist das eine große/kleine Stadt?	Is it a big/small town?
Wieviele Einwohner gibt es?	How many inhabitants are there?
Es gibt zweihunderttausend Einwohner.	There are 200,000 inhabitants.
Was gibt es in deinem Stadtteil?	What is there in your part of town?
Es gibt eine Kirche, ein Kino und viele Geschäfte.	There is a church, a cinema and many shops.
Was gibt es in der Stadt zu sehen?	What is there to see in town?
Was kann man in Northampton machen?	What is there to do in Northampton?
Man kann den Markt besuchen und das Museum besichtigen.	One can visit the market and see the museum.
Welche Sporteinrichtungen gibt es?	Which sports facilities are there?
Es gibt ein Schwimmbad und ein Stadion.	There is a swimming pool and a stadium.
Was machst du, wenn du in die Stadt gehst?	What do you do when you go into town?
Ich mache einen Schaufensterbummel oder treffe meine Freunde im Jugendclub.	I go window shopping or meet my friends in the youth club.

Wie komme ich am besten ...? / How do I get to ...?

Die Wegbeschreibung / Road directions

die Ampel (n)	traffic lights
die Brücke (n)	bridge
die Bushaltestelle (n)	bus stop
die Ecke (n)	corner
die Einbahnstraße (n)	one way street
das Einkaufszentrum (-zentren)	shopping centre
die Fußgängerzone (n)	pedestrian precinct

das	Industriegebiet (e)	industrial estate
der	Kreisel (-)	roundabout
die	Kreuzung (en)	cross-roads
der	Schnellimbiß	snack bar
die	Stadtmitte	town centre
die	Telefonzelle (n)	phone box
	abbiegen	to turn
	fahren*	to go (by vehicle), to drive
	gehen*	to go
	nehmen	to take
	überqueren	to cross (road)
	an der Ecke	on the corner
	gegenüber (+ Dat)	opposite
	gegenüber dem Rathaus	opposite the townhall
	hinter (+ Dat)	behind
	hinter der Kirche	behind the church
	nach (+ Dat)	after
	nach der Ampel	after the lights
	neben (+ Dat)	next to
	neben dem Theater	next to the theatre
	um die Ecke	round the corner
	vor (+ Dat)	in front of
	vor dem Kino	in front of the cinema
	zwischen (+ Dat)	in between
	zwischen der Bank und dem Kino	between the bank and the cinema

Phrases

Entschuldigung, wie komme ich am besten zum Bahnhof, bitte?	Excuse me, what's the best way to the station, please?
Gehen Sie hier geradeaus und nehmen Sie die zweite Straße links.	Go straight on here, and take the second street on the left.
Gehen Sie über die Kreuzung.	Go across the junction.
Nehmen Sie die erste Straße rechts, dann gehen Sie am Fluß entlang bis zur Ampel.	Take the first street on the right, then go along the river as far as the lights.
Ist hier in der Nähe ein Café?	Is there a café near here?
Ja, gegenüber der Bank.	Yes, opposite the bank.
Ist das weit von hier?	Is it far from here?
Das ist gleich hier um die Ecke.	It is just round the corner.
Das sind nur fünf Minuten zu Fuß.	It is only five minutes on foot.
Sind Sie zu Fuß oder mit dem Wagen hier.	Are you here on foot or in a car?
Am besten nehmen Sie den Bus, Nummer 7.	You'd best take the number 7 bus.
Ich suche das Hotel Miramar.	I am looking for the Hotel Miramar.
Wo ist das bitte?	Where is it, please?

Das Land — The country

Auf dem Lande — In the country

der	Bach (Bäche)	brook
der	Bauernhof (-höfe)	farm
der	Berg (e)	mountain
das	Dorf (Dörfer)	village
das	Feld (er)	field
der	Fluß (Flüsse)	river
der	Hain (e)	copse
der	Hügel (-)	hill
die	Insel (n)	island
das	Land (Länder)	country
der	Landkreis (e)	district
die	Landstraße (n)	country road
der	See (n)	lake
das	Tal (Täler)	valley
der	Teich (e)	pond
der	Wald (Wälder)	forest, wood
das	Waldstück (e)	wood
die	Wiese (n)	meadow
	10 km entfernt	10 km away
	abseits	out of the way
	entlang (+ Acc.)	along
	ganz in der Nähe	very near
	gegenüber	opposite
	gelegen	situated
	hinter	behind
	in der Nähe von	near
	in der Mitte	in the middle
	links neben	to the left of
	neben	beside
	rechts neben	to the right of
	vor	in front of
	weit weg von	far from
	im Norden	in the north
	nördlich von	north of
	im Osten	in the east
	östlich von	east of
	im Süden	in the south
	südlich von	south of
	im Westen	in the west
	westlich von	west of
	besichtigen	to visit (a monument)
	schwimmen	to swim
	sehen	to see
	spielen	to play
	wandern*	to hike

Phrases

Ich wohne in Newchurch. Das ist ein Dorf in der Nähe von Newport.	I live in Newchurch. It is a village near Newport.

Im Dorf gibt es eine alte Kirche, eine Post und eine Kneipe.	In the village there is an old church, a post office and a pub.
Der Fluß ist in der Nähe des Dorfes.	The river is near the village.
Ich wohne gern auf dem Lande, weil es sehr ruhig ist. Die Luft ist auch weniger verschmutzt.	I like living in the country because it is so quiet. The air is also less polluted.
Ich wohne nicht gerne auf dem Lande.	I don't like living in the country.
Es ist langweilig; die Verkehrsverbindungen sind schlecht.	It is boring; the public transport is bad.
Es gibt nichts für junge Leute.	There is nothing for young people.

Das Wetter / Weather

der Frost	frost
das Gewitter (-)	thunderstorm
der Nebel	fog
der Regen	rain
der Schnee	snow
die Sonne	sun
der Wind (e)	wind
die Wolke (n)	cloud
bewölkt	cloudy
gefroren	frozen
heiß	hot
kalt	cold
neblig	foggy
sonnig	sunny
windig	windy
regnen	to rain
scheinen	to shine
schneien	to snow

Phrases

Es regnet.	It is raining.
Die Sonne scheint.	The sun is shining.
Es schneit.	It is snowing.
Es ist windig.	It is windy.
Es donnert.	It is thundering.
Es blitzt.	There is lightning.
Die Temperatur beträgt 30 Grad.	The temperature is 30 degrees.
Wie ist das Wetter in Schottland?	What is the weather like in Scotland?
Wie war das Wetter in den Ferien?	What was the weather like during the holidays?
Gestern hat es den ganzen Tag geregnet.	Yesterday it rained all day long.
Am Nachmittag war es heiß.	In the afternoon it was hot.
Im Dezember hat es geschneit.	It snowed in December.
Morgen scheint die Sonne wieder.	Tomorrow it will be sunny again.

Schule / School

In der Schule / At school

die Gesamtschule (n)	comprehensive school
die Grundschule (n)	primary school
das Gymnasium (Gymnasien)	grammar school
die Hauptschule (n)	secondary school
die Herbstferien (pl)	autumn half-term holiday
der Kindergarten (-gärten)	nursery school
die Oberstufe (n)	sixth form
die Osterferien (pl)	Easter holidays
die Pause (n)	break
die Pfingstferien (pl)	summer half-term
die Realschule (n)	secondary (modern) school
die Schule (n)	school
die Schulferien (pl)	school holidays
die Sommerferien (pl)	summer holidays
die Stunde (n)	lesson
das Trimester (-)	term
der Unterricht	teaching, lesson
die Unterrichtsstunde (n)	lesson
die Versammlung (en)	assembly
die Weihnachtsferien (pl)	Christmas holidays

Das Personal / Staff

der Direktor (en)	headmaster
die Direktorin (nen)	headmistress
der Hausmeister (-)	caretaker
der Lehrer (-)	teacher (male)
die Lehrerin (nen)	teacher (female)
die Sekretärin (nen)	secretary

Die Fächer (pl) / School subjects

Biologie	biology
Chemie	chemistry
Deutsch	German
Englisch	English
Erdkunde	geography
Französisch	French
Geschichte	history
Hauswirtschaft	home economics
Informatik	computing/IT
Kunst	art
Latein	Latin
Mathe/Mathematik	maths/mathematics
die Naturwissenschaft (en)	science
Physik	physics
Religion	religious studies
Spanisch	Spanish
Sport	games/PE
Töpfern	pottery

einfach	easy
interessant	interesting
langweilig	boring
nützlich	useful
nutzlos	useless
schwer	difficult
es macht Spaß	it is fun

Die Gebäude (pl) — Buildings

die Bibliothek	library
die Kantine	canteen
das Klassenzimmer (-)	classroom
das Labor (s)	laboratory
das Lehrerzimmer (-)	staff room
die Lehrmittelsammlung (en)	resource centre
der Schulhof (-höfe)	playground
die Toiletten (pl)	toilets
die Turnhalle	gymnasium
der Umkleideraum (-räume)	changing room
alt	old
aus Backstein	made of brick
aus Beton	made of concrete
gemischt	mixed
für Jungen	for boys
für Mädchen	for girls
modern	modern

Schulverben — School verbs

abschreiben	to copy
anfangen	to begin
antworten	to answer
anwesend sein	to be present
aussuchen	to select
bestehen	to pass (an exam)
bestrafen	to punish
dauern	to last
die Hausaufgaben machen	to do homework
durchfallen*	to fail
einen Versuch machen	to do an experiment
enden	to end
erklären	to explain
fragen (nach)	to ask (for)
lernen	to learn
malen	to paint
musizieren	to make music
nachsitzen	to have a detention
rechnen	to calculate
reden	to talk
schreiben	to write
singen	to sing
sitzenbleiben*	to repeat a year
spielen	to play
vergessen	to forget
versetzt werden*	to move on to the next year
wählen	to choose
wiederholen	to repeat
zählen	to count
zeichnen	to draw
zuhören	to listen

Phrases

Wann stehst du auf?	When do you get up?
Ich stehe um halb sieben auf.	I get up at half past six.
Wann gehst du aus dem Haus?	When do you leave your house?
Ich verlasse das Haus um halb acht.	I leave home at half past seven.
Wann kommst du in der Schule an?	When do you arrive at school?
Ich komme um Viertel nach acht in der Schule an.	I arrive at school at quarter past eight.
Wie kommst du in die Schule?	How do you get to school?
Ich gehe zu Fuß.	I go on foot.
Ich fahre mit dem Bus/Zug/Rad/Wagen.	I go by bus/train/bike/car.
Ich fahre mit der Straßenbahn/U-Bahn.	I go by tram/underground.
Wann beginnt die erste Stunde?	When does the first lesson start?
Die Schule fängt um neun Uhr an.	School starts at nine o'clock.
Wie lange dauert eine Stunde?	How long is a lesson?
Die Stunden dauern fünfundvierzig Minuten.	Lessons last 45 minutes.
Was machst du in der Pause?	What do you do during break?
Ich spiele Fußball und plaudere mit meinen Freunden.	I play football and chat with my friends.
Wo ißt du zu Mittag?	Where do you eat lunch?
Ich esse in der Kantine.	I eat in the canteen.
Was ißt du zu Mittag?	What do you eat for lunch?
Ich esse belegte Brote.	I eat sandwiches.
Wann ist die Schule aus?	When does school finish?
Die Schule endet um vier Uhr.	School finishes at four o'clock.
Wie kommst du nach Hause?	How do you get home?
Meine Mutter/mein Vater holt mich von der Schule ab.	My mum/dad picks me up from school.
Wieviele Schüler sind in deiner Klasse?	How many pupils are in your class?
Es gibt 30 Schüler in meiner Klasse.	There are 30 pupils in my class.
Welche Fächer lernst du?	Which subjects do you study?
Ich lerne Deutsch, natürlich, Englisch, Mathe und Biologie.	I study German, of course, English, maths and biology.

Was ist dein Lieblingsfach?	What is your favourite subject?
Mein Lieblingsfach ist Deutsch.	My favourite subject is German.
Welches Fach gefällt dir nicht?	Which subject don't you like?
Ich mache Mathe nicht gern.	I don't like doing maths.
Wie findest du Erdkunde?	What do you think of geography?
Ich finde Erdkunde nützlich.	I think geography is useful.
Wieviel Hausaufgaben hast du pro Woche?	How much homework do you have per week?
Ich habe etwa zwei Stunden Hausaufgaben	I have about two hours' homework.
Bist du Mitglied einer Schulmannschaft?	Are you a member of a school team?
Ich bin Mitglied der Fußballmannschaft.	I am a member of the football team.
Welche Klubs gibt es in deiner Schule?	What clubs are there in your school?
Es gibt einen Schachklub und eine Theatergruppe.	There is a chess club and a drama group.
Ich singe im Schulchor.	I sing in the school choir.
Wieviele Wochen Ferien bekommst du?	How many weeks' holiday do you get?
Ich habe zwei Wochen Osterferien, zehn Tage über Weihnachten und sechs Wochen im Sommer.	I get two weeks' Easter holidays, ten days at Christmas, and six weeks in the summer.

Gesundheit und Fitneß / Health and fitness

Die Körperteile / Parts of the body

der Arm (Arme)	arm
das Auge (n)	eye
der Bauch (Bäuche)	stomach
das Bein (e)	leg
das Blut	blood
der Finger (-)	finger
der Fuß (Füße)	foot
der Hals (Hälse)	neck, throat
die Hand (Hände)	hand
das Knie (e)	knee
der Kopf (Köpfe)	head
der Mund (Münder)	mouth
die Nase (n)	nose
das Ohr (en)	ear
der Zahn (Zähne)	tooth

Beim Arzt, beim Zahnarzt / At the doctor's, at the dentist's

die Arznei	medicine
der Arzt (Ärzte)	doctor (male)
die Arzthelferin (nen)	doctor's receptionist
die Ärztin (nen)	doctor (female)
der Krankenpfleger (-)	nurse (male)
die Krankenschwester (n)	nurse (female)
die Krankheit (en)	illness
das Medikament (e)	medicine
die Plombe (n)	filling
das Rezept (e)	prescription
der Schmerz (en)	pain
die Sprechstunde (n)	surgery time
das Sprechzimmer (-)	consulting room
die Spritze (n)	injection
der Termin (e)	appointment
der Verband (-bände)	bandage
das Wartezimmer (-)	waiting room
der Zahnarzt (-ärzte)	dentist (male)
die Zahnärztin (nen)	dentist (female)

Phrases

Könnte ich bitte einen Termin haben?	May I have an appointment, please?
Geht es am nächsten Montag um drei Uhr?	Can you come next Monday at three o'clock?
Wo tut es weh?	Where does it hurt?
Ich habe Ohrenschmerzen/ Zahnschmerzen/ Halsschmerzen.	I've got ear-ache/ tooth-ache/ a sore throat.
Mein Fuß tut weh.	My foot hurts.
Meine Arme tun weh.	My arms hurt.
Mir geht es schlecht.	I feel poorly.
Ich habe mich erbrochen.	I was sick.
Mir ist übel.	I feel sick.
Mir ist heiß.	I am hot.
Mir ist kalt.	I am cold.
Ihr ist heiß.	She is hot.
Ich habe meinen Fuß verstaucht.	I have twisted my ankle.
Gehen Sie mit diesem Rezept zur Apotheke.	Take this prescription to the chemist.
Nehmen Sie die Tropfen dreimal täglich.	Take the drops three times a day.

In der Apotheke / At the chemist's

die Binde (n)	bandage, dressing
die Damenbinde (n)	sanitary towel
der Durchfall	diarrhoea
die Erkältung	cold
das Fieber	high temperature
die Grippe	flu
das Hustenbonbon (s)	cough sweet
der Hustensaft (-säfte)	cough medicine
der Insektenstich (e)	insect bite
die Magenschmerzen (pl)	stomach-ache
die Magenverstimmung (en)	stomach upset
das Pflaster (-)	sticking plaster
die Reisekrankheit (en)	travel sickness
die Salbe (n)	cream
die Seife (n)	soap

der Sonnenbrand	sun burn
der Sonnenstich (e)	sun stroke
die Tablette (n)	tablet
die Tube (n)	tube
die Watte	cotton wool
die Zahnpasta	toothpaste

Phrases

Haben Sie ein Mittel gegen Halsschmerzen?	Have you got anything for a sore throat?
Haben Sie etwas gegen Kopfschmerzen?	Have you got something for a headache?
Ich bin allergisch gegen Aspirin.	I am allergic to aspirin.
Muß ich für das Rezept bezahlen?	Do I have to pay for the prescription?
Verkaufen Sie Sonnencreme?	Do you sell sun tan lotion?
Können Sie mir etwas gegen Heuschnupfen geben?	Can you give me something for hay fever?

Das Familienleben — Family life

Die Wohnung — Housing

der Bungalow (s)	bungalow
das Doppelhaus (-häuser)	semi-detached house
die Eigentumswohnung (en)	owner-occupied flat
das Einfamilienhaus (-häuser)	detached house
das Haus (Häuser)	house
die Mietwohnung (en)	rented flat
das Reihenhaus (-häuser)	terraced house
der Wohnblock (s)	block of flats
die Wohnung (en)	flat

Zimmer — Rooms

das Arbeitszimmer (-)	study
der Aufzug (-züge)/Lift (s)	lift
das Bad(ezimmer) (-)	bathroom
das Eßzimmer (-)	dining room
der Flur (e)	corridor
das Gästezimmer (-)	guestroom
der Keller (-)	cellar
die Küche (n)	kitchen
das Schlafzimmer (-)	bedroom
der Speicher (-)	loft
die Terrasse (n)	patio
die Toilette (n)	toilet
die Treppe (n)	staircase
das Wohnzimmer (-)	living room

Teile des Gebäudes — Parts of the building

das Dach (Dächer)	roof
der Eingang (Eingänge)	entrance
das Erdgeschoß	ground floor
der Fensterladen (-läden)	shutter
das Gas	gas
der Heizkörper (-)	radiator
der offene Kamin (e)	open fireplace
der Rolladen (-läden)	rolling shutter
der Schlüssel (-)	key
der Schornstein (e)	chimney
der Stock (Stockwerke)	floor, storey
der Strom	electricity
die Tür (en)	door
die Zentralheizung (en)	central heating

Im Badezimmer — In the bathroom

das Badetuch (-tücher)	bath towel
die Badewanne (n)	bath tub
das Bidet	bidet
die Dusche (n)	shower
das Handtuch (-tücher)	towel
der Schwamm (Schwämme)	sponge
die Seife (n)	soap
der Spiegel (-)	mirror
das Waschbecken (-)	sink/basin
der Waschlappen (-)	face cloth
das Wasser	water
heißes/kaltes Wasser	hot/cold water
der Wasserhahn (-hähne)	tap
die Zahnbürste (n)	toothbrush
die Zahnpasta	toothpaste

Im Schlafzimmer — In the bedroom

das Bett (en)	bed
die Bettdecke (n)	duvet
die Gardine (n)	net curtain
der Kleiderschrank (-schränke)	wardrobe
das Kopfkissen (-)	pillow
die Lampe (n)	lamp
der Nachttisch (e)	bedside table
die Nachttischlampe (n)	bedside light
das Regal (e)	shelf
der Schreibtisch (e)	desk
der Stuhl (Stühle)	chair
der Teppich (e)	carpet, rug
der Teppichboden (-böden)	fitted carpet
der Vorhang (-hänge)	curtain
der Wecker (-)	alarm clock

Im Wohnzimmer — In the living room

das Bild (er)	picture
der Blumenstrauß (-sträuße)	bunch of flowers
der Bücherschrank (-schränke)	bookcase
der Couchtisch (e)	coffee-table
das Familienfoto (s)	family photo
der Fernseher (-)	TV set
der Heizkörper (-)	radiator
der Sessel (-)	armchair

das Sofa (s)	sofa
die Stereoanlage (n)	stereo
die Vase (n)	vase
die Zimmerpflanze (n)	house plant

Im Eßzimmer — In the dining room

das Besteck (e)	cutlery
das Geschirr	crockery
das Glas (Gläser)	glass
der Stuhl (Stühle)	chair
der Teller (-)	plate
der Tisch (e)	table
die Tischdecke (n)	tablecloth
das Tischtuch (-tücher)	tablecloth
die Wanduhr (en)	wall clock

In der Küche — In the kitchen

der Backofen (-öfen)	oven
der Besen (-)	broom
die Bratpfanne (n)	frying pan
der Gefrierschrank (-schränke)	freezer
der Herd (e)	cooker
der Kochtopf (-töpfe)	saucepan
der Kühlschrank (-schränke)	fridge
der Mikrowellenherd (e)	microwave oven
der Mülleimer (-)	rubbish bin
der Schrank (Schränke)	cupboard
die Spülmaschine (n)	dishwasher
der Spülstein (e)	sink
das Spülbecken (-)	sink
der Staubsauger (-)	vacuum cleaner
die Waschmaschine (n)	washing-machine

Im Garten — In the garden

der Apfelbaum (-bäume)	apple tree
die Bank (Bänke)	bench
der Baum (Bäume)	tree
die Birke (n)	birch
die Blume (n)	flower
das Blumenbeet (e)	flower bed
der Busch (Büsche)	bush
das Gemüse	vegetable
der Gemüsegarten (-gärten)	vegetable garden
das Gewächshaus (-häuser)	greenhouse
der Rasen (-)	lawn
die Rose (n)	rose
die Tanne (n)	fir tree
die Tulpe (n)	tulip

abtrocknen	to dry up
aufräumen	to tidy up
den Rasen mähen	to mow the lawn
den Tisch decken	to lay the table
gießen	to water
helfen	to help
klingeln	to ring (door bell)
kochen	to cook
putzen	to clean
spülen	to wash up
staubsaugen	to hoover
tapezieren	to hang wall paper
teilen	to share
umziehen*	to move house
wohnen	to live

Phrases

Wohnst du in einem Haus oder in einer Wohnung?	Do you live in a house or a flat?
Ich wohne in einem Haus am Stadtrand.	I live in a house on the edge of town.
Ich wohne in einer Wohnung im dritten Stock.	I live in a flat on the third floor.
Ich wohne nur drei Kilometer von der Schule.	I live only three kilometres from school.
Ist dein Haus alt oder modern?	Is your house old or modern?
Wie ist dein Haus?	What is your house like?
Mein Haus ist ziemlich neu. Es ist aus Backstein und hat zwei Stock, das Erdgeschoß und den ersten Stock.	My house is rather new. It is built of brick and has two storeys, the ground floor and the first floor.
Um das Haus herum gibt es einen kleinen Garten.	Around the house is a small garden.
Hast du dein eigenes Zimmer?	Do you have your own room?
Nein, ich teile mein Zimmer mit meinem Bruder/ meiner Schwester.	No, I share my room with my brother/my sister.
Wie ist dein Zimmer?	What is your room like?
Mein Zimmer ist mittelgroß, mit Zentralheizung. Die Wände sind gelb tapeziert, der Teppichboden ist grau. Die Vorhänge sind auch grau.	My room is medium sized, with central heating. The walls are papered in yellow, the fitted carpet is grey. The curtains are also grey.
Welche Möbel hast du in deinem Zimmer?	What sort of furniture do you have in your room?
Ich habe ein Bett, einen Schreibtisch, einen Stuhl und einen Schrank. Unter dem Fenster steht ein kleines Sofa, und an der Wand hängt ein Regal mit meiner Stereoanlage.	I have a bed, a desk, a chair and a wardrobe. Under the window is a small sofa and on the wall hangs a shelf with my stereo.
Hat dein Haus einen Garten?	Does your house have a garden?
Ja, es gibt einen kleinen Garten vor dem Haus und einen größeren hinter dem Haus.	Yes, there is a small garden in front of the house and a bigger one at the back of the house.
Im Vorgarten gibt es Blumenbeete und einen Rasen, hinter dem Haus sind ein Gemüsegarten und Obstbäume.	In the front garden there are flower beds and a lawn, at the back of the house are a vegetable patch and fruit trees.

Wo ist die Toilette bitte?	Where is the toilet, please?
Die Toilette ist hier links, neben der Haustür.	The toilet is on the left, next to the front door.
Darf ich bitte baden?	May I have a bath?
Darf ich mich bitte duschen?	May I have a shower?
Hast du alles, was du brauchst?	Have you got everything you need?
Nein, ich habe mein Handtuch vergessen.	No, I have forgotten my towel.
Wann frühstückst du?	When do you eat breakfast?
Ich frühstücke um sieben Uhr.	I eat breakfast at seven o'clock.
Wann ißt du zu Mittag?	When do you eat lunch?
Ich esse um zwölf Uhr zu Mittag.	I eat lunch at twelve o'clock.
Wann gibt es Abendessen?	When do you have your evening meal?
Hilfst du deiner Vater/deinen Mutter/deinem Eltern im Haus?	Do you help your mother/your father/your parents in the house?
Ich decke den Tisch.	I lay the table.
Ich arbeite im Garten, mähe den Rasen und gieße die Blumen.	I work in the garden, mow the lawn and water the flowers.
Ich gehe einmal in der Woche einkaufen.	I go shopping once a week.
Ich putze jeden Tag die Küche.	I clean the kitchen every day.
Ich bügle für die ganze Familie.	I iron for the whole family.
Ich koche das Mittagessen.	I cook lunch.
Kann ich dir/Ihnen helfen?	May I help you?
Kann ich für dich/Sie spülen?	May I wash up for you?
Soll ich den Tisch decken?	Shall I lay the table?

Der Alltag — Everyday routines

Der Alltag	Everyday routines
der Abend (e)	evening
das Abendessen (-)	evening meal
die Arbeit (en)	work
das Frühstück (e)	breakfast
die Hausarbeit (en)	housework
die Hausaufgabe (n)	homework
das Mittagessen (-)	lunch
der Morgen (-)	morning
der Tag (e)	day
früh	early
langsam	slow
pünktlich	punctually
rechtzeitig	in time
in Ruhe	calmly
schnell	fast, quickly
spät	late
sich **an**ziehen	to get dressed
aufstehen*	to get up
aufwachen*	to wake up
sich **aus**ziehen	to get undressed
baden	to take a bath
sich die Zähne putzen	to brush one's teeth
sich duschen	to shower
essen	to eat
fernsehen	to watch TV
frühstücken	to have breakfast
sich kämmen	to comb one's hair
sich rasieren	to shave
schlafen	to sleep
schlafen gehen*	to go to bed
nach Hause kommen*	to come home
die Hausaufgabe machen	to do homework
nach unten gehen*	to go downstairs
zu Bett gehen*	to go to bed
nach oben gehen*	to go upstairs
aus dem Haus gehen*	to leave the house
Radio hören	to listen to the radio
sich mit Freunden treffen	to meet friends
sich **um**ziehen	to get changed
verlassen	to leave
sich waschen	to wash
zurückkommen*	to come back

Das Taschengeld — Pocket money

Das Taschengeld	Pocket money
die Bank (en)	bank
das Geld	money
die Münze (n)	coin
der Schein (e)	bank-note
die Sparkasse (n)	savings bank
das Sparschwein (e)	piggy bank
das Stück (e)	coin
arm	poor
großzügig	generous
preiswert	cheap, good value for money
pro Woche	per week
pro Monat	per month
reich	rich
sparsam	careful with money
teuer	expensive
viel	a lot
wenig	a little
ausgeben	to spend
brauchen für (+ Acc)	to spend on, need for
kaufen	to buy
kosten	to cost
sparen	to save

Phrases

Wieviel Taschengeld bekommst du?	How much pocket money do you get?

Ich bekomme sechs Pfund pro Woche.	I get £6 per week.
Wofür brauchst du dein Taschengeld?	What do you spend your pocket money on?
Ich brauche es für Comics und Schreibwaren.	I spend it on comics and stationery.
Ich spare für ein Fahrrad.	I am saving up for a bike.
Ich kaufe Bücher und Kleidung.	I buy books and clothes.

Im Café, in der Konditorei — In the café

Getränke — Drinks

der Apfelsaft	apple juice
der Apfelwein	cider
das Bier (e)	beer
der Kaffee	coffee
die Limonade (n)	lemonade
der Orangensaft (-säfte)	orange juice
der Saft (Säfte)	juice
der Schnaps (Schnäpse)	spirit
die (heiße) Schokolade	hot chocolate
der Tee	tea
der Wein (e)	wine

Essen — Food

der Apfelkuchen (-)	apple cake
das Besteck (e)	cutlery
die Bestellung (en)	order
das Gebäck	biscuits
das Kaffeestückchen (-)	Danish pastry
das Kännchen (-)	little pot
der Käsekuchen (-)	cheese cake
der Kellner (-)	waiter
die Kellnerin (nen)	waitress
der Kuchen (-)	cake
die Sahnetorte (n)	cream cake
die Schwarzwälderkirschtorte (-)	Black Forest gateau
die Tasse (n)	cup
der Teller (-)	plate
die Theke (n)	counter
die Torte (n)	gateau
der Zettel (-)	receipt

Phrases

Was möchten Sie, bitte?	What would you like?
Wählen Sie bitte die Kuchen an der Theke.	Please choose the cakes at the counter.
Nehmen Sie den Zettel mit zu ihrem Tisch.	Take the receipt to your table.
Bestellen Sie die Getränke beim Kellner.	Order your drinks with the waiter.
Welche Kuchensorten haben Sie?	What types of cake do you have?
Ich lade dich ein. Was möchtest du?	I'm paying. What would you like?
Zahlen, bitte.	The bill, please.
Geht das zusammen oder getrennt?	Do you want to pay together or separately?

An der Imbißstube — At the snack bar

die Bockwurst (-würste)	boiled sausage
die Bratwurst (-würste)	fried sausage
die Frikadelle (n)	hamburger
der Kartoffelsalat (e)	potato salad
mit Mayonnaise	with mayonnaise
die Pommes Frites	chips
die Portion (en)	portion
eine große/kleine Portion	a large/small portion
das Schaschlik (s)	kebab
ohne Senf	without mustard

Im Restaurant — In the restaurant

Vorspeisen — Starters

russische Eier	stuffed eggs
die Gemüsesuppe (n)	vegetable soup
die Hühnerpastete (n)	chicken vol-au-vent
die Tagessuppe (n)	soup of the day

Hauptgerichte — Main courses

Brathähnchen, Pommes Frites und Salat	roast chicken, chips and salad
Brathähnchen und Brötchen Bratwurst, Kartoffeln	roast chicken and bread roll, fried sausage and potatoes
Jägerschnitzel, Salzkartoffeln, Erbsen	schnitzel with mushrooms, boiled potatoes and peas
Kalbsbraten, Knödel und Salat	roast veal, dumplings and salad
Schnitzel, Pommes Frites, Salat	schnitzel, chips and salad

Nachspeisen — Desserts

gemischtes Eis mit Sahne	mixed ice cream with cream
Obstteller	fruit platter
Vanillepudding	vanilla flavour whipped pudding
Bedienung und Mehrwertsteuer inklusive	service and VAT included.

Phrases

Einen Tisch für vier am Fenster bitte.	A table for four near the window, please.
Die Speisekarte, bitte.	The menu, please.
Haben Sie schon gewählt?	Have you already chosen?
Einmal Jägerschnitzel und einmal Brathähnchen, bitte.	One mushroom schnitzel and one roast chicken, please.
Zum Nachtisch hätte ich gern zweimal Eis, bitte.	As dessert, I'd like two ice creams, please.
Entschuldigen Sie, aber das Schnitzel ist hart.	Excuse me, the schnitzel is tough.

Können Sie uns einen sauberen Teller bringen?	Could you bring us a clean plate?
'Forelle blau', was ist das?	What is 'blue trout'?

Einkaufen / Shopping

die Abteilung (en)	department
im Angebot	on special offer
die Apotheke (n)	chemist's
der Aufzug (-züge)	lift
die Bäckerei (en)	baker's shop
das Bekleidungshaus (-häuser)	clothes shop
die Buchhandlung (en)	bookshop
der Eingang (-gänge)	entrance
der Einkaufskorb (-körbe)	shopping basket
der Einkaufswagen (-)	shopping trolley
die Eisenwarenhandlung (en)	ironmonger's shop
der Friseursalon (s)	hairdresser's
der Gemüseladen (-läden)	greengrocer's shop
das Geschäft (e)	shop
der Händler (-)	trader
die Kasse	cash register, till
das Kaufhaus (-häuser)	department store
die Konditorei (en)	cake shop
der Kunde (n)	customer (male)
die Kundin (nen)	customer (female)
der Laden (Läden)	shop
das Lebensmittelgeschäft (e)	general food shop
der Markt (Märkte)	market
die Metzgerei (en)	butcher's shop
der Notausgang (-gänge)	emergency exit
die Öffnungszeiten (pl)	opening times
der Preis (e)	price
die Rolltreppe (n)	escalator
das Schaufenster (-)	shop window
die Selbstbedienung (en)	self-service
das Sonderangebot (e)	special offer
der Supermarkt (-märkte)	supermarket
das Tabakwarengeschäft (e)	tobacconist's shop
der Verkäufer (-)	shop assistant (male)
die Verkäuferin (nen)	shop assistant (female)
die Ware (n)	goods
Bitte an der Kasse bezahlen.	Please pay at the till.

drücken	push
geschlossen	closed
zu verkaufen	for sale
ziehen	pull

Beim Kleiderkauf / Buying clothes

die Bluse (n)	blouse
der Gürtel (-)	belt
die Handschuhe	gloves
das Hemd (en)	shirt
die Hose (n)	trousers
der Hut (Hüte)	hat
die Jacke (n)	jacket
das Kleid (er)	dress
der Regenmantel (-mäntel)	raincoat
der Rock (Röcke)	skirt
der Schal (s)	scarf
der Schlafanzug (-züge)	pyjamas
die Stiefel	boots
die Strumpfhose (n)	tights
das T-shirt (s)	T-shirt
die Turnschuhe	trainers

aus Baumwolle	made of cotton
aus Kunstfaser	made of artificial fibre
aus Leder	made of leather
aus Leinen	made of linen
aus Seide	made of silk
aus Wolle	made of wool

Phrases

Kann ich Ihnen helfen?	Can I help you?
Nein, ich möchte mich nur umschauen.	I'm just looking.
Ja, ich suche einen Pullover, bitte.	Yes, I'm looking for a jumper.
Welche Größe haben Sie?	What size do you take?
Ich brauche Größe M oder 40.	I need size M or 40.
Haben Sie denselben/dieselbe/dasselbe auch in grün?	Do you have the same also in green?
Wo kann ich den Pullover anprobieren?	Where can I try the jumper on?
Die Kabinen sind dort drüben.	The changing rooms are over there.
Dieser Pullover ist zu klein. Haben Sie ihn etwas größer, bitte?	This jumper is too small. Do you have a slightly bigger one?
Behalten Sie den Kassenzettel, dann können Sie es umtauschen.	Keep the till receipt, then you can change it.

Im Lebensmittelgeschäft / In the food shop

Das Fleisch / Meat

der Aufschnitt	sliced sausage selection
der Braten	joint of meat, roast
das Geflügel	poultry
das Hähnchen	chicken
das Hammelfleisch	mutton
das Lammfleisch	lamb
das Rindfleisch	beef
der Schinken	ham
das Schweinefleisch	pork

Das Gemüse / Vegetables

der Blumenkohl	cauliflower
die Bohne (n)	bean
die Erbse (n)	pea
die Karotte (n)	carrot

die Kartoffel (n)	potato
der Kohl	cabbage
der Kopfsalat (e)	lettuce
der Pilz (e)	mushroom
der Rosenkohl	sprout
der Spinat	spinach
die Zwiebel (n)	onion

Das Obst — Fruit

Das Obst	Fruit
die Ananas	pineapple
der Apfel (Äpfel)	apple
die Apfelsine (n)	orange
die Banane (n)	banana
die Birne (n)	pear
die Erdbeere (n)	strawberry
die Himbeere (n)	raspberry
die Johannisbeere (n)	blackcurrant
die Kirsche (n)	cherry
die Melone (n)	melon
der Pfirsich (e)	peach
die Pflaume (n)	plum
die Tomate (n)	tomato
die Traube (n)	grape
die Zitrone (n)	lemon

Phrases

Was darf es sein?	What would you like?
Wer ist der Nächste, bitte?	Who is next please?
Wer ist an der Reihe?	Whose turn is it?
Ich möchte .../Ich hätte gern ...	I'd like ...
ein Pfund Bananen	a pound of bananas
ein Kilo Äpfel	a kilo of apples
zweihundertfünfzig Gramm Aufschnitt	250 grams of sliced sausage
drei Scheiben Schinken	three slices of ham
einen Liter Milch	a litre of milk
eine Dose Erbsen	a tin of peas
ein Paket Zucker	a bag/packet of sugar
eine Flasche Limonade	a bottle of lemonade
Am Stück oder geschnitten?	In one piece or sliced?
Darf es ein bißchen mehr sein?	Do you mind if it's a little over?
Sonst noch etwas?	Anything else?

Getränke und Snacks — Drinks and snacks

Getränke und Snacks	Drinks and snacks
der Apfelsaft	apple juice
der Apfelwein	cider
das Bier	beer
das Brot (e)	bread
das Brötchen (-)	bread roll
die Chips (pl)	crisps
das Ei (er)	egg
das Eis	ice cream
der Kaffee	coffee
der Käse (-)	cheese
der Kuchen (-)	cake
die Marmelade	jam
die Milch	milk
das Mineralwasser	mineral water
die Nudeln (pl)	pasta
der Saft	juice
der Sprudel	fizzy mineral water, lemonade
die Tafel (n) Schokolade	bar of chocolate
der Tee	tea
die Torte (n)	gateau
der Wein	wine

Die Reiseandenken — Souvenirs

Die Reiseandenken	Souvenirs
der Bierkrug (-krüge)	beer mug
der Bildband (-bänder)	book with photographs
die Briefmarke (n)	stamps
das Halstuch (-tücher)	scarf
die Kassette (n)	cassette
der Kugelschreiber (-)	biro
die Mütze (n)	cap, hat
die Postkarte (n)	postcard
die Trachtenpuppe (n)	doll in folk costume

aussuchen	to choose
bezahlen	to pay
fragen nach + Dat	to demand/to ask for
kaufen	to buy
kosten	to cost
mögen	to like
nehmen	to take
öffnen	to open
schließen	to close
suchen	to look for
tragen	to wear
verkaufen	to sell
versuchen	to try

Phrases

Ich suche ein Geschenk für meine Mutter.	I am looking for a present for my Mum.
Wieviel kostet die Puppe, bitte?	How much is the doll, please?
Ich nehme sie.	I'll take it.
Ich habe nur einen Hundertmarkschein.	I've only got a 100 Mark note.
Können Sie das wechseln?	Have you got change for this?
Geben Sie mir bitte eine Mütze.	Can I have a cap, please?
Bezahlen Sie bitte an der Kasse.	Please pay at the till.
Können Sie das bitte als Geschenk einpacken?	Could you please wrap it as a present?

Bank und Post / Bank and post office

In der Bank / At the Bank

das Geld (er)	money
der Geldautomat (en)	cashpoint
die Kasse (n)	cash till
das Kleingeld	change
das Konto (en)	bank account
die Mark	mark
der Pfennig (e)	pfennig
das Pfund	pound sterling
der Reisescheck (s)	traveller's cheque
der Scheck (s)	cheque
der Wechselkurs (e)	exchange rate
einlösen	to cash (cheque)
umtauschen	to change (money)
wechseln	to change (money)

Phrases

Ich möchte 100 Pfund wechseln.	I'd like to change £100.
Ich möchte einen Reisescheck einlösen.	I'd like to cash a traveller's cheque.
Wie steht das Pfund heute?	What is the rate for the pound today?

Auf der Post / At the post office

der (Post)beamte (n)	post office worker
der Brief (e)	letter
der Briefkasten (-kästen)	letter box
die Briefmarke (n)	stamp
der Briefträger (-)	postman
per Eilbote	by express
per Luftpost	by airmail
das Päckchen (-)	small package
das Paket (e)	parcel
die Post	post office, mail
das Postamt (-ämter)	post office
die Postkarte (n)	postcard
der Schalter (-)	counter
einwerfen	to put into a letter box
schicken	to send
senden	to send (often electronically)

Phrases

Was kostet ein Brief nach England?	How much is a letter to England?
Ich hätte gern zwei Briefmarken zu einer Mark.	I'd like two one-mark stamps.
Kann ich von hier telefonieren?	Can I phone from here?
Gehen Sie bitte zu Zelle drei.	Please go to booth three.
Wann ist die nächste Leerung?	When is the next collection?

Bus, Bahn und Auto / Bus, train and car

Transportmittel / Transport

das Auto (s)	car
der Bus (se)	bus
das Fahrrad (-räder)	bicycle
der Lastwagen (-)	lorry
der Lieferwagen (-)	van
das Mofa (s)	moped
das Motorrad (-räder)	motorbike
der Reisebus (se)	coach
die Straßenbahn (en)	tram
die U-Bahn (en)	underground
das Verkehrsmittel (n)	means of transport
der Wagen (-)	car
das Wohnmobil (e)	motorhome, camper
der Zug (Züge)	train
reisen*	to travel
fahren*	to drive, to travel

Mit der Bahn / By train

die Abfahrt (en)	departure
das Abteil (e)	compartment
die Ankunft (Ankünfte)	arrival
der Anschluß (Anschlüsse)	connecting train
der Bahnhof (-höfe)	station
der Bahnsteig (e)	platform
der Eilzug (-züge)	fast train
die einfache Fahrkarte (n)	single ticket
die Fahrkarte (n)	ticket
der Fahrplan (-pläne)	timetable
die Gepäckaufbewahrung	luggage locker
das Gleis (e)	track/platform
der Hauptbahnhof (-höfe)	main station
der Nichtraucher	non-smoker
der Personenzug (-züge)	local train
der Raucher	smoker
der Reisende (n)	traveller
die Reservierung (en)	reservation
die Rückfahrkarte (n)	return ticket
der Schnellzug (-züge)	express train
die Verspätung	delay
der Warteraum (-räume)	waiting room
erster Klasse	first class
zweiter Klasse	second class
abfahren*	to depart
ankommen*	to arrive
durchfahren*	to go through/direct
umsteigen*	to change trains
warten	to wait

Phrases

Wann fährt der nächste Zug nach ...?	When is the next train to ...?
Wo fährt er ab?	Which platform?
Auf Gleis drei.	On platform three.
Wann kommt er in ... an?	When does it arrive in ...?
Einmal nach Bonn, hin und zurück.	One return ticket to Bonn.
Zweimal einfach nach Berlin.	Two single tickets to Berlin.
Ich möchte einen Platz reservieren.	I'd like to reserve a seat.
Muß ich umsteigen?	Do I have to change?
Ja, Sie müssen in Bern umsteigen.	Yes, you have to change in Bern.
Nein, der Zug fährt durch.	No, it's a through train.

Mit dem Bus — By bus

der Automat (en)	ticket machine
der Busbahnhof (-höfe)	bus station
der Entwerter (-)	machine to date-stamp tickets
die Haltestelle (n)	bus stop
die Linie (n)	line
die Streifenkarte (n)	strip of tickets

Phrases

Ist hier in der Nähe eine Haltestelle?	Is there a bus stop near here?
Welcher Bus fährt zum Schwimmbad?	Which bus goes to the swimming pool?
Nehmen Sie die Linie drei.	Take bus (line) number three.
Wie oft fahren die Busse zum Theater?	How often do the buses go to the theatre?
Sie fahren alle zwanzig Minuten.	They are every twenty minutes.
Fährt dieser Bus nach Neumaden?	Does this bus go to Neumaden?

Mit dem Flugzeug — By plane

der Abflug	departure of plane
der Flug (Flüge)	flight
der Flughafen (-häfen)	airport
das Flugzeug (e)	plane
die Gepäckrückgabe	baggage reclaim
der Pilot (en)	pilot
der Reisepaß (-pässe)	passport
die Stewardeß (Stewardessen)	stewardess
der Ticket (s)	plane ticket
die Zollkontrolle (n)	customs control
abfliegen*	to take off
dauern	to last
fliegen*	to fly
landen*	to land
verpassen	to miss

Phrases

Ich möchte einen Flug buchen.	I'd like to book a flight.
Wann ist der nächste Flug nach London?	When is the next flight to London?
Gibt es morgen eine Maschine nach Edinburgh?	Is there a plane to Edinburgh tomorrow?
Wo sind die Kofferkulis?	Where are the luggage trolleys?
Gibt es einen Flughafenbus?	Is there a coach to the airport?

Die Überfahrt — The channel crossing

die Fähre (n)	ferry
der Fährhafen (-häfen)	ferry port
der Hafen (Häfen)	port, harbour
der Kanaltunnel	Channel Tunnel
das Luftkissenboot (e)	hovercraft
das Meer (e)	sea
planmäßig	on time
ruhig	calm
stürmisch	stormy
verspätet	delayed

Phrases

Wie war die Überfahrt?	What was the crossing like?
Es war sehr angenehm.	It was very pleasant.
Was hast du während der Überfahrt gemacht?	What did you do during the crossing?
Ich habe gelesen und geschlafen.	I read and slept.
Ich bin auf Deck gegangen.	I went on deck.
Bist du mit der Fähre von Dover gekommen?	Did you come on the ferry from Dover?
Nein, ich habe das Luftkissenboot von Folkestone genommen.	No, I took the hovercraft from Folkestone.

Ausflüge — Excursions

Ausgehen — Going out

der Ausflug (-flüge)	outing
die Ausstellung (en)	exhibition
der Balkon (e)	balcony
die Disco (s)	disco
die Eintrittskarte (n)	ticket
die Eisbahn (en)	ice-rink
das Eisstadion (-stadien)	ice-rink
die Feier (n)	party
die Fete (n)	party
der Film (e)	film
das Freizeitzentrum (-zentren)	leisure centre
die Galerie (n)	gallery
das Hotel (s)	hotel
die Karte (n)	ticket
das Kino (s)	cinema

der Klub (s)	club
die Kneipe (n)	pub
das Konzert (e)	concert
die Milchbar (s)	milk bar
der Nachtklub (s)	night club
der Originalton (-töne)	original soundtrack
die Party (s)	party
das Programm	TV channel
das Restaurant (s)	restaurant
der Schauspieler (-)	actor
die Schauspielerin (nen)	actress
der Schnellimbiß (sse)	snack bar
das Schwimmbad (bäder)	swimming pool
der Sperrsitz (e)	stalls
der Sportplatz (-plätze)	sportsground
das Sportzentrum (-zentren)	sportscentre
das Stadion (Stadien)	stadium
das Theater (-)	theatre
das Theaterstück (e)	play
der Untertitel (-)	subtitle
die Vorführung (en)	performance
ausgezeichnet	excellent
einfach Klasse	great
großartig	great
interessant	interesting
langweilig	boring
mittelmäßig	mediocre
schlecht	bad
uninteressant	not interesting
beginnen	to begin
buchen	to book
dauern	to last
enden	to finish
kosten	to cost
reservieren	to reserve

Phrases

Wollen wir heute abend ausgehen?	Shall we go out tonight?
Ja gerne.	Yes, please.
Nein danke.	No, thank you.
Leider kann ich heute nicht.	Sorry, I can't make it today.
Ich habe viele Hausaufgaben.	I have a lot of homework.
Ich muß auf meinen kleinen Bruder aufpassen.	I have to babysit my little brother.
Ich bin schon verabredet.	I have already got another engagement.
Ich muß erst meinen Austauschpartner/ meine Austauschpartnerin fragen.	I have to ask my exchange partner first.
Ich darf heute nicht ausgehen.	I am not allowed to go out today.
Ich habe Hausarrest.	I am grounded.
Was möchtest du heute abend machen?	What would you like to do tonight?
Wo möchtest du hingehen?	Where would you like to go?
Was können wir heute abend machen?	What can we do tonight?
Willst du in die Disco gehen?	Do you want to go to the disco?
Wollen wir ein Video leihen?	Shall we hire a video?
Ich würde gern ins Kino gehen.	I'd like to go to the cinema.
Was hast du am letzten Samstag gemacht?	What did you do last Saturday?
Ich bin am Vormittag in die Stadt gegangen, am Nachmittag habe ich mit meinen Freunden Fußball gespielt.	I went to town on Saturday morning, in the afternoon I played football with my friends.
Am Abend habe ich ferngesehen.	In the evening I watched TV.
Was hast du gestern abend gemacht?	What did you do yesterday evening?
Ich habe meine Hausaufgaben gemacht.	I did my homework.

Kino/Theater	**Cinema/Theatre**
Was gibt es heute im Kino?	What is showing in the cinema today?
Man zeigt einen Liebesfilm.	There is a romantic film.
Was steht auf dem Theaterprogramm?	What's on at the theatre?
Es gibt ein Stück von Agatha Christie.	There is a play by Agatha Christie.
Hast du schon *Apollo 13* gesehen?	Have you seen *Apollo 13*?
Gibt es das schon als Video?	Is it already out on video?
Wann treffen wir uns?	When shall we meet?
Treffen wir uns bei mir um 7 Uhr.	Let's meet at 7 o'clock at my house.
Wo treffen wir uns?	Where shall we meet?
Treffen wir uns vor dem Kino um halb acht.	Let's meet in front of the cinema at half past seven.
Bis um halb acht.	See you at half past seven.
Sei bitte pünktlich.	Please be on time.
Wann beginnt der Film/das Stück?	When does the film/the play begin?
Wann ist der Film/das Stück zu Ende?	When does the film/the play finish?
Was kostet eine Karte?	How much is a ticket?
Eine Schülerkarte kostet 10,— DM.	A ticket for a student is 10,— DM.
Gibt es noch Plätze im Parkett?	Are there any seats left in the stalls?
Zwei Plätze im Parkett, bitte.	Two seats in the stalls, please.
Gibt es eine Ermäßigung für Schüler?	Is there a reduction for students?

Feiertage — Special days

der heilige Abend	Christmas Eve
der Feiertag (e)	bank holiday
der Geburtstag (e)	birthday
das Geschenk (e)	present
der Kuchen (-)	cake, gateau
der Namenstag (e)	saint's day
Neujahr	New Year's Day
das jüdische Neujahr	Jewish New Year
Ostern	Easter
das Passa	Passover
der Ramadan	Ramadan
der Sabbat	Sabbath
Sylvester	New Year´s Eve
Weihnachten	Christmas
der erste Weihnachtstag	Christmas Day
der zweite Weihnachtstag	Boxing Day
der Weihnachtsbaum (-bäume)	Christmas tree
der Weihnachtsmann (-männer)	Father Christmas
einpacken	to wrap
feiern	to celebrate
kaufen	to buy
schenken	to give as a present
schicken	to send

Phrases

Ich kaufe ein Geschenk für meine Schwester.	I buy/am buying a present for my sister.
Ich suche eine Geburtstagskarte für meinen Cousin.	I am looking for a birthday card for my cousin.
Ich werde meinem Großvater eine Flasche Wein schenken.	I am going to give my grandad a bottle of wine.
Mein Geburtstag ist der 16. Juni.	My birthday is June 16th.

Die Ferien — Holidays

der Aufenthalt (e)	stay
der Ausflug (-flüge)	excursion, outing
der Austausch (e)	exchange
der Besuch (e)	visit
die Broschüre (n)	brochure
das Foto (s)	photo
das Informationsbüro (s)	tourist information office
der Koffer (-)	suitcase
die Landkarte (n)	map
die Reise (n)	journey
das Reisebüro (s)	travel agency
der Reisescheck (s)	traveller's cheque
der Rucksack (-säcke)	rucksack
der Stadtplan (-pläne)	map of town
der Tourist (en)	tourist
die Unterkunft (-künfte)	accommodation
der Urlaub (e)	holiday
das Verkehrsamt (-ämter)	tourist information office
sich amüsieren	to enjoy oneself
sich **aus**ruhen	to rest
bleiben*	to stay
sich entspannen	to relax
fahren*	to go, travel
fliegen*	to travel by plane
reisen*	to travel
auf Urlaub sein	to be on holiday
übernachten	to stay overnight
verbringen	to spend (time)

Phrases

Wohin fährst du in Urlaub?	Where are you going on holiday?
Ich verbringe vierzehn Tage in Spanien.	I am going to spend a fortnight in Spain.
Mit wem fährst du in Urlaub?	Who are you going on holiday with?
Wie lange bleibst du?	How long are you staying?
Wie fährst du nach Spanien?	How are you travelling to Spain?
Ich fahre mit meiner Familie nach Frankreich.	I am travelling to France with my family.
Ich werde nach Berlin fliegen.	I am going to fly to Berlin.

Camping — Camping

die Campingausrüstung (en)	camping equipment
der Campingplatz (-plätze)	camp-site
der Dosenöffner (-)	tin opener
der Empfang (Empfänge)	reception
die Gasflasche (n)	gas bottle
der Gaskocher (-)	gas cooker
das Lagerfeuer (-)	camp fire
die Lebensmittel (pl)	food
die Luftmatratze (n)	air bed
der Schlafsack (-säcke)	sleeping bag
der Stellplatz (-plätze)	pitch
die Streichhölzer (pl)	matches
der Strom	electricity
die Taschenlampe (n)	torch
das Taschenmesser (-)	penknife
der Waschraum (-räume)	toilet block
der Wohnwagen (-)	caravan
das Zelt (e)	tent
das ganze Jahr geöffnet	open all year
in der Nähe von + Dat	near to
sauber	clean
im Schatten	in the shade
schmutzig	dirty
in der Sonne	in the sun

voll	full
das Zelt **auf**schlagen	to pitch a tent
austauschen	to exchange
bezahlen	to pay
kochen	to cook
suchen	to look for
zelten	to camp (in a tent)

In der Jugendherberge — In the youth hostel

der Aufenthaltsraum (-räume)	day room
der Ausweis (e)	ID
die Bettwäsche	sheets
die Decke (n)	blanket
die Dusche (n)	shower
der Eßraum (-räume)	dining room
der Gruppenleiter (-)	party leader, organiser
die Herbergsmutter (-mütter)	warden (female)
die Herbergsregeln (pl)	rules of the youth hostel
der Herbergsvater (-väter)	warden (male)
der Keller	cellar
der Leinenschlafsack (-säcke)	sheet sleeping bag
die Nacht (Nächte)	night
die Nachtruhe	silence at night, lights out
der Schlafsaal (-säle)	dormitory
außer	except
gestattet	permitted
das ganze Jahr über	for the whole year
verboten	forbidden
voll	full
abräumen	to clear (table)
aufräumen	to tidy up
helfen	to help
kehren	to sweep
leihen	to hire
öffnen	to open
reservieren	to book
schließen	to shut

Phrases

Haben Sie noch Platz frei?	Have you got any beds left?
Für wieviele Personen?	For how many persons?
Wir sind vier, zwei Mädchen und zwei Jungen.	There are four of us, two girls and two boys.
Welche Mahlzeiten möchten Sie?	Which meals would you like?
Wir nehmen Frühstück und Abendessen.	We want breakfast and evening meal.
Brauchen Sie Bettwäsche?	Do you need bed linen?
Ja, wir hätten gern zwei Leinenschlafsäcke.	Yes, we'd like two sheet sleeping bags.
Die Schlafräume sind im ersten Stock.	The dormitories are on the first floor.

Im Hotel — At the hotel

der Aufzug (-züge)	lift
mit Bad	with bath
das Doppelzimmer (-)	double room (with one big bed)
mit Dusche (n)	with shower
das Einzelzimmer (-)	single room
der Empfang	reception
das Erdgeschoß	groundfloor
der Fernseher (-)	TV set
die Übernachtung mit Frühstück	bed and breakfast
das Gasthaus (-häuser)	guesthouse, inn
die Halbpension	half board (bed, breakfast and evening meal)
das Hotelverzeichnis (e)	list of hotels
der Kellner (-)	waiter
die Kellnerin (nen)	waitress
der Lift (s)	lift
der Notausgang (-gänge)	emergency exit
der Parkplatz (-plätze)	car park
die Pension (en)	guesthouse
der Preis (e)	price
der Schlüssel (-)	key
der Strand (Strände)	beach
das Telefon (e)	telephone
die Treppe (n)	staircase
die Vollpension	full board
das Zweibettzimmer (-)	twin-bedded room
allein	alone
ander	other
belegt	occupied
bequem	comfortable
dunkel	dark
frei	free
gemütlich	cosy
groß	big
inbegriffen	included
klein	small
laut	noisy
luxuriös	luxurious
preiswert	good value for money
sauber	clean
schmutzig	dirty
teuer	expensive
für + Acc	for
mit + Dat	with
ohne + Acc	without
sich beschweren	to complain
bestellen	to order
buchen	to book
sich erkundigen	to ask for information
fragen (nach + Dat)	to ask (for)
reservieren	to reserve

Phrases

Das Wasser in meinem Zimmer ist nur lauwarm.	The water in my room is only lukewarm.
Kann ich mit dem Direktor sprechen?	May I speak to the manager?
Kann ich noch eine Decke haben?	May I have another blanket?
Der Kopfkissenbezug ist schmutzig.	The pillowcase is dirty.
Ich habe zwei Doppelzimmer reserviert, auf den Namen Smith.	I reserved two double rooms in the name of Smith.
Wann gibt es Abendessen?	When is the evening meal served?
Ist die Mehrwertsteuer im Preis inbegriffen?	Is VAT included in the price?
Nehmen Sie Euroschecks?	Do you accept Eurocheques?

Am Meer — At the seaside

der Badeanzug (-züge)	bathing suit
die Badehose (n)	swimming trunks
das Dingi (s)	dinghy
die Ebbe	low tide
das Eis	ice cream
die Flut	high tide
das Meer (e)	sea
der Sand	sand
die Sandburg (en)	sandcastle
das Schlauchboot (e)	inflatable boat
der Schwimmring (e)	rubber ring
das Segelboot (e)	sailing boat
der Sonnenbrand (-brände)	sunburn
das Sonnenöl	sun tan lotion
der Sonnenschirm (e)	parasol
der Strand (Strände)	beach
der Yachthafen (-häfen)	yacht marina
heiß	hot
ruhig	calm
sonnig	sunny
still	calm
stürmisch	stormy
windig	windy
baden	to bathe in the sea
eine Sandburg bauen	to build a sandcastle
Wasserski fahren*	to waterski
in der Sonne liegen	to sunbathe
segeln	to sail
Wasserball spielen	to play waterball
windsurfen	to windsurf

Auf dem Land — In the country

der Bauernhof (-höfe)	farm
der Baum (Bäume)	tree
der Berg (e)	mountain
das Bergsteigen	mountaineering
die Blume (n)	flower
das Dorf (Dörfer)	village
das Feld (er)	field
die Landschaft (en)	landscape
der Pfad (e)	path
das Tal (Täler)	valley
der Urlaub auf dem Bauernhof	farm holiday
der Wald (Wälder)	forest
die Wiese (n)	meadow
spazierengehen*	to go for a walk
wandern*	to hike

Phrases

Wo verbringst du deine Ferien?	Where are you spending your holidays?
Ich fahre ans Meer.	I am going to the seaside.
Ich fahre in die Berge.	I am going to the mountains.
Wir zelten.	We camp (in a tent).
Ich werde meine Kusine besuchen.	I am going to visit my cousin.
Wie lange wirst du am Meer bleiben?	How long are you going to stay at the seaside?
Ich bleibe vierzehn Tage am Meer.	I am staying at the seaside for a fortnight.
Wie ist das Wetter?	What is the weather like?
Es ist heiß/sonnig/kalt.	It is hot/sunny/cold.
Es regnet die ganze Zeit.	It is raining the whole time.
Was machst du am Strand?	What do you do at the beach?
Ich liege in der Sonne, schwimme und windsurfe.	I sunbathe, swim and windsurf.
Was machst du abends?	What do you do in the evenings?
Ich gehe spazieren oder bleibe in meinem Hotelzimmer.	I go for walks or stay in my hotel room.
Was wirst du in den Osterferien machen?	What are you going to do in the Easter holidays?
Ich werde nach Deutschland fahren.	I'm going to Germany.
Ich werde meinen Austauschpartner besuchen.	I'm visiting my exchange partner.
Ich mache eine Schülerfahrt nach Berlin.	I'm going on a school trip to Berlin.
Was hast du in den Sommerferien gemacht?	What did you do in the summer holidays?
Ich bin mit meinen Eltern nach Schottland gefahren.	I went to Scotland with my parents.
Ich bin zu Hause geblieben.	I stayed at home.
Hast du ein Museum besichtigt?	Did you visit a museum?
Nein, ich mag Museen nicht.	No, I don't like museums.

Die Medien | The media

Medien | Media types

das Fernsehen	TV
das Kino (s)	cinema
die Presse	press
das Radio (s)	radio
das Theater (-)	theatre
die Zeitschrift (en)	magazine
die Zeitung (en)	newspaper

Geräte | Equipment

die Antenne (n)	aerial
der Compact-Disc-Spieler (-)	CD player
die Fernbedienung (en)	remote control
der Fernseher (-)	TV set
die Fernsehzeitung (en)	TV magazine
das Kabelfernsehen	cable TV
die Satellitenschüssel (n)	satellite dish
die Stereoanlage (n)	stereo system
der Videorekorder (-)	video cassette recorder
der Walkman	walkman

Im Kino | In the cinema

der Abenteuerfilm/ Spielfilm(e)	adventure film
der Heimatfilm (e)	film set in a specific region
der Horrorfilm (e)	horror film
die Komödie (n)	comedy
der Kriminalfilm (e)	detective film
der Liebesfilm (e)	romantic film
der Science-fictionfilm (e)	science fiction film
der Spionagefilm (e)	spy film
der Thriller (-)	thriller
der Zeichentrickfilm (e)	cartoon

Phrases

Gehen wir heute abend ins Kino?	Shall we go to the cinema tonight?
Was läuft?	What's on?
Wann beginnt der Film?	When does the film begin?
Wann ist der Film zu Ende?	When does the film end?
Gibt es eine Ermäßigung für Schüler?	Is there a reduction for students?
Es ist ein englischer Film im Originalton.	It is an English film with the original soundtrack.
Ist der Film auf englisch?	Is the film in English?
Nein, aber es gibt Untertitel.	No, but there are subtitles.

Im Fernsehen, im Radio | On TV, on the radio

der Filmstar (s)	filmstar
der Komödiant (en)	comedian
der Schauspieler (-)	actor
die Schauspielerin (nen)	actress

Sendungen | Programme types

der Dokumentarfilm (e)	documentary
das Hörspiel (e)	radio play
die Musiksendung (en)	music show
die Nachrichten (pl)	news
das Nachrichtenmagazin (e)	news magazine
das Quiz	quiz
die Quizsendung (en)	quiz programme
die Seifenoper (n)	soap opera
die Serie (n)	serial
die Sportschau	sports programme
das Theaterstück (e)	theatre play
die Werbung (en)	advertisements
der Wetterbericht (e)	weather forecast
die Wettervorhersage (n)	weather forecast

abspielen	to replay
anschalten	to turn on
aufnehmen	to record
ausschalten	to turn off
hören	to listen to
umschalten	to switch over (TV channel)
gern sehen	to like watching

Phrases

Siehst du manchmal fern?	Do you sometimes watch TV?
Ja, ich sehe jeden Tag eine Stunde fern.	Yes, I watch TV every day for an hour.
Nein, ich sehe nicht oft fern.	No, I don't watch TV very often.
Was ist deine Lieblingssendung?	What is your favourite programme?
Ich sehe gern Kriminalfilme.	I like watching detective films.
Welche Sendungen siehst du nicht gern?	Which programmes don´t you like?
Ich mag Liebesfilme nicht.	I don't like romantic films.
Ich finde die Nachrichten langweilig.	I think the news is boring.
Darf ich ein bißchen fernsehen, bitte?	May I watch some TV?
Darf ich Radio hören, bitte?	May I listen to the radio?
Könntest du den Fernseher etwas leiser/lauter schalten?	Could you please turn the volume down/up?

Bücher | Books

der Abenteuerroman (e)	adventure novel
das Buch (Bücher)	book
der Comic (s)	comic strip
die Frauenzeitschrift (en)	women's magazine
der Kriminalroman (e)	detective novel
der Roman (e)	novel
die Wochenzeitschrift (en)	weekly (political) magazine

Phrases

Liest du gerne?	Do you like reading?
Ja, ich bin ein richtiger Bücherwurm.	Yes, I am a real bookworm.
Welche Bücher liest du?	What sort of books do you read?
Ich lese gern Romane, besonders Detektivromane.	I like reading novels, especially detective novels.

Section five

Mini-dictionary

In this section you can find both an German–English dictionary and an English–German dictionary.

Before each German word in the German–English dictionary you are given, where appropriate, the **gender**, and after the word the **plural ending** in brackets, followed by the English translation. For example:

die	Adresse (n)	address

After each English word in the English–German dictionary you are given, where appropriate, the **gender** of the German word and its **plural ending** in brackets. For example:

address	die	Adresse (n)

German–English

Mini-Dictionary

	abbiegen	to	turn
der	Abend (e)		evening
das	Abendessen (-)		evening meal
der	Abenteuerfilm (e)		adventure film
der	Abenteuerroman (e)		adventure novel
	abfahren*	to	depart
die	Abfahrt (en)		departure
	abfliegen*	to	take off (plane)
der	Abflug		departure of plane
	abräumen	to	clear (table)
der	Absatz (Absätze)		paragraph
	abschreiben	to	copy
	abseits		out of the way
	abspielen	to	replay
das	Abteil (e)		compartment
die	Abteilung (en)		department
	abtrocknen	to	dry up
die	Adresse(n)		address
die	Allee (n)		avenue
	allein		alone
	Alles Gute!		Best wishes! All the best!
	Alles Gute im neuen Jahr!		Happy New Year!
	Allgemeines		general
der	Alltag		daily routine
das	Alphabet		Alphabet
	alt		old
das	Alter		age
die	Ampel (n)		traffic lights
sich	amüsieren	to	enjoy oneself
	an		at
die	Ananas		pineapple
	ander		other
	anfangen	to	begin
die	Anführungstriche		speech marks
im	Angebot		on special offer
	angeln	to	fish
	angestellt		employed
der	Angestellte (n)		office worker
	ankommen*	to	arrive
die	Ankunft (Ankünfte)		arrival
	anschalten	to	turn on
der	Anschluß (Anschlüsse)		connecting train
	anschmiegsam		affectionate
die	Anschrift (en)		address
die	Antenne (n)		aerial

die	Antwort (en)		answer
	antworten	to	answer
	anwesend		present
sich	**an**ziehen	to	get dressed
der	Apfel (Äpfel)		apple
der	Apfelbaum (-bäume)		apple tree
der	Apfelkuchen (-)		apple cake
der	Apfelsaft		apple juice
die	Apfelsine (n)		orange
der	Apfelwein		cider
in der	Apotheke		at the chemist's
die	Apotheke (n)		chemist's
die	Arbeit (en)		work
	arbeiten	to	work
der	Arbeiter (-)		worker
	arbeitslos		unemployed
das	Arbeitszimmer (-)		study
	arm		poor
der	Arm (Arme)		arm
die	Arznei		medicine
beim	Arzt		at the doctor's
der	Arzt (Ärzte)		doctor (male)
die	Arzthelferin (nen)		doctor's receptionist
die	Ärztin (nen)		doctor (female)
	auf		on
	auf Urlaub		on holiday
der	Aufenthalt (e)		stay
der	Aufenthaltsraum (-räume)		day room
	aufnehmen	to	record
	aufräumen	to	tidy up
das Zelt	**auf**schlagen	to	pitch a tent
der	Aufschnitt		sliced sausage selection
	aufstehen*	to	get up
	aufwachen*	to	wake up
der	Aufzug (-züge)		lift
das	Auge (n)		eye
	aus		from
der	Ausflug (-flüge)		outing, excursion
	ausgeben	to	spend
das	Ausgehen		going out
	ausgehen*	to	go out
	ausgezeichnet		excellent
gut/schlecht	**aus**kommen mit	to	get on well/badly with someone
	ausmisten	to	muck out
sich	**aus**ruhen	to	rest

	ausschalten	to	turn off
	außer		except
die	Ausstellung (en)		exhibition
	aussuchen	to	choose, select
der	Austausch (e)		exchange
	austauschen		exchange
der	Ausweis (e)		identity card
der	Ausweis (e)		ID
	auswendig lernen	to	learn by heart
sich	**aus**ziehen	to	get undressed
das	Auto (s)		car
der	Automat (en)		ticket machine
das	Baby (s)		baby
der	Bach (Bäche)		brook
die	Bäckerei (en)		baker's shop
der	Backofen (-öfen)		oven
aus	Backstein		made of brick
mit	Bad		with bath
das	Bad(ezimmer) (-)		bathroom
der	Badeanzug (-züge)		bathing suit
die	Badehose (n)		swimming trunks
	baden	to	take a bath, to swim
das	Badetuch (tücher)		bath towel
die	Badewanne (n)		bath tub
das	Badezimmer		bathroom
der	Bahnhof (-höfe)		railway station
der	Bahnsteig (e)		platform
der	Balkon (e)		balcony
die	Banane (n)		banana
die	Bank (Bänke)		bench
die	Bank (en)		bank
	basteln	to	do DIY
der	Bauch (Bäuche)		stomach
	bauen	to	build
der	Bauernhof (-höfe)		farm
der	Baum (Bäume)		tree
aus	Baumwolle		made of cotton
	bearbeiten	to	edit
die	Bedienung		service
	beginnen	to	begin
	bei		at the house of
das	Bein (e)		leg
das	Beispiel (e)		example
der	Bekannte (n)		friend/acquaintance
das	Bekleidungshaus (-häuser)		clothes shop

	belegt		occupied
	bequem		comfortable
der	Berg (e)		mountain
das	Bergsteigen		mountaineering
der	Beruf (e)		job
sich	beschweren	to	complain
der	Besen (-)		broom
	besichtigen	to	visit (a monument)
das	Besteck (e)		cutlery
	bestehen	to	pass (an exam)
	bestellen	to	order
die	Bestellung (en)		order
	bestrafen	to	punish
der	Besuch (e)		visit
aus	Beton		made of concrete
das	Bett (en)		bed
zu/ins	Bett gehen*	to	go to bed
die	Bettdecke (n)		duvet
die	Bettwäsche		sheets
	bewölkt		cloudy
	bezahlen	to	pay
der	Bezirk (e)		district
die	Bibliothek (en)		library
das	Bidet (s)		bidet
das	Bier (e)		beer
der	Bierdeckel (-)		beer mat
der	Bierkrug (-krüge)		beer mug
das	Bild (er)		picture
der	Bildband (-bänder)		book with photographs
der	Bildschirm (e)		screen
die	Binde (n)		bandage, dressing
der	Bindestrich		hyphen
	Biologie		biology
die	Birke (n)		birch
die	Birne (n)		pear
	Bis bald!		See you soon!
	Bis dann!		See you later!
	Bis morgen!		See you tomorrow!
	bissig		liable to bite
	bitte		please
	blau		blue
	bleiben*	to	stay
der	Bleistift (e)		pencil
die	Blockflöte (n)		recorder
die	Blume (n)		flower

das	Blumenbeet (e)		flower bed
der	Blumenkohl		cauliflower
der	Blumenstrauß (-sträuße)		bunch of flowers
die	Bluse (n)		blouse
das	Blut		blood
die	Bockwurst (würste)		boiled sausage
der	Boden (Böden)		floor
die	Bohne (n)		bean
	bösartig		vicious
der	Braten		roast, joint of meat
	Brathähnchen und Brötchen		roast chicken and bread roll
	Brathähnchen, Pommes Frites und Salat		roast chicken, chips and salad
die	Bratpfanne (n)		frying pan
die	Bratwurst (-würste)		fried sausage
	Bratwurst, Kartoffeln		fried sausage and potatoes
	brauchen für (+ Acc)	to	spend on, need for
	braun		brown
der	Brief (e)		letter
der	Brieffreund (e)		penfriend (male)
die	Brieffreundin (nen)		penfriend (female)
der	Briefkasten (-kästen)		letter box
die	Briefmarke (n)		stamp
der	Briefträger (-)		postman
die	Broschüre (n)		brochure
das	Brot (e)		bread
das	Brötchen (-)		bread roll
die	Brücke (n)		bridge
der	Bruder (Brüder)		brother
das	Buch (Bücher)		textbook, book
	buchen	to	book
der	Bücherschrank (-schränke)		bookcase
die	Buchhandlung (en)		bookshop
	buchstabieren	to	spell
der	Bungalow (s)		bungalow
der	Buntstift (e)		coloured pencil
	bürsten	to	brush
der	Bus (se)		bus
der	Busbahnhof (-höfe)		bus station
der	Busch (Büsche)		bush
die	Bushaltestelle (n)		bus stop
das	Café		café
das	Camping		camping
die	Campingausrüstung (en)		camping equipment
der	Campingplatz (-plätze)		camp-site

das	Cello (s)		cello
	Chemie		chemistry
die	Chips (pl)		crisps
der	Chor (Chöre)		choir
der	Comic (s)		comic strip
der	Compact-Disc-Spieler (-)		CD player
die	Compact Disc/CD		CD
der	Computer (-)		computer
das	Computerspiel (e)		computer game
der	Computervirus (viren)		computer virus
der	Couchtisch (e)		coffee-table
der	Cousin (s)		cousin (male)
das	Dach (Dächer)		roof
die	Dame (n)		lady
die	Damenbinde (n)		sanitary towel
	danke		thank you
	Darf ich ...		May I ...
die	Datei		file, data base
	dauern	to	last
die	Decke (n)		ceiling
die	Decke (n)		blanket
	Deutsch		German
der	Dingi (s)		dinghy
der	Direktor (en)		headmaster
der	Direktor/die Direktorin		manager
die	Direktorin (nen)		headmistress
die	Disco (s)		disco
die	Diskette		disk
der	Dokumentarfilm (e)		documentary
der	Dom (e)		cathedral
das	Doppelhaus (-häuser)		semi-detached house
das	Doppelzimmer (-)		double room (with one big bed)
das	Dorf (Dörfer)		village
der	Dosenöffner (-)		tin opener
	drücken		push
der	Drucker (-)		printer
	dunkel...		dark ...
	dunkelblau		dark blue
	dunkelgrün		dark green
	durchfahren*	to	go through/direct
der	Durchfall		diarrhoea
	durchfallen*	to	fail
die	Dusche		shower
mit	Dusche (n)		with shower
sich	duschen	to	shower

die	Ebbe		low tide
an der	Ecke		on the corner
die	Ecke (n)		corner
	editieren	to	edit
das ist mir	egal		I don't mind
das	Ei (er)		egg
russische	Eier		stuffed eggs
die	Eigentumswohnung (en)		owner-occupied flat
per	Eilbote		by express
der	Eilzug (-züge)		fast train
	Einbahnstraße (n)		one way street
	einfach		easy
	einfach Klasse		great
die	einfache Fahrkarte (n)		single ticket
das	Einfamilienhaus (-häuser)		detached house
der	Eingang (-gänge)		entrance
	einkaufen	to	shop
das	Einkaufen		shopping
	einkaufen gehen*	to	go shopping
einen	Einkaufsbummel machen	to	go round the shops
der	Einkaufskorb (körbe)		shopping basket
der	Einkaufswagen (-)		shopping trolley
das	Einkaufszentrum (-zentren)		shopping centre
	einlösen	to	cash (cheque)
	einpacken	to	wrap
die	Eintrittskarte (n)		ticket
	einverstanden		agreed
	einwerfen	to	put into a letter box
das	Einzelzimmer (-)		single room
das	Eis		ice cream
die	Eisbahn (en)		ice-rink
die	Eisenwarenhandlung (en)		ironmonger's shop
das	Eisstadion (-stadien)		ice-rink
der	Elektriker/die Elektrikerin		electrician
die	Eltern (pl)		parents
der	Empfang (Empfänge)		reception
	enden	to	end, finish
	Englisch		English
der	Enkel (n)		grandson
die	Enkelin (nen)		granddaughter
	entlang (+ Acc)		along
	entschuldigen Sie		excuse me, sorry
	Entschuldigung		excuse me, sorry
sich	entspannen	to	relax
der	Entwerter (-)		machine to date-stamp tickets

die	Erbse (n)		pea
die	Erdbeere (n)		strawberry
das	Erdgeschoß		ground floor
	Erdkunde		geography
die	Erkältung		cold
	erklären	to	explain
sich	erkundigen	to	ask for information
	erster Klasse		first class
der/die	Erwachsene (n)		adult
	essen	to	eat
das	Essen		food
der	Eßraum (-räume)		dining room
das	Eßzimmer (-)		dining room
die	Fabrik (en)		factory
die	Fächer (pl)		school subjects
die	Fähre (n)		ferry
	fahren*	to	go (by vehicle), drive
der	Fahrer (-)		driver (male)
die	Fahrerin (nen)		driver (female)
der	Fährhafen (-häfen)		ferry port
die	Fahrkarte (n)		ticket
der	Fahrplan (-pläne)		timetable
das	Fahrrad (-räder)		bicycle
die	Familie (n)		family
das	Familienfoto (s)		family photo
das	Familienleben		family life
das	Familienmitglied (er)		family member
der	Familienname (n)		surname
die	Farbe (n)		colour
	faxen	to	fax
der	Fehler (-)		mistake
die	Feier (n)		party
	feiern	to	celebrate
der	Feiertag (e)		bank holiday
das	Feld (er)		field
das	Fenster (-)		window
der	Fensterladen (-läden)		shutter
die	Ferien (plural only)		holidays
die	Fernbedienung (en)		remote control
	fernsehen	to	watch TV
das	Fernsehen		TV
im	Fernsehen		on TV
der	Fernseher (-)		TV set
die	Fernsehzeitung (en)		TV magazine
die	Fete (n)		party

das	Fieber		high temperature
der	Film (e)		film
der	Filmstar (s)		filmstar
der	Filzstift (e)		felt-tip
	finden	to	find
der	Finger (-)		finger
der	Fisch (e)		fish
	Fische		Pisces
der	Fitneß		fitness
das	Fleisch		meat
	fliegen*	to	travel by plane, fly
die	Flöte		flute
der	Flug (Flüge)		flight
der	Flughafen (-häfen)		airport
das	Flugzeug (e)		plane
der	Flur (e)		corridor
der	Fluß (Flüsse)		river
die	Flut		high tide
	formatieren	to	format
das	Foto (s)		photo
der	Fotoapparat (e)		camera
	fotografieren	to	take photos
die	Frage (n)		question
	fragen (nach)	to	ask (for)
das	Fragewort (-wörter)		question word
das	Fragezeichen		question mark
	Französisch		French
die	Frau (en)		Mrs, Ms
die	Frau (en)		woman/wife
die	Frauenzeitschrift (en)		women's magazine
das	Fräulein (-)		Miss, young girl
	frei		free
die	Freizeit		free time
das	Freizeitzentrum (-zentren)		leisure centre
der	Freund (e)		friend (male)
sich mit	Freunden treffen	to	meet friends
die	Freundin (nen)		friend (female)
die	Frikadelle (n)		hamburger
der	Friseursalon (s)		hairdresser's
der	Frisör/die Friseuse		hairdresser
	Frohe Ostern!		Happy Easter!
	Frohe Weihnachten!		Happy Christmas!
der	Frost		frost
	früh		early
das	Frühstück (e)		breakfast

	frühstücken	to	have breakfast
der	Füller (-)		ink pen
	für + Acc		for
der	Fuß (Füße)		foot
der	Fußball		football
die	Fußgängerzone (n)		pedestrian precinct
	füttern	to	feed
die	Galerie (n)		gallery
	ganz		quite
	ganz in der Nähe		very near
das	ganze Jahr über		for the whole year
die	Gardine (n)		net curtain
der	Garten (Gärten)		garden
das	Gas		gas
die	Gasflasche (n)		gas bottle
der	Gaskocher (-)		gas cooker
die	Gasse (n)		alley, lane
das	Gästezimmer (-)		guestroom
das	Gasthaus (-häuser)		guesthouse, inn
das	Gebäck		biscuits
das	Gebäude (n)		building
der	Geburtsort (e)		place of birth
der	Geburtstag (e)		birthday
das	Geflügel		poultry
der	Gefrierschrank (-schränke)		freezer
	gefroren		frozen
	gegenüber (+ Dat)		opposite
	gegenüber dem Rathaus		opposite the townhall
	gehen*	to	go
	gehorsam		obedient
die	Geige (n)		violin
	gelb		yellow
das	Geld		money
der	Geldautomat (en)		cashpoint
	gelegen		situated
	gemischt		mixed
	gemischtes Eis mit Sahne		mixed ice cream with cream
das	Gemüse		vegetable
der	Gemüsegarten (-gärten)		vegetable garden
der	Gemüseladen (-läden)		greengrocer's shop
die	Gemüsesuppe (n)		vegetable soup
	gemütlich		cosy
die	Gepäckaufbewahrung		luggage locker
die	Gepäckrückgabe		baggage reclaim
	gepflegt		tidy

das	Gerät (e)		equipment
die	Gesamtschule (n)		comprehensive school
das	Geschäft (e)		shop
der	Geschäftsmann/die Geschäftsfrau		businessman/woman (self employed)
das	Geschenk (e)		present
	Geschichte		history
die	Geschichte (n)		story
	geschieden		divorced
das	Geschirr		crockery
	geschlossen		closed
die	Geschwister (pl)		brothers and sisters
das	Gesellschaftsspiel (e)		board game
	gestattet		permitted
die	Gesundheit		health
das	Getränk (e)		drink
das	Gewächshaus (-häuser)		greenhouse
	gewinnen	to	win
das	Gewitter (-)		thunderstorm
	gibt es		is there, are there
	gießen	to	water
die	Gitarre (n)		guitar
das	Glas (Gläser)		glass
das	Gleis (e)		track, platform
Viel	Glück!		Good luck!
	Glückwünsche		best wishes
	grau		grey
die	Grippe		flu
	groß		big
	großartig		great
die	Großeltern (pl)		grandparents
die	Großmutter (-mütter)		grandmother
	großschreiben	to	write with a capital letter
der	Großvater (-väter)		grandfather
	großzügig		generous
	grün		green
die	Grundschule (n)		primary school
die	Gruppe (n)		group
der	Gruppenleiter (-)		party leader, organiser
	Grüß Gott!		good day! (in South Germany)
	Grüße		greetings
der	Gürtel (-)		belt
	Gute Nacht!		Good night!
	Gute Reise!		Have a good journey!
	Guten Abend!		Good evening!
	Guten Morgen!		Good morning!

	Guten Tag!		Good day! Good afternoon!
das	Gymnasium (Gymnasien)		grammar school
die	Gymnastik		gymnastics
der	Hafen (Häfen)		port, harbour
das	Hähnchen		chicken
der	Hain (e)		copse
	häkeln	to	crochet
die	Halbpension		half board (bed, breakfast and evening meal)
	halbtags		part-time
der	Hals (Hälse)		neck, throat
das	Halstuch (-tücher)		scarf
die	Haltestelle (n)		bus stop
das	Hammelfleisch		mutton
der	Hamster (-)		hamster
die	Hand (Hände)		hand
die	Handarbeit (en)		needlework
der	Händler (-)		trader
die	Handschuhe		gloves
das	Handtuch (-tücher)		towel
der	Hauptbahnhof (-höfe)		main station
das	Hauptgericht (e)		main course
die	Hauptschule (n)		secondary school
das	Haus (Häuser)		house
aus dem	Haus gehen*	to	leave the house
die	Hausarbeit (en)		housework
die	Hausaufgabe (n)		homework
die	Hausaufgabe machen	to	do homework
nach	Hause kommen*	to	come home
der	Hausmeister (-)		caretaker
das	Haustier (e)		pet
	Hauswirtschaft		home economics
das	Heft (e)		exercise book
der	heilige Abend		Christmas Eve
der	Heimatfilm (e)		film set in a specific region
	heiß		hot
	heißen	to	be called
der	Heizkörper (-)		radiator
	helfen	to	help
	hell...		light ...
	hellblau		light blue
	hellgrün		light green
das	Hemd (en)		shirt
der/die	Heranwachsende (n)		adolescent
die	Herbergsmutter (-mütter)		warden (female)

die	Herbergsregeln (pl)		rules of the youth hostel
der	Herbergsvater (-väter)		warden (male)
die	Herbstferien (pl)		autumn half-term holiday
der	Herd (e)		cooker
der	Herr (en)		Mr, Sir, gentleman
	Herzlichen Glückwunsch zum Geburtstag!		Happy Birthday!
die	Himbeere (n)		raspberry
	hinter (+ Dat)		behind
	hinter der Kirche		behind the church
	historisch		historical
der	Hit (s)		hit song
das	Hobby (s)		hobby
der	Hocker (-)		stool
	hören	to	listen to
der	Horrorfilm (e)		horror film
das	Hörspiel (e)		radio play
die	Hose (n)		trousers
das	Hotel (s)		hotel
das	Hotelverzeichnis (e)		list of hotels
der	Hügel (-)		hill
die	Hühnerpastete (n)		chicken vol-au-vent
der	Hund (e)		dog
das	Hustenbonbon (s)		cough sweet
der	Hustensaft (-säfte)		cough medicine
der	Hut (Hüte)		hat
	Ich finde		I think
	Ich glaube nicht		I don't think
	Ich glaube/denke		I think
	Ich hasse		I hate
	Ich liebe		I adore
	Ich mag		I like
	Ich mag ... nicht.		I don't like ...
	im Schatten		in the shade
die	Imbißstube (n)		snack bar
	in		in
	in der Nähe von		near
	in der Sonne		in the sun
	in die Stadt gehen*	to	go into town
	inbegriffen		included
das	Industriegebiet (e)		industrial estate
der	Industriekaufmann/die Industriekauffrau		businessman/woman
die	Industriestadt (-städte)		industrial town
die	Informatik		IT

das	Informationsbüro (s)		tourist information office
der	Ingenieur		engineer
	inklusive		included
der	Insektenstich (e)		insect bite
die	Insel (n)		island
das	Instrument (e)		instrument
	interessant		interesting
	ja, natürlich		yes, of course
die	Jacke (n)		jacket
	Jägerschnitzel, Salzkartoffeln, Erbsen		schnitzel with mushrooms, potatoes and peas
die	Johannisbeere (n)		blackcurrant
das	jüdische Neujahr		Jewish New Year
die	Jugend		youth, young people
der	Jugendclub (s)		youth club
die	Jugendherberge (e)		Youth Hostel
der/die	Jugendliche (n)		youngster
das	Jugendzentrum (-zentren)		youth centre
der	Junge (n)		boy
für	Jungen		for boys
	Jungfrau		Virgo
das	Kabelfernsehen		cable TV
der	Kaffee		coffee
das	Kaffeestückchen (-)		Danish pastry
	Kalbsbraten, Knödel und Salat		roast veal, dumplings and salad
	kalt		cold
sich	kämmen	to	comb one's hair
der	Kanaltunnel		Channel Tunnel
der	Kanarienvogel (-vögel)		canary
das	Kännchen (-)		little pot
die	Kantine		canteen
die	Karotte (n)		carrot
die	Karte (n)		ticket
	Karten spielen	to	play cards
die	Kartoffel (n)		potato
der	Kartoffelsalat (e)		potato salad
der	Käse (-)		cheese
der	Käsekuchen (-)		cheese cake
die	Kasse (n)		cash till
die	Kassette (n)		cassette
der	Kassettenrekorder (-)		cassette recorder
	kastanienbraun		chestnut brown
die	Katze (n)		cat
das	Kaufhaus (-häuser)		department store
	kehren	to	sweep

der	Keller (-)		cellar
der	Kellner (-)		waiter
die	Kellnerin (nen)		waitress
das	Kind (er)		child
der	Kindergarten (-gärten)		nursery school
das	Kino (s)		cinema
die	Kirche (n)		church
die	Kirsche (n)		cherry
die	Klarinette (n)		clarinet
das	Klassenzimmer (-)		classroom
das	Klavier (e)		piano
das	Kleid (er)		dress
der	Kleiderkauf		buying clothes
der	Kleiderschrank (-schränke)		wardrobe
	klein		small
das	Kleingeld		change
	kleinschreiben	to	write with a lower case (small) letter
	klingeln	to	ring (door bell)
der	Klub (s)		club
die	Kneipe (n)		pub
das	Knie (e)		knee
	kochen	to	cook
der	Kochtopf (-töpfe)		saucepan
der	Koffer (-)		suitcase
der	Kohl		cabbage
das	Komma (s)		comma
der	Komödiant (en)		comedian
die	Komödie (n)		comedy
die	Konditorei (en)		cake shop
das	Konto (en)		bank account
das	Konzert (e)		concert
der	Kopf (Köpfe)		head
das	Kopfkissen (-)		pillow
der	Kopfsalat (e)		lettuce
der	Körperteil (e)		part of the body
	kosten	to	cost
	Krach haben mit	to	have an argument with
das	Krankenhaus (-häuser)		hospital
der	Krankenpfleger (-)		nurse (male)
die	Krankenschwester (n)		nurse (female)
die	Krankheit (en)		illness
	Krebs		Cancer
die	Kreide (n)		chalk
der	Kreisel (-)		roundabout
dic	Kreuzung (en)		cross-roads

das	Kreuzworträtsel (-)		crossword
das	Kricket		cricket
der	Kricketspieler (-)		cricket player
der	Kriminalfilm (e)		detective film
der	Kriminalroman (e)		detective novel
die	Küche (n)		kitchen
der	Kuchen (-)		cake, gateau
der	Kugelschreiber (-)		biro
der	Kühlschrank (-schränke)		fridge
der	Kuli (s)		biro
der	Kunde (n)		customer (male)
die	Kundin (nen)		customer (female)
	Kunst		art
aus	Kunstfaser		made of artificial fibre
die	Kusine (n)		cousin (female)
das	Labor (s)		laboratory
	laden	to	load
der	Laden (Läden)		shop
das	Lagerfeuer (-)		camp fire
das	Lammfleisch		lamb
die	Lampe (n)		lamp
das	Land		countryside
das	Land (Länder)		country
auf dem	Lande		in the country
	landen*	to	land
die	Landkarte (n)		map
der	Landkreis (e)		district
die	Landschaft (en)		landscape
die	Landstraße (n)		country road
	langsam		slow
	langweilig		boring
der	Lastwagen (-)		lorry
	Latein		Latin
	laut		noisy
die	Lebensmittel (pl)		food
das	Lebensmittelgeschäft (e)		grocer's
aus	Leder		made of leather
der	Lehrer (-)		teacher (male)
die	Lehrerin (nen)		teacher (female)
das	Lehrerzimmer (-)		staff room
die	Lehrmittelsammlung (en)		resource centre
die	Leichtathletik		athletics
	leihen	to	hire
aus	Leinen		made of linen
der	Leinenschlafsack (-säcke)		sheet sleeping bag

	lernen	to	learn
	lesen	to	read
der	Liebesfilm (e)		romantic film
die	Lieblingsgruppe (n)		favourite group
der	Lieblingssänger (-)		favourite singer
das	Lied (er)		song
der	Lieferwagen (-)		van
der	Lift (s)		lift
die	Limonade (n)		lemonade
das	Lineal (e)		ruler
die	Linie (n)		line
	links neben	to	the left of
	löschen	to	delete
	Löwe		Leo
das	Luftkissenboot (e)		hovercraft
die	Luftmatratze (n)		air bed
per	Luftpost		by airmail
	luxuriös		luxurious
das	macht nichts		it doesn't matter
das	Mädchen (-)		girl
für	Mädchen		for girls
die	Magenschmerzen (pl)		stomach ache
die	Magenverstimmung (en)		stomach upset
	malen	to	paint (a picture)
der	Mann (Männer)		man, husband
die	Mannschaft (en)		team
das	Mäppchen (-)		pencil case
	marineblau		navy blue
die	Mark		mark
der	Marker (-)		marker pen
der	Markt (Märkte)		market
die	Marmelade		jam
die	Mathe/Mathematik		maths/mathematics
der	Maurer/die Maurerin		bricklayer/builder
die	Maus (Mäuse)		mouse
mit	Mayonnaise		with mayonnaise
der	Mechaniker/die Mechanikerin		mechanic
die	Medien (pl)		the media
das	Medikament (e)		medicine
am	Meer		at the seaside
das	Meer (e)		sea
das	Meerschweinchen (-)		guinea-pig
die	Mehrwertsteuer		VAT
die	Meinung (en)		opinion
die	Melone (n)		melon

die	Metzgerei (en)		butcher's shop
die	Mietwohnung (en)		rented flat
der	Mikrowellenherd (e)		microwave oven
die	Milch		milk
die	Milchbar (s)		milk bar
das	Mineralwasser		mineral water
	mit + Dat		with
das	Mitglied (er)		member
das	Mittagessen (-)		lunch
in der	Mitte		in the middle
	mittelmäßig		mediocre
der	Modellbau		making models
	modern		modern
das	Mofa (s)		moped
	mögen	to	like
der	Monat (e)		month
der	Monitor (e)		monitor
der	Morgen (-)		morning
das	Motorrad (-räder)		motorbike
der	Mülleimer (-)		rubbish bin
der	Mund (Münder)		mouth
die	Münze (n)		coin
das	Museum (Museen)		museum
die	Musik		music
die	klassische Musik		classical music
die	Musiksendung (en)		music show
	musizieren	to	make music
die	Mutter (Mütter)		mother
die	Mutti (s)		mummy
die	Mütze (n)		cap, hat
	nach (+ Dat)		after
	nach der Ampel		after the lights
der	Nachmittag (e)		afternoon
die	Nachrichten (pl)		news
das	Nachrichtenmagazin (e)		news magazine
	nachsitzen	to	have a detention
die	Nachspeise (n)		dessert
die	Nacht (Nächte)		night
der	Nachtklub (s)		night club
die	Nachtruhe		silence at night, lights out
der	Nachttisch (e)		bedside table
die	Nachttischlampe (n)		bedside light
in der	Nähe von (+ Dat)		near
	nähen	to	sew
der	Name (n)		name

der	Namenstag (e)		saint's day
die	Nase (n)		nose
die	Naturwissenschaft (en)		science
der	Nebel		fog
	neben (+ Dat)		next to
	neben dem Theater		next to the theatre
	neblig		foggy
	nehmen	to	take
	Neujahr		New Year's Day
der	Nichtraucher		non-smoker
im	Norden		in the north
	nördlich von (+ Dat)		north of
der	Notausgang (-gänge)		emergency exit
die	Note (n)		mark, grade
die	Nudeln (pl)		pasta
	nützlich		useful
	nutzlos		useless
nach	oben gehen*	to	go upstairs
die	Oberstufe (n)		sixth form
das	Obst		fruit
das	Obstteller		fruit platter
der	offene Kamin (e)		open fireplace
die	öffentlichen Verkehrsmittel (pl)		public transport
	öffnen	to	open
die	Öffnungszeiten (pl)		opening times
	ohne (+ Acc)		without
das	Ohr (en)		ear
die	Oma (s)		granny
der	Onkel (s)		uncle
der	Opa (s)		grandad
der	Orangensaft (-säfte)		orange juice
das	Orchester (-)		orchestra
der	Originalton (-töne)		original soundtrack
im	Osten		in the east
die	Osterferien (pl)		Easter holidays
	Ostern		Easter
	östlich von (+ Dat)		east of
das	Päckchen (-)		small package
das	Paket (e)		parcel
der	Papi		daddy
das	Papier		paper
das	Parkhaus (-häuser)		multi-story car park
der	Parkplatz (-plätze)		car park
die	Party (s)		party
das	Passa		Passover

die	Pause (n)		break
die	Pension (en)		guesthouse
das	Personal		staff
die	Personalien (pl)		personal details
der	Personenzug (-züge)		local train
der	Pfad (e)		path
der	Pfennig (e)		pfennig
das	Pferd (e)		horse
die	Pfingstferien (pl)		summer half-term
der	Pfirsich (e)		peach
das	Pflaster (-)		sticking plaster
die	Pflaume (n)		plum
das	Pfund		pound sterling
die	Physik		physics
der	Pilot (en)		pilot
der	Pilz (e)		mushroom
	planmäßig		on time
der	Plattenspieler (-)		record player
der	Platz (Plätze)		square, place
die	Plombe (n)		filling
der	Polizist/die Polizistin		police officer
die	Pommes Frites		chips
das	Pony (Ponys)		pony
die	Popmusik		pop music
die	Portion (en)		portion
die	Post		post office, mail
das	Postamt (-ämter)		post office
der	Postbeamte/die Postbeamtin		post office worker
das	Poster (-)		poster
das	Postfach (-fächer)		PO box
die	Postkarte (n)		post card
die	Postleitzahl (en)		postcode
die	Präposition (en)		prepositions
der	Preis (e)		price
	preiswert		cheap, good value for money
die	Presse		press
	pro Monat		per month
	pro Woche		per week
das	Problem (e)		problem
das	Programm		TV channel
der	Projektor (en)		projector
der	Punkt		full stop
	pünktlich		punctually
	putzen	to	clean
die	Putzfrau		cleaner

die	Querflöte (n)		flute
das	Quiz		quiz
die	Quizsendung (en)		quiz programme
	radfahren*	to	cycle
der	Radiergummi (s)		rubber
im	Radio		on the radio
das	Radio (s)		radio
	Radio hören	to	listen to the radio
der	Ramadan		Ramadan
der	Rasen (-)		lawn
den	Rasen mähen	to	mow the lawn
sich	rasieren	to	shave
das	Rathaus		town hall
die	Ratte (n)		rat
der	Raucher		smoker
die	Realschule (n)		secondary (modern) school
	rechnen	to	calculate
	rechts neben (+ Dat)	to	the right of
	rechtzeitig		in time
	reden	to	talk
	Redewendungen		fillers (in conversation)
das	Regal (e)		shelf
der	Regen		rain
der	Regenmantel (-mäntel)		raincoat
	regnen	to	rain
	reich		rich
das	Reihenhaus (-häuser)		terraced house
die	Reise (n)		journey
das	Reiseandenken		souvenir
das	Reisebüro (s)		travel agency
der	Reisebus (se)		coach
die	Reisekrankheit (en)		travel sickness
	reisen*	to	travel
der	Reisende (n)		traveller
der	Reisepaß (-pässe)		passport
der	Reisescheck (s)		traveller's cheque
das	Reiten		riding
	reiten*	to	ride
	Religion		religious studies
	renovieren	to	renovate
	reservieren	to	reserve
die	Reservierung (en)		reservation
das	Restaurant (s)		restaurant
	restaurieren	to	restore
das	Rezept (e)		prescription

das	Rindfleisch		beef
der	Rock (Röcke)		skirt
der	Rolladen (-läden)		rolling shutter
	Rollschuh laufen*	to	roller-skate
die	Rolltreppe (n)		escalator
der	Roman (e)		novel
	rosa		pink
die	Rose (n)		rose
der	Rosenkohl		sprout
	rot		red
die	Rückfahrkarte (n)		return ticket
der	Rucksack (-säcke)		rucksack
in	Ruhe		calmly
	ruhig		quiet
der	Sabbat		Sabbath
die	Sackgasse (n)		cul-de-sac
der	Saft (Säfte)		juice
die	Sahnetorte (n)		cream cake
die	Salbe (n)		cream
	sammeln	to	collect
die	Sammlung (en)		collection
der	Sand		sand
die	Sandburg (en)		sandcastle
eine	Sandburg bauen	to	build a sandcastle
der	Sänger (-)		singer (male)
die	Sängerin (nen)		singer (female)
die	Satellitenschüssel (n)		satellite dish
der	Satz (Sätze)		sentence
	sauber		clean
	saubermachen	to	clean
	Schach spielen	to	play chess
der	Schal (s)		scarf
der	Schalter (-)		counter
das	Schaschlik (s)		kebab
das	Schaufenster (-)		shop window
einen	Schaufensterbummel machen	to	go window shopping
der	Schauspieler (-)		actor
die	Schauspielerin (nen)		actress
der	Scheck (s)		cheque
der	Schein (e)		bank-note
	scheinen	to	shine
	schenken	to	give as a present
	schicken	to	send
die	Schildkröte (n)		tortoise
der	Schinken		ham

der	Schlafanzug (züge)		pyjamas
	schlafen	to	sleep
	schlafen gehen*	to	go to bed
der	Schlafsaal (-säle)		dormitory
der	Schlafsack (-säcke)		sleeping bag
das	Schlafzimmer (-)		bedroom
der	Schlager (-)		hit song (in German)
das	Schlagzeug		drum kit
die	Schlange (n)		snake
das	Schlauchboot (e)		inflatable boat
	schlecht		bad
	schließen	to	shut, close
	Schlitt schuhlaufen*	to	ice-skate
ein	Schloß besichtigen	to	visit a stately home
der	Schlüssel (-)		key
der	Schmerz (en)		pain
	schmutzig		dirty
der	Schnaps (Schnäpse)		spirit
der	Schnee		snow
	schneien	to	snow
	schnell		fast, quickly
der	Schnellimbiß (sse)		snack bar
der	Schnellzug (-züge)		express train
	Schnitzel, Pommes Frites, Salat		schnitzel, chips and salad
die	Schokolade		chocolate
der	Schornstein (e)		chimney
der	Schrank (Schränke)		cupboard
	schreiben	to	write
der	Schreibtisch (e)		desk
die	Schule (n)		school
der	Schüler (-)		pupil (male)
die	Schülerin (nen)		pupil (female)
die	Schulferien (pl)		school holidays
der	Schulhof (-höfe)		playground
	Schütze		Sagittarius
der	Schwamm (Schwämme)		sponge
	schwarz		black
die	Schwarzwälderkirschtorte (-)		Black Forest gateau
das	Schweinefleisch		pork
	schwer		difficult
die	Schwester (n)		sister
das	Schwimmbad (-bäder)		swimming pool
	schwimmen	to	swim
das	Schwimmen		swimming
der	Schwimmring (e)		rubber ring

der	Science-fictionfilm (e)		science fiction film
der	See (n)		lake
das	Segelboot (e)		sailing boat
	segeln	to	sail
	sehen	to	see
gern	sehen	to	like watching
	sehr		very
aus	Seide		made of silk
die	Seife (n)		soap
die	Seifenoper (n)		soap opera
die	Sekretärin (nen)		secretary
die	Selbstbedienung (en)		self-service
	senden	to	send (often electronically)
die	Sendung (en)		programme
ohne	Senf		without mustard
die	Serie (n)		serial
der	Sessel (-)		armchair
	singen	to	sing
	sitzenbleiben*	to	repeat a year
	skifahren*	to	ski
	skilaufen*	to	ski
	Skorpion		Scorpio
das	Sofa (s)		sofa
der	Sohn (Söhne)		son
die	Sommerferien (pl)		summer holidays
das	Sonderangebot (e)		special offer
die	Sonne		sun
in der	Sonne liegen	to	sunbathe
der	Sonnenbrand (-brände)		sunburn
das	Sonnenöl		sun tan lotion
der	Sonnenschirm (e)		parasol
der	Sonnenstich (e)		sun stroke
	sonnig		sunny
	Spanisch		Spanish
	sparen	to	save
die	Sparkasse (n)		bank
	sparsam		careful with money
das	Sparschwein (e)		piggy bank
es macht	Spaß		it is fun
viel	Spaß!		Enjoy yourself!
	spät		late
	spazierenführen	to	take for a walk
	spazierengehen*	to	go for a walk
der	Speicher (-)		loft
	speichern	to	save

der	Sperrsitz (e)		stalls
der	Spiegel (-)		mirror
das	Spiel		game, match
	spielen	to	play
der	Spielfilm (e)		feature film
der	Spinat		spinach
der	Spionagefilm (e)		spy film
	Sport		games/PE
der	Sport (die Sportarten)		sport (s)
	Sport treiben	to	do sport
der	Sportplatz (-plätze)		sportsground
die	Sportschau		sports programme
das	Sportzentrum (-zentren)		sportscentre
die	Sprechstunde (n)		surgery time
das	Sprechzimmer (-)		consulting room
die	Spritze (n)		injection
der	Sprudel		fizzy mineral water, lemonade
das	Spülbecken (-)		sink
	spülen	to	wash up
die	Spülmaschine (n)		dish-washer
der	Spülstein (e)		sink
das	Stadion (Stadien)		stadium
die	Stadt (Städte)		town
die	Stadtmitte		town centre
der	Stadtplan (-pläne)		map of town
der	Stadtteil (e)		district, part of a town
	staubsaugen	to	hoover
der	Staubsauger (-)		vacuum cleaner
	Steinbock		Capricorn
der	Stellplatz (-plätze)		pitch
die	Stereoanlage (n)		stereo system
das	Sternzeichen (-)		star sign
die	Stewardeß (Stewardessen)		stewardess
der	Stiefbruder (-brüder)		half-brother, stepbrother
die	Stiefel		boots
die	Stiefmutter (-mütter)		stepmother
die	Stiefschwester (n)		half-sister, stepsister
der	Stiefvater (-väter)		stepfather
	Stier		Taurus
	still		calm
der	Stock (Stockwerke)		floor, storey
der	Strand (Strände)		beach
die	Straße (n)		street, road
die	Straßenbahn (en)		tram
die	Streichhölzer (pl)		matches

die	Streifenkarte (n)		strip of tickets
sich	streiten	to	argue
	stricken	to	knit
der	Strom		electricity
die	Strumpfhose (n)		tights
das	Stück (e)		coin
der	Stuhl (Stühle)		chair
die	Stunde (n)		lesson
der	Stundenplan (-pläne)		timetable
	stundenweise		hourly
	stürmisch		stormy
	suchen	to	look for
im	Süden		in the south
	südlich von		south of
der	Supermarkt (-märkte)		supermarket
	Sylvester		New Year´s Eve
das	T-shirt (s)		T-shirt
das	Tabakwarengeschäft (e)		tobacconist's shop
das	Tabellenprogramm		spreadsheet
die	Tablette (n)		tablet
die	Tafel (n)		blackboard
die	Tafel Schokolade		bar of chocolate
der	Tag (e)		day
die	Tagessuppe (n)		soup of the day
das	Tal (Täler)		valley
die	Tankstelle (n)		filling station
die	Tanne (n)		fir tree
die	Tante (n)		aunt
	tanzen	to	dance
	tapezieren	to	hang wall paper
das	Taschengeld		pocket money
die	Taschenlampe (n)		torch
das	Taschenmesser (-)		penknife
die	Tasse (n)		cup
die	Tastatur (en)		keyboard
der	Tee		tea
der	Teich (e)		pond
	teilen	to	share
das	Telefon (e)		telephone
die	Telefonnummer (n)		telephone number
die	Telefonzelle (n)		phone box
der	Teller (-)		plate
das	Tennis		tennis
der	Tennisplatz (-plätze)		tennis court
der	Teppich (e)		carpet, rug

der	Teppichboden (-böden)		fitted carpet
der	Termin (e)		appointment
die	Terrasse (n)		patio
	teuer		expensive
die	Textverarbeitung		word processing
das	Theater (-)		theatre
das	Theaterstück (e)		play
die	Theke (n)		counter
der	Thriller (-)		thriller
der	Ticket (s)		plane ticket
der	Tisch (e)		table
den	Tisch decken	to	lay the table
die	Tischdecke (n)		tablecloth
das	Tischtuch (-tücher)		tablecloth
die	Tochter (Töchter)		daughter
die	Toilette (n)		toilet
die	Tomate (n)		tomato
	töpfern	to	do pottery
die	Torte (n)		gateau
der	Tourist (en)		tourist
die	Trachtenpuppe (n)		doll in folk costume
	tragen	to	wear
	trainieren	to	train
das	Training		training
das	Transportmittel (-)		means of transport
die	Traube (n)		grape
die	Treppe (n)		staircase
das	Trimester (-)		term
die	Trompete (n)		trumpet
	tschüß		cheerio
die	Tube (n)		tube
die	Tulpe (n)		tulip
die	Tür (en)		door
das	Turnen		gymnastics
die	Turnhalle (n)		gym
die	Turnschuhe		trainers
die	U-Bahn (en)		underground
	üben	to	practise
	über		over
die	Überfahrt		the channel crossing
	übernachten	to	stay overnight
die	Übernachtung mit Frühstück		bed and breakfast
	überqueren	to	cross (road)
	um die Ecke		round the corner
	um wieviel Uhr		at what time

der	Umkleideraum (-räume)		changing room
	umschalten		to switch over (TV channel)
	umsteigen	to	change trains
	umtauschen	to	change (money)
sich	**um**ziehen*	to	get changed
	umziehen	to	move house
die	Uniform (en)		uniform
	uninteressant		not interesting
nach	unten gehen*	to	go downstairs
	unter		under
die	Unterkunft (-künfte)		accommodation
der	Unterricht		teaching, lesson
die	Unterrichtsstunde (n)		lesson
	unterschreiben	to	sign
die	Unterschrift (en)		signature
der	Untertitel (-)		subtitle
der	Urlaub auf dem Bauernhof		farm holiday
der	Urlaub (e)		holiday
der	Vanillepudding		vanilla flavour whipped pudding
die	Vase (n)		vase
der	Vater (Väter)		father
der	Vati		daddy
der	Verband (-bände)		bandage
	verbessern	to	correct
	verboten		forbidden
	verbringen	to	spend time
der	Verein (e)		club
	vergessen	to	forget
	verheiratet		married
	verkaufen	to	to sell
zu	verkaufen		for sale
der	Verkäufer (-)		shop assistant (male)
die	Verkäuferin (nen)		shop assistant (female)
das	Verkehrsamt (-ämter)		tourist information office
das	Verkehrsmittel (-)		means of transport
	verlassen	to	leave
	verlieren	to	lose
	verlobt		engaged
der/die	Verlobte (n)		fiancé(e)
	verpassen	to	miss
die	Versammlung (en)		assembly
	verschmutzt		polluted
	versetzt werden	to	move on to the next year
	verspätet		delayed
die	Verspätung		delay

sich	verstehen mit	to	get on with someone
	versuchen	to	try
einen	Versuch machen	to	do an experiment
sich	vertragen mit (+ Dat)	to	get on
der	Vertreter/die Vertreterin		sales representative
der/die	Verwandte (n)		relative
	verwitwet		widowed
die	Videokamera (s)		video-camera, camrecorder
der	Videorekorder (-)		video cassette recorder
das	Videospiel (e)		video game
	viel		a lot
	vielleicht		perhaps
die	Volksmusik		folk music
	voll		full
die	Vollpension		full board
	von (+ Dat)		from
	vor (+ Dat)		in front of
	vor dem Kino		in front of the cinema
die	Vorführung (en)		performance
der	Vorhang (-hänge)		curtain
der	Vorname (n)		first name, christian name
der	Vorort (e)		suburb
die	Vorspeise		starter
	Waage		Libra
der	Wagen (-)		car
	wählen	to	choose
der	Wald (Wälder)		forest, wood
das	Waldstück (e)		wood
der	Walkman		walkman
die	Wand (Wände)		wall
	wandern*	to	hike
die	Wanduhr (en)		wall clock
	wann		when
die	Ware (n)		goods
	warten	to	wait
der	Warteraum (-räume)		waiting room
das	Wartezimmer (-)		waiting room
	warum		why
	was		what
das	Waschbecken (-)		sink, washbasin
sich	waschen	to	wash (oneself)
der	Waschlappen (-)		face cloth
die	Waschmaschine (n)		washing-machine
der	Waschraum (-räume)		toilet block
das	Wasser		water

	Wasserball spielen	to	play waterball
der	Wasserhahn (-hähne)		tap
	Wassermann		Aquarius
	Wasserski fahren*	to	waterski
der	Wassersport		watersport
die	Watte		cotton wool
der	Wechselkurs (e)		exchange rate
	wechseln	to	change (money)
der	Wecker (-)		alarm clock
der	Weg (e)		way, road, path
die	Wegbeschreibung		road directions
	Weihnachten (pl)		Christmas
der	Weihnachtsbaum (-bäume)		Christmas tree
die	Weihnachtsferien (pl)		Christmas holidays
der	Weihnachtsmann (-männer)		Father Christmas
der	erste Weihnachtstag		Christmas Day
der	zweite Weihnachtstag		Boxing Day
der	Wein (e)		wine
	weiß		white
	weit weg von		far from
	welcher, welche, welches		which
der	Wellensittich (e)		budgie
	wenig		a little
	wer		who
die	Werbung (en)		advertisements
im	Westen		in the west
	westlich von		west of
das	Wetter		weather
der	Wetterbericht (e)		weather forecast
die	Wettervorhersage (n)		weather forecast
	Widder		Aries
	wie		how
	Wie schade!		What a pity!
	wie viele		how many
	wiederholen	to	repeat
Auf	Wiedersehen!		Goodbye!
die	Wiese (n)		meadow
	wieviel		how much
der	Wind (e)		wind
	windig		windy
	windsurfen	to	windsurf
der	Wintersport		winter sport
	wo		where
das	Wochenende (n)		weekend
die	Wochenzeitschrift (en)		weekly (political) magazine

	wohin		where to
der	Wohnblock (s)		block of flats
	wohnen	to	live
das	Wohnmobil (e)		motorhome, camper
die	Wohnung (en)		flat
der	Wohnwagen (-)		caravan
das	Wohnzimmer (-)		living room
die	Wolke (n)		cloud
aus	Wolle		made of wool
der	Yachthafen (-häfen)		yacht marina
	zählen	to	count
der	Zahn (Zähne)		tooth
beim	Zahnarzt		at the dentist's
der	Zahnarzt (-ärzte)		dentist (male)
die	Zahnärztin (nen)		dentist (female)
die	Zahnbürste (n)		toothbrush
sich die	Zähne putzen	to	brush one's teeth
die	Zahnpasta		toothpaste
die	Zeichensetzung		punctuation
der	Zeichentrickfilm (e)		cartoon
	zeichnen	to	draw
die	Zeitschrift (en)		magazine
die	Zeitung (en)		newspaper
das	Zelt (e)		tent
	zelten	to	camp (in a tent)
die	Zentralheizung (en)		central heating
der	Zettel (-)		receipt
das	Zeugnis (se)		school report
	ziehen	to	pull
	zierlich		dainty, delicate
das	Zimmer (-)		room
die	Zimmerpflanze (n)		house plant
die	Zitrone (n)		lemon
die	Zollkontrolle (n)		customs control
	zu (+ Dat)		to
der	Zug (Züge)		train
	zuhören	to	listen to
	zurückkommen*	to	come back
das	Zweibettzimmer (-)		twin bedded room
	zweiter Klasse		second class
die	Zwiebel (n)		onion
	Zwilling		Gemini
	zwischen (+ Dat)		in between

English–German

Mini-Dictionary

	accommodation	die	Unterkunft (-künfte)
	actor	der	Schauspieler (-)
	actress	die	Schauspielerin (nen)
	address	die	Adresse (n)
	address	die	Anschrift (en)
	adolescent	der/die	Heranwachsende (n)
	adult	der/die	Erwachsene (n)
	adventure film	der	Abenteuerfilm (e)
	adventure novel	der	Abenteuerroman (e)
	advertisements	die	Werbung (en)
	aerial	die	Antenne (n)
	affectionate		anschmiegsam
	after		nach (+ Dat)
	after the lights		nach der Ampel
	afternoon	der	Nachmittag (e)
	age	das	Alter
	agreed		einverstanden
	air bed	die	Luftmatratze (n)
	airport	der	Flughafen (-häfen)
	alarm clock	der	Wecker (-)
	All the best!		Alles Gute!
	alley, lane	die	Gasse (n)
	alone		allein
	along		entlang (+ Acc)
	alphabet	das	Alphabet
	answer	die	Antwort (en)
to	answer		antworten
	apple	der	Apfel (Äpfel)
	apple cake	der	Apfelkuchen (-)
	apple juice	der	Apfelsaft
	apple tree	der	Apfelbaum (-bäume)
	appointment	der	Termin (e)
	Aquarius		Wassermann
to	argue	sich	streiten
	Aries		Widder
	arm	der	Arm (Arme)
	armchair	der	Sessel (-)
	arrival	die	Ankunft (Ankünfte)
to	arrive		**an**kommen*
	art		Kunst
made of	artificial fibre	aus	Kunstfaser
to	ask (for)		fragen (nach)
to	ask for information	sich	erkundigen
	assembly	die	Versammlung (en)
	at		an

	athletics	die	Leichtathletik
	aunt	die	Tante (n)
	autumn half-term holidays	die	Herbstferien (pl)
	avenue	die	Allee (n)
	baby	das	Baby (s)
	bad		schlecht
	baggage reclaim	die	Gepäckrückgabe
	baker's shop	die	Bäckerei (en)
	balcony	der	Balkon (e)
	banana	die	Banane (n)
	bandage	der	Verband (-bände)
	bandage, dressing	die	Binde (n)
	bank	die	Bank (en)
	bank	die	Sparkasse (n)
	bank account	das	Konto (en)
	bank holiday	der	Feiertag (e)
	bank-note	der	Schein (e)
	bar of chocolate	die	Tafel (n) Schokolade
with	bath	mit	Bad
	bath towel	das	Badetuch (-tücher)
	bath tub	die	Badewanne (n)
	bathing suit	der	Badeanzug (züge)
	bathroom	das	Bad (Bäder)
	bathroom	das	Badezimmer (-)
to	be called		heißen
	beach	der	Strand (Strände)
	bean	die	Bohne (n)
	bed	das	Bett (en)
	bed and breakfast	die	Übernachtung mit Frühstück
	bedroom	das	Schlafzimmer (-)
	bedside light	die	Nachttischlampe (n)
	bedside table	der	Nachttisch (e)
	beef	das	Rindfleisch
	beer	das	Bier (e)
	beer mat	der	Bierdeckel (-)
	beer mug	der	Bierkrug (-krüge)
to	begin		**an**fangen
to	begin		beginnen
	behind		hinter (+ Dat)
	behind the church		hinter der Kirche
	belt	der	Gürtel (-)
	bench	die	Bank (Bänke)
	Best wishes!		Alles Gute!
	best wishes		Glückwünsche
	bicycle	das	Fahrrad (-räder)

	bidet	das	Bidet (s)
	big		groß
	biology		Biologie
	birch	die	Birke (n)
	biro	der	Kugelschreiber (-)
	biro	der	Kuli (s)
	birthday	der	Geburtstag (e)
	biscuits	das	Gebäck
	black		schwarz
	Black Forest gateau	die	Schwarzwälderkirschtorte (-)
	blackboard	die	Tafel (n)
	blackcurrant	die	Johannisbeere (n)
	blanket	die	Decke (n)
	block of flats	der	Wohnblock (s)
	blood	das	Blut
	blouse	die	Bluse (n)
	blue		blau
	board game	das	Gesellschaftsspiel (e)
	boiled sausage	die	Bockwurst (-würste)
	book	das	Buch (Bücher)
to	book		buchen
	book with photographs	der	Bildband (-bänder)
	bookcase	der	Bücherschrank (-schränke)
	bookshop	die	Buchhandlung (en)
	boots	die	Stiefel
	boring		langweilig
	Boxing Day	der	zweite Weihnachtstag
	boy	der	Junge (n)
for	boys	für	Jungen
	bread	das	Brot (e)
	bread roll	das	Brötchen (-)
	break	die	Pause (n)
	breakfast	das	Frühstück (e)
	bricklayer/builder	der	Maurer/die Maurerin
	bridge	die	Brücke (n)
	brochure	die	Broschüre (n)
	brook	der	Bach (Bäche)
	broom	der	Besen (-)
	brother	der	Bruder (Brüder)
	brothers and sisters	die	Geschwister (pl)
	brown		braun
to	brush		bürsten
to	brush one's teeth	sich	die Zähne putzen
	budgie	der	Wellensittich (e)
to	build		bauen

to	build a sandcastle	eine	Sandburg bauen
	building	das	Gebäude (n)
	bunch of flowers	der	Blumenstrauß (-sträuße)
	bungalow	der	Bungalow (s)
	bus	der	Bus (se)
	bus station	der	Busbahnhof (-höfe)
	bus stop	die	Bushaltestelle (n)
	bus stop	die	Haltestelle (n)
	bush	der	Busch (Büsche)
	businessman/woman	der	Industiekaufmann/die Industriekauffrau
	businessman/woman(self employed)	der	Geschäftsmann/die Geschäftsfrau
	butcher's shop	die	Metzgerei (en)
	buying clothes	der	Kleiderkauf
	by airmail	per	Luftpost
	by express	per	Eilbote
	cabbage	der	Kohl
	cable TV	das	Kabelfernsehen
	café	das	Café
	cake, gateau	der	Kuchen (-)
	cake shop	die	Konditorei (en)
to	calculate		rechnen
	calm		still
	calmly	in	Ruhe
	camera	der	Fotoapparat (e)
to	camp (in a tent)		zelten
	camp fire	das	Lagerfeuer (-)
	camp-site	der	Campingplatz (-plätze)
	camping	das	Camping
	camping equipment	die	Campingausrüstung (en)
	canary	der	Kanarienvogel (-vögel)
	Cancer		Krebs
	canteen	die	Kantine
	cap, hat	die	Mütze (n)
	Capricorn		Steinbock
	car	das	Auto (s)
	car	der	Wagen (-)
	car park	der	Parkplatz (-plätze)
	caravan	der	Wohnwagen (-)
	careful with money		sparsam
	caretaker	der	Hausmeister (-)
	carpet, rug	der	Teppich (e)
	carrot	die	Karotte (n)
	cartoon	der	Zeichentrickfilm (e)
to	cash (cheque)		**ein**lösen

	cash till	die	Kasse (n)
	cashpoint	der	Geldautomat (en)
	cassette	die	Kassette (n)
	cassette recorder	der	Kassettenrekorder (-)
	cat	die	Katze (n)
	cathedral	der	Dom (e)
	cauliflower	der	Blumenkohl
	CD	die	Compact Disc/CD
	CD player	der	Compact-Disc-Spieler (-)
	ceiling	die	Decke (n)
to	celebrate		feiern
	cellar	der	Keller (-)
	cello	das	Cello (s)
	central heating	die	Zentralheizung (en)
	chair	der	Stuhl (Stühle)
	chalk	die	Kreide (n)
	change	das	Kleingeld
to	change (money)		**um**tauschen
to	change (money)		wechseln
to	change trains		**um**steigen*
	changing room	der	Umkleideraum (-räume)
the	channel crossing	die	Überfahrt
	Channel Tunnel	der	Kanaltunnel
	cheap, good value for money		preiswert
	cheerio		Tschüß
	cheese	der	Käse (-)
	cheese cake	der	Käsekuchen (-)
at the	chemist's	in der	Apotheke
	chemist's	die	Apotheke (n)
	chemistry		Chemie
	cheque	der	Scheck (s)
	cherry	die	Kirsche (n)
	chestnut brown		kastanienbraun
	chicken	das	Hähnchen
	chicken vol-au-vent	die	Hühnerpastete (n)
	child	das	Kind (er)
	chimney	der	Schornstein (e)
	chips	die	Pommes Frites
	chocolate	die	Schokolade
	choir	der	Chor (Chöre)
to	choose		**aus**suchen
to	choose		wählen
	Christmas		Weihnachten
	Christmas Day	der	erste Weihnachtstag
	Christmas Eve	der	heilige Abend

	Christmas holidays	die	Weihnachtsferien (pl)
	Christmas tree	der	Weihnachtsbaum (-bäume)
	church	die	Kirche (n)
	cider	der	Apfelwein
	cinema	das	Kino (s)
	clarinet	die	Klarinette (n)
	classical music	die	klassische Musik
	classroom	das	Klassenzimmer (-)
to	clean		putzen
	clean		sauber
to	clean		**sauber**machen
	cleaner (lady)	die	Putzfrau
to	clear (table)		**ab**räumen
to	close		schließen
	closed		geschlossen
	clothes shop	das	Bekleidungshaus (-häuser)
	cloud	die	Wolke (n)
	cloudy		bewölkt
	club	der	Klub (s)
	club	der	Verein (e)
	coach	der	Reisebus (se)
	coffee	der	Kaffee
	coffee-table	der	Couchtisch (e)
	coin	die	Münze (n)
	coin	das	Stück (e)
	cold	die	Erkältung
	cold		kalt
to	collect		sammeln
	collection	die	Sammlung (en)
	colour	die	Farbe (n)
	coloured pencil	der	Buntstift (e)
to	comb one's hair	sich	kämmen
to	come back		**zurück**kommen*
to	come home	nach	Hause kommen*
	comedian	der	Komödiant (en)
	comedy	die	Komödie (n)
	comfortable		bequem
	comic strip	der	Comic (s)
	comma	das	Komma (s)
	compartment	das	Abteil (e)
to	complain	sich	beschweren
	comprehensive school	die	Gesamtschule (n)
	computer	der	Computer (-)
	computer game	das	Computerspiel (e)
	computer virus	der	Computervirus (-viren)

	concert	das	Konzert (e)
made of	concrete	aus	Beton
	connecting train	der	Anschluß (Anschlüsse)
	consulting room	das	Sprechzimmer (-)
to	cook		kochen
	cooker	der	Herd (e)
	copse	der	Hain (e)
to	copy		**ab**schreiben
	corner	die	Ecke (n)
on the	corner	an der	Ecke
to	correct		verbessern
	corridor	der	Flur (e)
to	cost		kosten
	cosy		gemütlich
made of	cotton		aus Baumwolle
	cotton wool	die	Watte
	cough medicine	der	Hustensaft (-säfte)
	cough sweet	das	Hustenbonbon (s)
to	count		zählen
	counter	der	Schalter (-)
	counter	die	Theke (n)
	country	das	Land (Länder)
in the	country	auf dem	Lande
	country road	die	Landstraße (n)
	countryside	das	Land
	cousin (female)	die	Kusine (n)
	cousin (male)	der	Cousin (s)
	cream	die	Salbe (n)
	cream cake	die	Sahnetorte (n)
	cricket	das	Kricket
	cricket player	der	Kricketspieler (-)
	crisps	die	Chips (pl)
to	crochet		häkeln
	crockery	das	Geschirr
to	cross (road)		überqueren
	cross-roads	die	Kreuzung (en)
	crossword	das	Kreuzworträtsel (-)
	cul-de-sac	die	Sackgasse (n)
	cup	die	Tasse (n)
	cupboard	der	Schrank (Schränke)
	curtain	der	Vorhang (-hänge)
	customer (female)	die	Kundin (nen)
	customer (male)	der	Kunde (n)
	customs control	die	Zollkontrolle (n)
	cutlery	das	Besteck (e)

to	cycle		**rad**fahren*
	daddy	der	Papi
	daddy	der	Vati
	daily routine	der	Alltag
	dainty, delicate		zierlich
to	dance		tanzen
	Danish pastry	das	Kaffeestückchen (-)
	dark ...		dunkel...
	dark blue		dunkelblau
	dark green		dunkelgrün
	daughter	die	Tochter (Töchter)
	day	der	Tag (e)
	day room	der	Aufenthaltsraum (-räume)
	delay	die	Verspätung
	delayed		verspätet
to	delete		löschen
	dentist (female)	die	Zahnärztin (nen)
	dentist (male)	der	Zahnarzt (-ärzte)
at the	dentist's	beim	Zahnarzt
to	depart		**ab**fahren*
	department	die	Abteilung (en)
	department store	das	Kaufhaus (-häuser)
	departure	die	Abfahrt (en)
	departure of plane	der	Abflug
	desk	der	Schreibtisch (e)
	dessert	die	Nachspeise (n)
	detached house	das	Einfamilienhaus (-häuser)
	detective film	der	Kriminalfilm (e)
	detective novel	der	Kriminalroman (e)
	diarrhoea	der	Durchfall
	difficult		schwer
	dinghy	das	Dingi (s)
	dining room	der	Eßraum (-räume)
	dining room	das	Eßzimmer (-)
	dirty		schmutzig
	disco	die	Disco (s)
	dish-washer	die	Spülmaschine (n)
	disk	die	Diskette
	district	der	Bezirk (e)
	district	der	Landkreis (e)
	district, part of a town	der	Stadtteil (e)
	divorced		geschieden
to	do an experiment		einen Versuch machen
to	do DIY		basteln
to	do homework	die	Hausaufgabe machen

to	do sport		Sport treiben
	doctor (female)	die	Ärztin (nen)
	doctor (male)	der	Arzt (Ärzte)
at the	doctor's	beim	Arzt
	doctor's receptionist	die	Arzthelferin (nen)
	documentary	der	Dokumentarfilm (e)
	dog	der	Hund (e)
	doll in folk costume	die	Trachtenpuppe (n)
	door	die	Tür (en)
	dormitory	der	Schlafsaal (-säle)
	double room (with one big bed)	das	Doppelzimmer (-)
to	draw		zeichnen
	dress	das	Kleid (er)
	drink	das	Getränk (e)
	driver (female)	die	Fahrerin (nen)
	driver (male)	der	Fahrer (-)
	drum kit	das	Schlagzeug
to	dry up		**ab**trocknen
	duvet	die	Bettdecke (n)
	ear	das	Ohr (en)
	early		früh
in the	east	im	Osten
	east of		östlich von (+ Dat)
	Easter		Ostern
	Easter holidays	die	Osterferien (pl)
	easy		einfach
to	eat		essen
to	edit		bearbeiten
to	edit		editieren
	egg	das	Ei (er)
	electrician	der	Elektriker/die Elektrikerin
	electricity	der	Strom
	emergency exit	der	Notausgang (-gänge)
	employed		angestellt
to	end		enden
	engaged		verlobt
	engineer	der	Ingenieur
	English		Englisch
to	enjoy oneself	sich	amüsieren
	Enjoy yourself!		Viel Spaß!
	entrance	der	Eingang (-gänge)
	equipment	das	Gerät (e)
	escalator	die	Rolltreppe (n)
	evening	der	Abend (e)
	evening meal	das	Abendessen (-)

	example	das	Beispiel (e)
	excellent		ausgezeichnet
	except		außer
	exchange	der	Austausch (e)
to	exchange		**aus**tauschen
	exchange rate	der	Wechselkurs (e)
	excursion, outing	der	Ausflug (-flüge)
	excuse me, sorry		entschuldigen Sie
	excuse me, sorry		Entschuldigung
	exercise book	das	Heft (e)
	exhibition	die	Ausstellung (en)
	expensive		teuer
to	explain		erklären
	express train	der	Schnellzug (-züge)
	eye	das	Auge (n)
	face cloth	der	Waschlappen (-)
	factory	die	Fabrik (en)
to	fail		**durch**fallen*
	family	die	Familie (n)
	family life	das	Familienleben
	family member	das	Familienmitglied (er)
	family photo	das	Familienfoto (s)
	far from		weit weg von (+ Dat)
	farm	der	Bauernhof (-höfe)
	farm holiday	der	Urlaub auf dem Bauernhof
	fast train	der	Eilzug (-züge)
	fast, quickly		schnell
	father	der	Vater (Väter)
	Father Christmas	der	Weihnachtsmann (-männer)
	favourite group	die	Lieblingsgruppe (n)
	favourite singer	der	Lieblingssänger (-)
to	fax		faxen
	feature film	der	Spielfilm(e)
to	feed		füttern
	felt-tip	der	Filzstift (e)
	ferry	die	Fähre (n)
	ferry port	der	Fährhafen (-häfen)
	fiancé(e)	der/die	Verlobte (n)
	field	das	Feld (er)
	file, data base	die	Datei
	fillers (in conversation)		Redewendungen
	filling	die	Plombe (n)
	filling station	die	Tankstelle (n)
	film	der	Film (e)
	film set in a specific region	der	Heimatfilm (e)

	filmstar	der	Filmstar (s)
to	find		finden
	finger	der	Finger (-)
to	finish		enden
	fir tree	die	Tanne (n)
	first class		erster Klasse
	first name, christian name	der	Vorname (n)
to	fish		angeln
	fish	der	Fisch (e)
	fitness	der	Fitneß
	fitted carpet	der	Teppichboden (-böden)
	fizzy mineral water, lemonade	der	Sprudel
	flat	die	Wohnung (en)
	flight	der	Flug (Flüge)
	floor	der	Boden (Böden)
	floor, storey	der	Stock (Stockwerke)
	flower	die	Blume (n)
	flower bed	das	Blumenbeet (e)
	flu	die	Grippe
	flute	die	Flöte (n)
	flute	die	Querflöte (n)
to	fly		fliegen*
	fog	der	Nebel
	foggy		neblig
	folk music	die	Volksmusik
	food	das	Essen
	food	die	Lebensmittel (pl)
	foot	der	Fuß (Füße)
	football	der	Fußball
	for		für (+ Acc)
	for the whole year		das ganze Jahr über
	forbidden		verboten
	forest, wood	der	Wald (Wälder)
to	forget		vergessen
to	format		formatieren
	free		frei
	free time	die	Freizeit
	freezer	der	Gefrierschrank (-schränke)
	French		französisch
	fridge	der	Kühlschrank (-schränke)
	fried sausage	die	Bratwurst (-würste)
	fried sausage and potatoes		Bratwurst, Kartoffeln
	friend (female)	die	Freundin (nen)
	friend (male)	der	Freund (e)
	friend/acquaintance	der	Bekannte (n)

	from		aus (+ Dat)
	from		von (+ Dat)
	frost	der	Frost
	frozen		gefroren
	fruit	das	Obst
	fruit platter	das	Obstteller
	frying pan	die	Bratpfanne (n)
	full		voll
	full board	die	Vollpension
	full stop	der	Punkt
it is	fun	es macht	Spaß
	gallery	die	Galerie (n)
	game, match	das	Spiel
	games/PE		Sport
	garden	der	Garten (Gärten)
	gas	das	Gas
	gas bottle	die	Gasflasche (n)
	gas cooker	der	Gaskocher (-)
	gateau	die	Torte (n)
	Gemini		Zwilling
	general		Allgemeines
	generous		großzügig
	geography		Erdkunde
	German		Deutsch
to	get changed	sich	**um**ziehen
to	get dressed	sich	**an**ziehen
to	get on	sich	vertragen
to	get on with someone	sich	verstehen mit (+ Dat)
to	get on well/badly with someone	gut/schlecht	**aus**kommen* mit
to	get undressed	sich	**aus**ziehen
to	get up		**auf**stehen*
	girl	das	Mädchen (-)
for	girls	für	Mädchen
to	give as a present		schenken
	glass	das	Glas (Gläser)
	gloves	die	Handschuhe
to	go		gehen*
to	go (by vehicle), drive		fahren*
to	go downstairs	nach	unten gehen*
to	go for a walk		**spazieren**gehen*
to	go into town		in die Stadt gehen*
to	go out		**aus**gehen*
to	go round the shops		einen Einkaufsbummel machen
to	go shopping		einkaufen gehen*
to	go through/direct		**durch**fahren*

to	go to bed	zu/ins	Bett gehen*
to	go to bed		schlafen gehen*
to	go upstairs	nach	oben gehen*
to	go window shopping		einen Schaufensterbummel machen
	going out	das	Ausgehen
	Good day! (in South Germany)		Grüß Gott!
	Good day, hello, good afternoon!		Guten Tag!
	Good evening!		Guten Abend!
	Have a good journey!		Gute Reise!
	Good luck!		Viel Glück!
	Good morning!		Guten Morgen!
	Good night!		Gute Nacht!
	Goodbye!		Auf Wiedersehen!
	goods	die	Ware (n)
	grammar school	das	Gymnasium (Gymnasien)
	grandad	der	Opa (s)
	granddaughter	die	Enkelin (nen)
	grandfather	der	Großvater (-väter)
	grandmother	die	Großmutter (-mütter)
	grandparents	die	Großeltern (pl)
	grandson	der	Enkel (n)
	granny	die	Oma (s)
	grape	die	Traube (n)
	great		einfach Klasse
	great		großartig
	green		grün
	greengrocer's shop	der	Gemüseladen (-läden)
	greenhouse	das	Gewächshaus (-häuser)
	greetings		Grüße
	grey		grau
	grocer's	das	Lebensmittelgeschäft (e)
	ground floor	das	Erdgeschoß
	group	die	Gruppe (n)
	guesthouse	die	Pension (en)
	guesthouse, inn	das	Gasthaus (-häuser)
	guestroom	das	Gästezimmer (-)
	guinea-pig	das	Meerschweinchen (-)
	guitar	die	Gitarre (n)
	gym	die	Turnhalle (n)
	gymnastics	die	Gymnastik
	gymnastics	das	Turnen
	hairdresser	der	Frisör/die Friseuse
	hairdresser's	der	Friseursalon (s)
	half board (bed, breakfast and evening meal)	die	Halbpension
	half-brother	der	Stiefbruder (-brüder)

	half-sister	die	Stiefschwester (n)
	ham	der	Schinken
	hamburger	die	Frikadelle (n)
	hamster	der	Hamster (-)
	hand	die	Hand (Hände)
to	hang wall paper		tapezieren
	Happy Birthday!		Herzlichen Glückwunsch zum Geburtstag!
	Happy Christmas!		Frohe Weihnachten!
	Happy Easter!		Frohe Ostern!
	Happy New Year!		Alles Gute im neuen Jahr!
	hat	der	Hut (Hüte)
to	have a detention		**nach**sitzen
to	have an argument with		Krach haben mit (+ Dat)
to	have breakfast		frühstücken
	head	der	Kopf (Köpfe)
	headmaster	der	Direktor (en)
	headmistress	die	Direktorin (nen)
	health	die	Gesundheit
to	help		helfen
	high temperature	das	Fieber
to	hike		wandern*
	hill	der	Hügel (-)
to	hire		leihen
	historical		historisch
	history		Geschichte
	hit song	der	Hit (s)
	hit song (in German)	der	Schlager (-)
	hobby	das	Hobby (s)
	holiday	der	Urlaub (e)
on	holiday	auf	Urlaub
	holidays	die	Ferien (plural only)
	home economics		Hauswirtschaft
	homework	die	Hausaufgabe (n)
to	hoover		**staub**saugen
	horror film	der	Horrorfilm (e)
	horse	das	Pferd (e)
	hospital	das	Krankenhaus (-häuser)
	hot		heiß
	hotel	das	Hotel (s)
	hourly		stundenweise
	house	das	Haus (Häuser)
at the	house of		bei (+ Dat)
	house plant	die	Zimmerpflanze (n)
	housework	die	Hausarbeit (en)

	hovercraft	das	Luftkissenboot (e)
	how		wie
	how many		wie viele
	how much		wieviel
	hyphen	der	Bindestrich
	I adore		Ich liebe
	I don't like ...		Ich mag ... nicht.
	I don't mind		das ist mir egal
	I don't think		Ich glaube nicht
	I hate		Ich hasse
	I like		Ich mag
	I think		Ich finde
	I think		Ich glaube/denke
	ice cream	das	Eis
	ice-rink	die	Eisbahn (en)
	ice-rink	das	Eisstadion (-stadien)
to	ice-skate		Schlittschuh laufen*
	ID	der	Ausweis (e)
	identity card	der	Ausweis (e)
	illness	die	Krankheit (en)
	in		in
	in between		zwischen (+ Dat)
	in front of		vor (+ Dat)
	in front of the cinema		vor dem Kino
	in time		rechtzeitig
	included		inbegriffen
	included		inklusive
	industrial estate	das	Industriegebiet (e)
	industrial town	die	Industriestadt (-städte)
	inflatable boat	das	Schlauchboot (e)
	injection	die	Spritze (n)
	ink pen	der	Füller (-)
	insect bite	der	Insektenstich (e)
	instrument	das	Instrument (e)
	interesting		interessant
	ironmonger's shop	die	Eisenwarenhandlung (en)
	is there, are there		gibt es
	island	die	Insel (n)
	IT	die	Informatik
	it doesn't matter	das	macht nichts
	jacket	die	Jacke (n)
	jam	die	Marmelade
	Jewish New Year	das	jüdische Neujahr
	job	der	Beruf
	joint of meat	der	Braten

	journey	die	Reise (n)
	juice	der	Saft (Säfte)
	kebab	das	Schaschlik (s)
	key	der	Schlüssel (-)
	keyboard	die	Tastatur (en)
	kitchen	die	Küche (n)
	knee	das	Knie (e)
to	knit		stricken
	laboratory	das	Labor (s)
	lady	die	Dame (n)
	lake	der	See (n)
	lamb	das	Lammfleisch
	lamp	die	Lampe (n)
to	land		landen*
	landscape	die	Landschaft (en)
to	last		dauern
	late		spät
	Latin		Latein
	lawn	der	Rasen (-)
to	lay the table		den Tisch decken
to	learn		lernen
to	learn by heart		auswendig lernen
made of	leather	aus	Leder
to	leave		verlassen
to	leave the house	aus dem	Haus gehen*
	to the left of		links neben
	leg	das	Bein (e)
	leisure centre	das	Freizeitzentrum (-zentren)
	lemon	die	Zitrone (n)
	lemonade	die	Limonade (n)
	Leo		Löwe
	lesson	die	Stunde (n)
	lesson	die	Unterrichtsstunde (n)
	letter	der	Brief (e)
	letter box	der	Briefkasten (-kästen)
	lettuce	der	Kopfsalat (e)
	liable to bite		bissig
	Libra		Waage
	library	die	Bibliothek (en)
	lift	der	Aufzug (-züge)
	lift	der	Lift (s)
	light ...		hell...
	light blue		hellblau
	light green		hellgrün
to	like		mögen

to	like watching	gern	sehen
	line	die	Linie (n)
made of	linen	aus	Leinen
	list of hotels	das	Hotelverzeichnis (e)
to	listen to		hören
to	listen to		**zu**hören
to	listen to the radio		Radio hören
a	little		wenig
	little pot	das	Kännchen (-)
to	live		wohnen
	living room	das	Wohnzimmer (-)
to	load		laden
	local train	der	Personenzug (-züge)
	loft	der	Speicher (-)
to	look for		suchen
	lorry	der	Lastwagen (-)
to	lose		verlieren
a	lot		viel
	luggage locker	die	Gepäckaufbewahrung
	lunch	das	Mittagessen (-)
	luxurious		luxuriös
	magazine	die	Zeitschrift (en)
	main course	das	Hauptgericht (e)
	main station	der	Hauptbahnhof (-höfe)
to	make music		musizieren
	making models	der	Modelbau
	man, husband	der	Mann (Männer)
	manager	der	Direktor/die Direktorin
	map	die	Landkarte (n)
	map of town	der	Stadtplan (-pläne)
	mark	die	Mark
	mark, grade	die	Note (n)
	marker pen	der	Marker (-)
	market	der	Markt (Märkte)
	married		verheiratet
	matches	die	Streichhölzer (pl)
	maths/mathematics	die	Mathe/Mathematik
	may I ...		darf ich ...
with	mayonnaise	mit	Mayonnaise
	meadow	die	Wiese (n)
	means of transport	das	Transportmittel (-)
	means of transport	das	Verkehrsmittel (-)
	meat	das	Fleisch
	mechanic	der	Mechaniker/die Mechanikerin
the	media	die	Medien (pl)

	medicine	die	Arznei
	medicine	das	Medikament (e)
	mediocre		mittelmäßig
to	meet friends	sich mit	Freunden treffen
	melon	die	Melone (n)
	member	das	Mitglied (er)
	microwave oven	der	Mikrowellenherd (e)
in the	middle of	in der	Mitte von (+ Dat)
	milk	die	Milch
	milk bar	die	Milchbar (s)
	mineral water	das	Mineralwasser
	mirror	der	Spiegel (-)
to	miss		verpassen
	Miss, young girl	das	Fräulein (-)
	mistake	der	Fehler (-)
	mixed		gemischt
	mixed ice cream with cream		gemischtes Eis mit Sahne
	modern		modern
	money	das	Geld
	monitor	der	Monitor (e)
	month	der	Monat (e)
	moped	das	Mofa (s)
	morning	der	Morgen (-)
	mother	die	Mutter (Mütter)
	motorbike	das	Motorrad (-räder)
	motorhome, camper	das	Wohnmobil (e)
	mountain	der	Berg (e)
	mountaineering	das	Bergsteigen
	mouse	die	Maus (Mäuse)
	mouth	der	Mund (Münder)
to	move house		**um**ziehen*
to	move on to the next year		versetzt werden
to	mow the lawn		den Rasen mähen
	Mr, Sir, gentleman	der	Herr (en)
	Mrs, Ms, woman	die	Frau (en)
to	muck out		**aus**misten
	multi-story car park	das	Parkhaus (-häuser)
	mummy	die	Mutti (s)
	museum	das	Museum (Museen)
	mushroom	der	Pilz (e)
	music	die	Musik
	music show	die	Musiksendung (en)
without	mustard	ohne	Senf
	mutton	das	Hammelfleisch
	name	der	Name (n)

	navy blue		marineblau
	near	in der	Nähe von
	neck, throat	der	Hals (Hälse)
	needlework	die	Handarbeit (en)
	net curtain	die	Gardine (n)
	New Year's Day		Neujahr
	New Year´s Eve		Sylvester
	news	die	Nachrichten (pl)
	news magazine	das	Nachrichtenmagazin (e)
	newspaper	die	Zeitung (en)
	next to		neben (+ Dat)
	next to the theatre		neben dem Theater
	night	die	Nacht (Nächte)
	night club	der	Nachtklub (s)
	noisy		laut
	non-smoker	der	Nichtraucher
in the	north	im	Norden
	north of		nördlich von (+ Dat)
	nose	die	Nase (n)
	not interesting		uninteressant
	novel	der	Roman (e)
	nurse (female)	die	Krankenschwester (n)
	nurse (male)	der	Krankenpfleger (-)
	nursery school	der	Kindergarten (-gärten)
	obedient		gehorsam
	occupied		belegt
made of	brick	aus	Backstein
	office worker	der	Angestellte (n)
	old		alt
	on		auf
	one way street	die	Einbahnstraße (n)
	onion	die	Zwiebel (n)
to	open		öffnen
	open fireplace	der	offene Kamin (e)
	opening times	die	Öffnungszeiten (pl)
	opinion	die	Meinung (en)
	opposite		gegenüber (+ Dat)
	opposite the town hall		gegenüber dem Rathaus
	orange	die	Apfelsine (n)
	orange juice	der	Orangensaft (-säfte)
	orchestra	das	Orchester (-)
to	order		bestellen
	order	die	Bestellung (en)
	original soundtrack	der	Originalton (-töne)
	other		ander

	out of the way		abseits
	outing, excursion	der	Ausflug (-flüge)
	oven	der	Backofen (-öfen)
	over		über
	owner-occupied flat	die	Eigentumswohnung (en)
	pain	der	Schmerz (en)
to	paint (a picture)		malen
	paper	das	Papier
	paragraph	der	Absatz (Absätze)
	parasol	der	Sonnenschirm (e)
	parcel	das	Paket (e)
	parents	die	Eltern (pl)
	part of the body	der	Körperteil (e)
	part-time		halbtags
	party	die	Feier (n)
	party	die	Fete (n)
	party	die	Party (s)
	party leader, organiser	der	Gruppenleiter (-)
to	pass (an exam)		bestehen
	Passover	das	Passa
	passport	der	Reisepaß (-pässe)
	pasta	die	Nudeln (pl)
	path	der	Pfad (e)
	patio	die	Terrasse (n)
to	pay		bezahlen
	pea	die	Erbse (n)
	peach	der	Pfirsich (e)
	pear	die	Birne (n)
	pedestrian precinct	die	Fußgängerzone (n)
	pencil	der	Bleistift (e)
	pencil case	das	Mäppchen (-)
	penfriend (female)	die	Brieffreundin (nen)
	penfriend (male)	der	Brieffreund (e)
	penknife	das	Taschenmesser (-)
	per month		pro Monat
	per week		pro Woche
	performance	die	Vorführung (en)
	perhaps		vielleicht
	permitted		gestattet
	personal details	die	Personalien (pl)
	pet	das	Haustier (e)
	pfennig	der	Pfennig (e)
	phone box	die	Telefonzelle (n)
	photo	das	Foto (s)
	physics		Physik

	piano	das	Klavier (e)
	picture	das	Bild (er)
	piggy bank	das	Sparschwein (e)
	pillow	das	Kopfkissen (-)
	pilot	der	Pilot (en)
	pineapple	die	Ananas
	pink		rosa
	Pisces		Fische
	pitch	der	Stellplatz (-plätze)
to	pitch a tent	das Zelt	**auf**schlagen
	place of birth	der	Geburtsort (e)
	plane	das	Flugzeug (e)
	plane ticket	der	Ticket (s)
	plate	der	Teller (-)
	platform	der	Bahnsteig (e)
	platform	das	Gleis (e)
to	play		spielen
	play	das	Theaterstück (e)
to	play cards		Karten spielen
to	play chess		Schach spielen
to	play waterball		Wasserball spielen
	playground	der	Schulhof (-höfe)
	please		bitte
	plum	die	Pflaume (n)
	PO box	das	Postfach (-fächer)
	pocket money	das	Taschengeld
	police officer	der	Polizist/die Polizistin
	polluted		verschmutzt
	pond	der	Teich (e)
	pony	das	Pony (Ponys)
	poor		arm
	pop music	die	Popmusik
	pork	das	Schweinefleisch
	port, harbour	der	Hafen (Häfen)
	portion	die	Portion (en)
	post card	die	Postkarte (n)
	post office	das	Postamt (-ämter)
	post office, mail	die	Post
	post office worker	der	Postbeamte/die Postbeamtin
	postcode	die	Postleitzahl (en)
	poster	das	Poster (-)
	postman	der	Briefträger (-)
	potato	die	Kartoffel (n)
	potato salad	der	Kartoffelsalat (e)
to do	pottery		töpfern

	poultry	das	Geflügel
	pound sterling	das	Pfund
to	practise		üben
	preposition	die	Präposition (en)
	prescription	das	Rezept (e)
	present		anwesend
	present	das	Geschenk (e)
	press	die	Presse
	price	der	Preis (e)
	primary school	die	Grundschule (n)
	printer	der	Drucker (-)
	problem	das	Problem (e)
	programme	die	Sendung (en)
	projector	der	Projektor (en)
	pub	die	Kneipe (n)
	public transport	die	öffentlichen Verkehrsmittel (pl)
	pull		ziehen
	punctually		pünktlich
	punctuation	die	Zeichensetzung
to	punish		bestrafen
	pupil (female)	die	Schülerin (nen)
	pupil (male)	der	Schüler (-)
	push		drücken
to	put into a letter box		**ein**werfen
	pyjamas	der	Schlafanzug (züge)
	question	die	Frage (n)
	question mark	das	Fragezeichen (-)
	question word	das	Fragewort (-wörter)
	quiet		ruhig
	quite		ganz
	quiz	das	Quiz
	quiz show	die	Quizsendung (en)
	radiator	der	Heizkörper (-)
on the	radio	im	Radio
	radio	das	Radio (s)
	radio play	das	Hörspiel (e)
	railway station	der	Bahnhof (-höfe)
	rain	der	Regen
to	rain		regnen
	raincoat	der	Regenmantel (-mäntel)
	Ramadan	der	Ramadan
	raspberry	die	Himbeere (n)
	rat	die	Ratte (n)
to	read		lesen
	receipt	der	Zettel (-)

	reception	der	Empfang (Empfänge)
to	record		**auf**nehmen
	record player	der	Plattenspieler (-)
	recorder	die	Blockflöte (n)
	red		rot
	relative	der/die	Verwandte (n)
to	relax	sich	entspannen
	religious studies		Religion
	remote control	die	Fernbedienung (en)
to	renovate		renovieren
	rented flat	die	Mietwohnung (en)
to	repeat		wiederholen
to	repeat a year		**sitzen**bleiben*
to	replay		**ab**spielen
	reservation	die	Reservierung (en)
to	reserve		reservieren
	resource centre	die	Lehrmittelsammlung (en)
to	rest	sich	**aus**ruhen
	restaurant	das	Restaurant (s)
to	restore		restaurieren
	return ticket	die	Rückfahrkarte (n)
	rich		reich
to	ride		reiten*
	riding	das	Reiten
to the	right of		rechts neben
to	ring (door bell)		klingeln
	river	der	Fluß (Flüsse)
	road directions	die	Wegbeschreibung
	roast	der	Braten
	roast chicken and bread roll		Brathähnchen und Brötchen
	roast chicken, chips and salad		Brathähnchen, Pommes Frites und Salat
	roast veal, dumplings and salad		Kalbsbraten, Knödel und Salat
to	roller-skate		Rollschuh laufen*
	rolling shutter	der	Rolladen (-läden)
	romantic film	der	Liebesfilm (e)
	roof	das	Dach (Dächer)
	room	das	Zimmer (-)
	rose	die	Rose (n)
	round the corner		um die Ecke
	roundabout	der	Kreisel (-)
	rubber	der	Radiergummi (s)
	rubber ring	der	Schwimmring (e)
	rubbish bin	der	Mülleimer (-)
	rucksack	der	Rucksack (-säcke)

	ruler	das	Lineal (e)
	Sabbath	der	Sabbat
	Sagittarius		Schütze
to	sail		segeln
	sailing boat	das	Segelboot (e)
	saint's day	der	Namenstag (e)
for	sale	zu	verkaufen
	sales representative	der	Vertreter/die Vertreterin
	sand	der	Sand
	sandcastle	die	Sandburg (en)
	sanitary towel	die	Damenbinde (n)
	satellite dish	die	Satellitenschüssel (n)
	saucepan	der	Kochtopf (-töpfe)
to	save		sparen
to	save		speichern
	scarf	der	Schal (s)
	scarf	das	Halstuch (-tücher)
	schnitzel with mushrooms, potatoes and peas		Jägerschnitzel, Salzkartoffeln, Erbsen
	schnitzel, chips and salad		Schnitzel, Pommes Frites, Salat
	school	die	Schule (n)
	school holidays	die	Schulferien (pl)
	school report	das	Zeugnis (se)
	school subjects	die	Fächer (pl)
	science	die	Naturwissenschaft (en)
	science fiction film	der	Science-fictionfilm (e)
	Scorpio		Skorpion
	screen	der	Bildschirm (e)
	sea	das	Meer (e)
at the	seaside	am	Meer
	second class		zweiter Klasse
	secondary (modern) school	die	Realschule (n)
	secondary school	die	Hauptschule (n)
	secretary	die	Sekretärin (nen)
to	see		sehen
	See you later!		Bis dann!
	See you soon!		Bis bald!
	See you tomorrow!		Bis morgen!
to	select		**aus**suchen
	self-service	die	Selbstbedienung (en)
	sell		verkaufen
	semi-detached house	das	Doppelhaus (-häuser)
to	send		schicken
to	send (often electronically)		senden
	sentence	der	Satz (Sätze)

	serial	die	Serie (n)
	service	die	Bedienung
to	sew		nähen
in the	shade		im Schatten
to	share		teilen
to	shave	sich	rasieren
	sheet sleeping bag	der	Leinenschlafsack (-säcke)
	sheets	die	Bettwäsche
	shelf	das	Regal (e)
to	shine		scheinen
	shirt	das	Hemd (en)
to	shop		**ein**kaufen
	shop	das	Geschäft (e)
	shop	der	Laden (Läden)
	shop assistant (female)	die	Verkäuferin
	shop assistant (male)	der	Verkäufer (-)
	shop window	das	Schaufenster (-)
	shopping	das	Einkaufen
	shopping basket	der	Einkaufskorb (-körbe)
	shopping centre	das	Einkaufszentrum (-zentren)
	shopping trolley	der	Einkaufswagen (-)
	shower	die	Dusche (n)
to	shower	sich	duschen
with	shower	mit	Dusche (n)
to	shut		schließen
	shutter	der	Fensterladen (-läden)
to	sign		unterschreiben
	signature	die	Unterschrift (en)
	silence at night, lights out	die	Nachtruhe
made of	silk	aus	Seide
to	sing		singen
	singer (female)	die	Sängerin (nen)
	singer (male)	der	Sänger (-)
	single room	das	Einzelzimmer (-)
	single ticket	die	einfache Fahrkarte (n)
	sink	das	Spülbecken (-)
	sink	der	Spülstein (e)
	sink, washbasin	das	Waschbecken (-)
	sister	die	Schwester (n)
	situated		gelegen
	sixth form	die	Oberstufe (n)
to	ski		**ski**fahren*
to	ski		**ski**laufen*
	skirt	der	Rock (Röcke)
to	sleep		schlafen

	sleeping bag	der	Schlafsack (-säcke)
	sliced sausage selection	der	Aufschnitt
	slow		langsam
	small		klein
	small package	das	Päckchen (-)
	smoker	der	Raucher
	snack bar	die	Imbißstube (n)
	snack bar	der	Schnellimbiß (sse)
	snake	die	Schlange (n)
	snow	der	Schnee
to	snow		schneien
	soap	die	Seife (n)
	soap opera	die	Seifenoper (n)
	sofa	das	Sofa (s)
	son	der	Sohn (Söhne)
	song	das	Lied (er)
	soup of the day	die	Tagessuppe (n)
in the	South	im	Süden
	South of		südlich von (+ Dat)
	souvenir	das	Reiseandenken
	Spanish		Spanisch
on	special offer	im	Angebot
	special offer	das	Sonderangebot (e)
	speech marks	die	Anführungstriche
to	spell		buchstabieren
to	spend		**aus**geben
to	spend on, need for		brauchen für (+ Acc)
to	spend time		verbringen
	spinach	der	Spinat
	spirit	der	Schnaps (Schnäpse)
	sponge	der	Schwamm (Schwämme)
	sport (s)	der	Sport (die Sportarten)
	sports centre	das	Sportzentrum (-zentren)
	sports ground	der	Sportplatz (-plätze)
	sports programme	die	Sportschau
	spreadsheet	das	Tabellenprogramm
	sprout	der	Rosenkohl
	spy film	der	Spionagefilm (e)
	square, place	der	Platz (Plätze)
	stadium	das	Stadion (Stadien)
	staff	das	Personal
	staff room	das	Lehrerzimmer (-)
	staircase	die	Treppe (n)
	stalls	der	Sperrsitz (e)
	stamp	die	Briefmarke (n)

	star sign	das	Sternzeichen (-)
	starter	die	Vorspeise
	stay	der	Aufenthalt (e)
to	stay		bleiben*
to	stay overnight		übernachten
	stepbrother	der	Stiefbruder (-brüder)
	stepfather	der	Stiefvater (-väter)
	stepmother	die	Stiefmutter (-mütter)
	stepsister	die	Stiefschwester (n)
	stereo system	die	Stereoanlage (n)
	stewardess	die	Stewardeß (Stewardessen)
	sticking plaster	das	Pflaster (-)
	stomach	der	Bauch (Bäuche)
	stomach ache	die	Magenschmerzen (pl)
	stomach upset	die	Magenverstimmung (en)
	stool	der	Hocker (-)
	stormy		stürmisch
	story	die	Geschichte (n)
	strawberry	die	Erdbeere (n)
	street, road	die	Straße (n)
	strip of tickets	die	Streifenkarte (n)
	study	das	Arbeitszimmer (-)
	stuffed eggs	russische	Eier
	subtitle	der	Untertitel (-)
	suburb	der	Vorort (e)
	suitcase	der	Koffer (-)
	summer half-term	die	Pfingstferien (pl)
	summer holidays	die	Sommerferien (pl)
in the	sun	in der	Sonne
	sun	die	Sonne
	sun stroke	der	Sonnenstich (e)
	suntan lotion	das	Sonnenöl
to	sunbathe	in der	Sonne liegen
	sunburn	der	Sonnenbrand (-brände)
	sunny		sonnig
	supermarket	der	Supermarkt (-märkte)
	surgery time	die	Sprechstunde (n)
	surname	der	Familienname (n)
to	sweep		kehren
to	swim		baden
to	swim		schwimmen
	swimming	das	Schwimmen
	swimming pool	das	Schwimmbad (-bäder)
	swimming trunks	die	Badehose (n)
to	switch over (TV channel)		**um**schalten

	T-shirt	das	T-shirt (s)
	table	der	Tisch (e)
	tablecloth	die	Tischdecke (n)
	tablecloth	das	Tischtuch (-tücher)
	tablet	die	Tablette (n)
to	take		nehmen
to	take a bath		baden
to	take for a walk		**spazieren**führen
to	take off (plane)		**ab**fliegen*
to	take photos		fotografieren
to	talk		reden
	tap	der	Wasserhahn (-hähne)
	Taurus		Stier
	tea	der	Tee
	teacher (female)	die	Lehrerin (nen)
	teacher (male)	der	Lehrer (-)
	teaching, lesson	der	Unterricht
	team	die	Mannschaft (en)
	telephone	das	Telefon (e)
	telephone number	die	Telefonnummer (n)
	tennis	das	Tennis
	tennis court	der	Tennisplatz (-plätze)
	tent	das	Zelt (e)
	term	das	Trimester (-)
	terraced house	das	Reihenhaus (-häuser)
	textbook	das	Buch (Bücher)
	thank you		danke
	theatre	das	Theater (-)
	thriller	der	Thriller (-)
	thunderstorm	das	Gewitter (-)
	ticket	die	Eintrittskarte (n)
	ticket	die	Fahrkarte (n)
	ticket	die	Karte (n)
	ticket cancelling machine	der	Entwerter (-)
	ticket machine	der	Automat (en)
	low tide	die	Ebbe
	high tide	die	Flut
	tidy		gepflegt
to	tidy up		**auf**räumen
	tights	die	Strumpfhose (n)
on	time		planmäßig
	timetable	der	Fahrplan (-pläne)
	timetable	der	Stundenplan (-pläne)
	tin opener	der	Dosenöffner (-)
	to		zu (+ Dat)

	tobacconist's shop	das	Tabakwarengeschäft (e)
	toilet	die	Toilette (n)
	toilet block	der	Waschraum (-räume)
	tomato	die	Tomate (n)
	tooth	der	Zahn (Zähne)
	toothbrush	die	Zahnbürste (n)
	toothpaste	die	Zahnpasta
	torch	die	Taschenlampe (n)
	tortoise	die	Schildkröte (n)
	tourist	der	Tourist (en)
	tourist information office	das	Informationsbüro (s)
	tourist information office	das	Verkehrsamt (-ämter)
	towel	das	Handtuch (-tücher)
	town	die	Stadt (Städte)
	town centre	die	Stadtmitte
	town hall	das	Rathaus
	track	das	Gleis (e)
	trader	der	Händler (-)
	traffic lights	die	Ampel (n)
to	train		trainieren
	train	der	Zug (Züge)
	trainers	die	Turnschuhe
	training	das	Training
	tram	die	Straßenbahn (en)
to	travel		reisen*
	travel agency	das	Reisebüro (s)
to	travel by plane		fliegen*
	travel sickness	die	Reisekrankheit (en)
	traveller	der	Reisende (n)
	traveller's cheque	der	Reisescheck (s)
	tree	der	Baum (Bäume)
	trousers	die	Hose (n)
	trumpet	die	Trompete (n)
to	try		versuchen
	tube	die	Tube (n)
	tulip	die	Tulpe (n)
to	turn		**ab**biegen
to	turn off		**aus**schalten
to	turn on		**an**schalten
on	TV	im	Fernsehen
	TV	das	Fernsehen
	TV channel	das	Programm
	TV set	der	Fernseher (-)
	TV magazine	die	Fernsehzeitung (en)
	twin-bedded room	das	Zweibettzimmer (-)

	uncle	der	Onkel (s)
	under		unter
	underground	die	U-Bahn (en)
	unemployed		arbeitslos
	uniform	die	Uniform (en)
	useful		nützlich
	useless		nutzlos
	vacuum cleaner	der	Staubsauger (-)
	valley	das	Tal (Täler)
	van	der	Lieferwagen (-)
	vanilla flavour whipped pudding	der	Vanillepudding
	vase	die	Vase (n)
	VAT	die	Mehrwertsteuer
	vegetable	das	Gemüse
	vegetable garden	der	Gemüsegarten (-gärten)
	vegetable soup	die	Gemüsesuppe (n)
	very		sehr
	very near		ganz in der Nähe
	vicious		bösartig
	video game		das Videospiel (e)
	video-camera, camrecorder	die	Videokamera (s)
	video cassette recorder	der	Videorekorder (-)
	village	das	Dorf (Dörfer)
	violin	die	Geige (n)
	Virgo		Jungfrau
	visit	der	Besuch (e)
to	visit (a monument)		besichtigen
to	visit a stately home		ein Schloß besichtigen
to	wait		warten
	waiter	der	Kellner (-)
	waiting room	der	Warteraum (-räume)
	waiting room	das	Wartezimmer (-)
	waitress	die	Kellnerin (nen)
to	wake up		**auf**wachen*
	walkman	der	Walkman
	wall	die	Wand (Wände)
	wall clock	die	Wanduhr (en)
	warden (female)	die	Herbergsmutter (-mütter)
	warden (male)	der	Herbergsvater (-väter)
	wardrobe	der	Kleiderschrank (-schränke)
to	wash (oneself)	sich	waschen
to	wash up		spülen
	washing-machine	die	Waschmaschine (n)
to	watch TV		**fern**sehen
to	water		gießen

	water	das	Wasser
to	waterski		Wasserski fahren*
	watersport	der	Wassersport
	way, road, path	der	Weg (e)
to	wear		tragen
	weather	das	Wetter
	weather forecast	der	Wetterbericht (e)
	weather forecast	die	Wettervorhersage (n)
	weekend	das	Wochenende (n)
	weekly (political) magazine	die	Wochenzeitschrift (en)
in the	west		im Westen
	west of		westlich von
	what		was
	What a pity!		Wie schade!
at	what time		um wieviel Uhr
	when		wann
	where		wo
	where to		wohin
	which		welcher, welche, welches
	white		weiß
	who		wer
	why		warum
	widowed		verwitwet
to	win		gewinnen
	wind	der	Wind (e)
	window	das	Fenster (-)
to	windsurf		windsurfen
	windy		windig
	wine	der	Wein (e)
	winter sport	der	Wintersport
	with		mit (+ Dat)
	without		ohne (+ Acc)
	woman, wife	die	Frau (en)
	women's magazine	die	Frauenzeitschrift (en)
	wood	das	Waldstück (e)
made of	wool	aus	Wolle
	word processing	die	Textverarbeitung
	work	die	Arbeit (en)
to	work		arbeiten
	worker	der	Arbeiter (-)
to	wrap		**ein**packen
to	write		schreiben
to	write with a capital letter		**groß**schreiben
to	write with a lower case (small) letter		**klein**schreiben
	yacht marina	der	Yachthafen (häfen)

yellow		gelb
yes, of course		Ja, natürlich
youngster	der/die	Jugendliche (n)
youth centre	das	Jugendzentrum (zentren)
youth club	der	Jugendclub (s)
Youth Hostel	die	Jugendherberge (e)
youth hostel rules	die	Herbergsregeln (pl)
youth, young people	die	Jugend